CREATIONISM ON TRIAL

Evolution and God
at Little Rock

Langdon Gilkey

1817

HARPER & ROW, PUBLISHERS, SAN FRANCISCO

Cambridge, Hagerstown, New York, Philadelphia
London, Mexico City, São Paulo, Singapore, Sydney

*Dedicated
with love
to my sister
Mary Jane Gilkey
June 1917—February 1983*

Contents

Preface

This volume represents an account of my experiences as a "theological" witness for the American Civil Liberties Union (ACLU) at the "creationist" trial in Little Rock, Arkansas, December 7-9, 1981. Appended to that account are also reflections on the state of church, laboratory, and wider society in light of that controversy.

To my surprise, the contest enacted in that courtroom between fundamentalist "creation science" (aided by the State of Arkansas) on the one side, and scholarly religion, established science, and liberal teachers (aided by the ACLU and one of New York's most potent law firms) on the other side, proved to be more than the exciting spectacle I had expected—a spectacle worthy of extended and, where possible, humorous comment. More important, I found it opening up windows into the baffling complexity and frequently impenetrable obscurity of our present cultural life as an advanced scientific society. I realized that this case could help us *understand* in new ways how science and the religious manifest themselves in such a society, and the strange roles they perform and the bizarre ways they may there unite and interact. This realization has only grown as I have found myself speaking on this theme in the many colleges, universities, and laboratories I have visited since then. So, at the suggestion of my colleague Martin Marty, I embarked upon this account. My hope is that it may add to our present self-understanding as a society dedicated in large part *both* to science and to religion, and that it will encourage these two communities—

both of whom are in part "to blame" for this controversy—to spend more of their energy and time seeking
to understand each other.

I wish to thank first of all the lawyers of Skadden,
Arps (especially Tony Siano) and of the ACLU (especially Jack Novik), who "captained" our team; the Little
Rock chapter of the ACLU; the gallant, responsible, and
thoughtful plaintiffs from Little Rock; the Arkansas
teachers who bravely witnessed for the plaintiffs; and
all those persons interested in this controversy who
have subsequently invited me to speak on it, and who
have so hospitably received me. I wish also to thank
Martha Morrow for typing the original manuscript and
Michelle Harewood for typing it in its present form.

I have dedicated this book to my late sister, Mary
Jane, who died suddenly in February of 1983. A few
sentences cannot begin to express what such a lifelong
relationship means, or how vast the void is when the
earthly form of that relation ceases—so I will not try.
We all miss her, as a loving and loyal sister, an affection-
ate, understanding, and especially thoughtful aunt—
and simply lots of fun for all of us in the family to be
with, whether in deMeye, in Nara, or playing canasta
and Uno in Boothbay.

PART I

The Trial

1
The Initiation of a Witness

It began, as far as I was concerned, on Wednesday, September 15, 1981. The phone rang in my office and a warm yet efficient voice said, "Professor Gilkey, this is Skadden, Arps, Slate, Maegher, and Flom of New York calling. Can you speak to our Mr. Siano?"

Realizing at once that such a series of incredible names could only mean that some big New York law firm was not only after me but had, so to speak, already cornered me, I mumbled a miserable assent and waited, telling myself that it couldn't be as bad as I already feared.

"Professor Gilkey," a brisk, strong voice broke in, "this is Tony Siano of Skadden, Arps. I'm for the moment representing the American Civil Liberties Union in relation to an upcoming creation-science case in Arkansas. Have you heard of the case? Good. We would like to receive some advice from you, and possibly some further help. Could I come to see you in your office on the coming Friday?"

Vastly relieved, I said certainly, and we arranged a time in the early afternoon.

"Good. I'll send some documents for you to read before we meet. Since they'll come by air courier, they'll be there first thing in the morning."

I was by now really excited. Here I was acting out, an actual part of, those ever-present TV ads showing important packages sent off from New York at 9 P.M. and arriving with the coffee at 7 A.M. on the Willamette River in Oregon!

Sure enough, on schedule the next morning a large package arrived. It contained a note from Siano; a copy of Arkansas Act 590 (the law requiring the teaching of creation science), which the ACLU was challenging; the official documentation of the case (listing plaintiffs, defendants, and stating the jurisdiction of the Federal Court in the Eastern district of Arkansas); and finally, some Little Rock newspaper reports concerning the introduction and passing of the Act in the Arkansas legislature, the governor's signing of it, and statements by the legislator who introduced it and the governor who signed it of their reasons as "Bible Christians" for supporting and implementing the Act. I read these documents, made some initial notes representing a theological reaction to the law and its provisions, and waited for the next day when Siano would arrive.

Like the package, Siano arrived on schedule—in fact, five minutes early. Immediately he was a vibrant presence in my office: wide-brimmed hat, trench coat with collar turned up, a couple of elegant leather shoulder bags, short dark beard, dapper vested suit with watch chain, and snapping dark eyes. He exuded energy, efficiency, and intelligence. After he had introduced himself, he introduced his business; he spoke quietly and warmly, with unmistakable charm.

"I'm a lawyer with Skadden, Arps. We are, let me say, the number one law firm dealing with mergers." (Later I discovered that they had been representing Conoco and Marathon, defending these large maidens against the even larger predatory monster, Mobil.) "If we don't represent one side of a big merger case, we feel we're slipping."

Just to make him feel quite at home, I said, "Perhaps you wouldn't know this, but that's just what we tell about ourselves at the University of Chicago Divinity School."

He smiled and went on: "There are twelve of us from Skadden who have been loaned out, so to speak, to work with the ACLU and an important Little Rock firm on

-4-

this creationist case. We've been at it since the middle of the summer; the case is to come to trial, we think, in early December. We're doing this, of course, without remuneration, *pro bono* as we say in the law, though naturally our expenses are paid. If you were to work with us on this case, and later to be a witness at the trial, you have clearly to understand that there will be no honorarium. Do you think you'd be willing to do this, as we are, only for expenses?"

I realized at once that Tony was a formidable lawyer: one could hardly say "No—I never do anything without a large fee" or "See my agent about my fee" after *that* presentation, even though his argument certainly tempted me to do so. So I again mumbled assent, and looked at him with the admiration and interest one feels for someone who has effortlessly but effectively backed one into a corner.

"We're in the process of building our case, and that means first of all finding the right witnesses. Your name has been suggested to us as a theologian and philosopher of religion—and that's why I'm here. Our team of lawyers is divided into two sections, one devoted to the 'religious' and the other to the 'scientific' side of the case. I'm in charge of the religion section. Today I've been talking with a Biblical scholar, an expert on Genesis; yesterday I was in Michigan interviewing an historian of fundamentalism. Later, if you join us, you'll learn just what our whole 'game plan' is, and your possible role in it. But meanwhile, why don't we talk a bit about the case and what you might contribute to it? You got the documents, did you?—and I presume you've already read them. What do you think—just as a starter—you'd say if you were called to testify?"

So I began outlining what, at that early point, I thought the main argument of a theologian might be in this case. I would, I said, begin with a discussion of what religion was, and so what religious ideas, doctrines, propositions were; I would then argue that creation science as defined in Act 590 was, contrary to its own claim to be science, a form of religious theory—in fact, an example of literalistic or fundamentalist Christian theory about the origins of the universe and of the forms of life within it. Secondly, I said, I would try to distinguish these kinds of "religious" statements from scientific ones—though I'd have to think a lot more carefully before I'd be able to say precisely how that argument would proceed. With that, I stopped for a moment.

Tony seemed satisfied enough with this. Then he surprised me by asking, "So you think their science is actually a case of apologetics?"

"My goodness," I said, "you certainly have been doing your homework! Where did you run into that term?"

"Oh, I remember it from my Catholic training as a boy—my family comes from Naples," said Tony with a smile. "But all of us have been reading day and night for three months now on the subjects and disciplines involved in this case, so we're getting used to some of your lingo."

I was impressed, then, and continued to be throughout the trial, with the vast variety of subjects that lawyers—and even more, judges—have to master in a hurry, and how extraordinarily well all the lawyers in this case succeeded in learning their way around the many academic disciplines involved there.

During this discussion, I noticed as I spoke that Tony was looking me carefully and systematically up and down, over and across, somewhat (I should imagine) the way one of the late Bear Bryant's assistants might size up, down to the smallest detail, a prospective tight end or linebacker. And I became suddenly conscious of what I must look like to this dapper New York lawyer: with my longish hair, white beard, open shirt collar, scarf, and beads, and, strangest of all, the earring in my left ear. So as I was outlining my argument, there was an accompanying stream-of-consciousness somewhat like this: "Since 1970, when I put it on (sailors in Holland, Portugal, and Greece wear earrings—as had the sea deity Poseidon—*and* I am a sailor), I have never taken that earring off, even for the most formal lectures and stiff receptions, or ever considered doing so, nor ever worn a necktie. But, to my surprise (I was saying to myself), I think I *would* in this case. How could I be a persuasive 'expert in theology,' a witness helpful to our common cause in Little Rock—or most anywhere else—if I kept it on?"

Having reached that decision, I found another immediately jostling my consciousness for attention: "But I'm too proud to tell this guy that at this point. Let him wonder about it for now, and if they *do* choose me, then I'll tell him that the earring will come off and tie go on."

After we had discussed somewhat further the kind of argument I might give, Tony said that the next thing for me to do was to set this argument into a more coherent, precise, and extended form—that is, to write it up for them in about twenty pages, and to send it off by Express first thing Monday morning (it was now Friday!). I should include in it, he said, (1) a careful definition of religion, (2) an argument as to why this law established religion—why creation science was religion, (3) a precise definition of apologetics and why this was an example of apologetics, and finally, (4) why and in what way creation science was *not* science. As soon as they had received my statement and digested it, I would hear from them about what I could do further to help their case. Then he asked me if he could please use my phone to call a cab. He had to catch an evening plane to Las Vegas to testify tomorrow for a client who had been involved in the MGM fire the preceding spring. He ordered the cab, donned his trench coat and hat, shouldered his various bags, shook my hand, and walked briskly out the office door.

I spent Friday night, Saturday, and Sunday rereading the law, making a new outline of my presentation, typing and then retyping twenty or so pages of extended argument, as Tony had directed. By Monday it was ready to send, and so once again, a courier was called in to whisk the package away. This argument, I was to discover, would be reworked again and again before final testimony was given in December, as I learned more about the logic of creation science and as new points to make struck us. What seems strange now, looking back, was that in the basic structure of the argument—that this was religion, why it was religion, and hence why it was not science—almost no change took place from that first raw conversation to the final carefully-tailored testimony.

*　　*　　*

Long before that weekend I can recall being alternately bemused and horrified that in some state in the Union a law such as Act 590 could actually be enacted and enforced in our day. Bemused because it seemed ironic that in an advanced scientific and technological culture such as ours, a sizeable enough portion of the population—all of whom admire and luxuriate in the technological know-how created by modern science— would question perhaps the most fundamental and pervasive theorem of modern science and, as a result, deliberately set out to dismantle the scientific edifice on which that technological eminence rests. And I was horrified that a particularly intolerant wing of my own Christian religious community should seek to control for its own doctrinal purposes the political and educational structures of our whole diverse and variegated society. Never before, however, had I sought to think through carefully the grounds for my deeply-felt opposition to laws such as Act 590, nor made explicit the reasons for my own obvious intention to do everything my powers and energy would allow to defeat such a bill as dangerous, if not lethal, to all that I, as a Christian

-8-

believer and as an active participant in a democratic society, held worthy and valuable. But now, having looked over this law with care, I found myself forced explicitly and precisely to formulate what I thought to be wrong, even dangerous, about it.

Very briefly, then, let me summarize this law (a copy of it is one of the Appendices) and explain, again briefly, why I opposed it. The law in effect required in every class in science in the school system of Arkansas "balanced treatment" (Section 2) of the "two scientific models" concerning the origin of "the universe, earth, life and man." More precisely, it mandated that wherever one model is taught, the other model must be given roughly the same time and attention (Section 5). It characterized (Section 4) these two models as "creation science" and "evolution science" and then proceeded to define them each by means of six or seven propositions. Carefully it specified that no religious instruction was to be permitted, nor reference to religious sources or doctrines made (Sections 2 and 5); rather, only the "scientific evidences and the inferences therefrom" (Section 2) in favor of both scientific models were to be taught.

The first thing on which it was important for me to become clear was the reason for my public opposition, and that of all those of us on the ACLU team, to this law. This opposition was not directed against either fundamentalism or creation science in itself. I agree with neither one of these two interrelated interpretations or forms of the Christian religion. Nevertheless, both on the basis of my own religious convictions (which hold that each of us must be free in conscience to choose and to determine the form that characterizes our own faith) and on the basis of my interpretation of democracy (which holds to the importance of the non-establishment by the State of religion or of any particular form of religion), the creationists have, it seems to me, a right under God and under our Constitution to preach, teach, and practice their faith in freedom as long as they do not interfere with the similar rights held by others.

I do not agree with their doctrines; nevertheless, the only counter to them which I would either employ or support is the force of persuasion, and not the force of legislative, judicial, or executive authority of the State. My aim in challenging creation science in Little Rock was, then, not at all the goal of silencing either creation science or fundamentalism, or of challenging their right to express either one. It was simply and solely to defeat *their* effort, which I believed Act 590 represented, to advance their own particular religious viewpoint through legislation—that is, to require through legislation that this particular religious view of our origins be taught as a science (and as *the* alternative to evolution) in the public schools.

But was this not, one might ask, a particularly democratic and fair piece of legislation? So it seemed. On the face of it, Act 590 appeared innocent and virtuous enough. It stated as its major intentions the protection of academic freedom by providing students genuine "choice," the protection of freedom of religious exercise and belief, and the prevention of the "establishment of religious instruction"—in fact, the very values we accused it of seeking to subvert. And it stated it would ensure these values of freedom, tolerance, and openness by a method long recognized in public affairs: that each side should have its adequate and fair "say," specifically the principle of balanced treatment in classroom discussion and in use of textbooks.

What, one might ask, could be more just or more "American" than to give the two models, or the two theories of origins, equal time in school, just as we give equal time to the two political parties and their candidates? So it seems to many.

During that initial reflection on the law, however, I came to the conclusion that this law and ones similar to it are, despite this appearance, in fact dangerous to the

health of our society; and that through its wide enactment it would represent a disaster to our common life,
especially our religious life. Further experience over
the following weeks prior to, during, and after the trial
would only deepen this conviction. Since for many it
comes as a surprise that a theologian and a "believer"
should resist this law, it may be well at the outset of this
account to explain further the reasons for my own personal antipathy to it.

First of all, the enactment of this sort of law—especially if it were to be widely adopted—would represent
a disaster for religion in our society. This was to me,
and to each of us representing religion among the
plaintiffs, the most important issue at stake. There can
be, I believe, no healthy, creative, or significant religious faith in a modern society unless, as I have noted,
the forms of that faith are free. A politically enforced or
supported religious faith becomes corrupt, dead, and
oppressive, encouraging inevitably in reaction a deep
personal distaste and moral disdain at such spiritual
imperialism. Enforced religion breeds precisely what it
most fears: rebellion against religion, cynicism about
religion, skepticism about its claims, and, as a consequence, indifference at best and outright antipathy at
worst. The First Amendment is important not only to
guarantee the rights of alternative religions and of non-
religious persons in society; it is also important in setting the only possible legal and social conditions for the
creative health of serious religion itself. This my own
tradition—the Baptist (as well as that of the Quaker and
the Unitarian)—has held from its own early beginnings
on this continent.

Freedom of religion in society, especially in any modern diversified culture, invariably means plurality of
religious viewpoints and even of religions within society; and so it entails widely diverse opinions regarding
all sorts of issues important to each set of religious
beliefs. If each community or group is to be free religiously to develop itself, it must allow the others equal

freedom, or else claim such freedom for itself alone, and be led thereby down the sinful slope of intolerance, inquisition, persecution, and, ultimately, the oppressive elimination of other religious groups. When society through its government, its public funds, or its public schools favors one form of religion, or identifies religion with that one form to the exclusion of others, it endangers all forms of religion. The First Amendment is the deepest constitutional or "worldly" base of whatever health our religious institutions and life may claim. This law, I was convinced—and this was my subsequent argument—would serve to establish a particular form of the Christian religion in the teaching program of the public schools; therefore, it represented a grave threat to the free religious life of our society.

So it was by no means accidental that most of the plaintiffs and one-half of the witnesses in this case represented religion. Many private individuals and a number of national and state-wide institutions who identified themselves as "religious" (that is, as concerned with the health of the Christian and the Jewish faiths) had hastened to stand up actively in opposition to this law. Specifically, twelve of the seventeen individuals who were plaintiffs were clergymen, and four of the six associations were religious associations (American Jewish Congress, e.g.). Among the ministers were representatives of the Presbyterian churches, the Disciples churches, the Methodist, Episcopal, and Roman Catholic bishops, and the Union of American Hebrew Congregations. Only one scientific group (The National Association of Biology Teachers) and one educational organization (the Arkansas Educational Association) joined these representatives of religion among the plaintiffs.

Although the media and most scientific commentators presented this trial as a continuation of the so-called "warfare between science and religion," the fact was, as the above shows, that in this case the legal defense of science and the legal opposition to fundamentalist control of education were instigated and executed largely by religious individuals and groups. When I asked as many of these staunch clerical plaintiffs as I could *why* they had so acted—often against their best interests in relation to their congregations—they all replied, "To save the Christian faith from an untrue and yet fatal identification with intolerant literalism on the one hand and an anti-scientific attitude on the other." I knew that this was why I was there (and the main reason I undertake this volume); I was interested to discover that the majority of the plaintiffs shared my motivation.

The defense of a responsible and intelligent religion in a scientific and technological society is of the utmost importance. So is the defense of science itself. Thus the second reason why the enactment of this law is a threat to our common life is that it would represent a disaster for the teaching of science and the training of future scientists in any state in which it was enforced. As anyone working creatively in science is aware (but as a layman I realized only as the trial unfolded), creation science represents a direct repudiation of perhaps the most general and pervasive theorem basic to all the physical and biological sciences. This is the concept of a universe in process, changing over vast stretches of time, interrelated and interacting in all of its aspects, out of whose developing interrelations novel forms of existence arise and come to be. This theorem far transcends the various theories and models of biological science alone, and certainly any concepts associated with Charles Darwin.

Actually, the thesis of a universe developing over immense stretches of time dominates every science from astrophysics through astronomy, physics, chemistry, biochemistry, geology, geophysics, microbiology, and on into biology, paleontology, zoology, botany, and meteorology. To counter the central theorem structuring these sciences, and to insert into their midst a set of alien theses unrelated to all other theories in these fields, would bring about a systematic destruction of American science far greater than that engineered so fatally by Stalin in the name of Lysenko on Soviet biology. As leading scientific groups, including the American Association for the Advancement of Science, have realized only slowly, such laws could well cripple American science for generations.

Finally, enacting this law would represent a disaster for academic freedom. It is not uncommon for a legislature to mandate *subjects* that must be included within the curricula of its public schools: so much science, so much civics, so much American and local history, so much technical training, health care, and so on. But it is a new precedent, and an ominous one, when a legislature requires what theories are to be taught within these mandated subjects, how much emphasis is to be given to each, and, by clear implication, what theories may not be taught.

Such authoritative interference by the State would be harmful enough in the crucial but relatively noncontroversial fields of natural science. But were this precedent to be followed in more sensitive areas of the school curriculum—in American history, in civics, in social theory—and, as a consequence, were the State to mandate in courses, say, on American society, *what* social views should be discussed and what should not, then academic freedom would be gravely endangered indeed. Wherever government has determined the *content* of a curriculum (as, for example, in the Soviet Union), free inquiry and free debate in education have vanished. It is, in short, one thing to mandate by legislation what subjects should be taught; it is quite another to legislate that certain specific theories or viewpoints should be represented there.[1] This is precisely the point of Act 590, and it is why it represents a threat to academic freedom.

As the full dimensions of this bizarre case took shape in the next weeks, I found myself intrigued by what, surprisingly enough, was revealed about our wider present cultural situation. In a new way it became evident that the relations between science and technology on the one hand and religion on the other were much more complex, ambiguous, and confusing than was conventionally assumed. At once it was plain that the controversy I was involved in was by no means merely one more battle in an endless "warfare of science and religion"—as the scientific community tended to see it and as the media more or less assumed. For after all, as we have noted, here were religious leaders and associations taking the leading role in defending science and academic freedom. And as I looked over the list of opposition witnesses, I saw to my surprise and amusement that over against these churchly plaintiffs, my colleagues in Scripture and church history, and me the theologian, and supporting the creationist cause, was arrayed a sequence of professional "scientists,"[2] each one replete with a scientific doctorate and a tenured position on a scientific faculty.

Here, then, was something novel and unexpected in our culture: a union of fundamentalist religion and self-proclaimed "science," a sort of "popular science" in league with popular religion, both of them juxtaposed to the "official" scientific community on the one hand and the "official" churchly and theological communities on the other. From the start this strange union of popular religion and popular science fascinated me; further reflection on the meaning of this unexpected union for an advanced scientific culture such as ours appears in Chapters 7 and 8.

Almost equally surprising for a theologian was to find himself for once a defender of the scientific establishment rather than its friendly if persistent critic.[3] Even stranger was the realization that I who had for so long spoken and written about the "religious pretensions" of much of the modern scientific community should now be involved not only in defending evolutionary theory as legitimate science but also in denying that such legitimate scientific theories were essentially naturalistic or atheistic. Even at that early stage this paradoxical role raised in my mind the questions, In what ways had we theologians been *right* to criticize science for these religious pretensions; and yet, as I now had to maintain, How at the same time was it not only legitimate but necessary to defend science against what seemed to be the same critique? Again the distinction between science *as a method of inquiry* and science as a *"religious phenomenon"* representing naturalistic humanism had to be thought through and clearly drawn if my participation as a theologian in this trial, not to mention my testimony, was to make sense.

*　　*　　*

During the three weeks after I sent in my projected testimony, Tony and I were in fairly regular communication by phone. Since no word was mentioned about the makeup of the team of witnesses to go to Little Rock, apparently that decision had not yet been made. From several of Tony's remarks I gathered that my colleague and friend Martin Marty had for some time been acting as an extremely important consultant for the ACLU lawyers—sort of like the coach at the top of the stadium who calls down plays to the other coaches on the sidelines. When we met in the hall shortly after my initial conversation with Tony, I said to Marty that I had something funny to tell him about my encounter with the New York lawyer. I said that during my talk with Tony, I had decided that in Arkansas I would take my earring off and wear a tie—but that I had been too proud to tell Tony at the time. Marty's eyes twinkled as if he knew lots of amusing things about all of this—and, as is his wont, hurried off to something else.

During the third week in October I was away for eight days in San Francisco. When I returned to my office, a letter was waiting there saying that I had been chosen as a witness for the plaintiffs at the trial. I was both very elated and extremely nervous: elated at the prospect of being involved in such a fascinating adventure as this, and nervous with the fear that I might on the stand foolishly blow this case which I now felt to be very important indeed. I got on the phone at once to report my acceptance to Skadden, Arps. Tony was out, and so I was put on the line with Trudy Kerr, the lawyer in general charge of the whole Skadden effort for the ACLU. When I gave my name, she at once replied: "Oh, Professor Gilkey, we understand that you're so anxious to be a witness for us in Arkansas that you're willing to take off your earring and shave off your beard!"

Somewhat startled at all this (Marty must have leaked this classified secret), I barely managed to protest, "Oh, no, I haven't *thought* of removing the beard. You must remember that Darwin had a big one, and we're on his side"—and warming up to my argument, I foolishly added, "And, after all, God has a beard!"

"Oh, no, She doesn't!" shot back Trudy. Fortunately, I got out a good laugh, even though I had been totally beaten, and, picking myself up from the floor, I tried to recover my aplomb: "You win; that's the last time I'll tangle with a lawyer!"

When I told Tony this whole story after the trial, he laughed and, looking (as usual) totally in command of the situation, added, "You know what I told them when I got back to New York after our first meeting? Well, I said there was a guy in Chicago who might well be an excellent witness.

"'Of course,' I added, 'he has long hair, a white beard, wears a scarf and beads, and totes an earring on his left ear. . . .'

"At that, the other Skadden, Arps lawyers all shouted, 'Jesus H. Christ, Siano—are you crazy? A guy on the witness stand in Little Rock looking like that will collapse the whole case!'

"So I told them, 'If a person is intelligent enough to be a good witness for us, he's intelligent enough to take that earring, beads, and scarf off for the trial. We'll just wait and see what he does.'

"And with that, Langdon, no one mentioned this matter from then on."

When Tony told me this story, I laughed at myself: And I had thought I had successfully kept something back from my lawyer!

2
Preparation for the Case

Soon after I had accepted the role of a witness, more packages of documents began to arrive from New York. There were books, articles, pamphlets, even comics—all presenting the arguments of creation science. As Tony had warned, my next task would be to absorb all of this material. Although the definition of creation science in the law itself would be the main target of our arguments, still it was important to have a clear and accurate —and not least, thoroughly documented—picture of this "theory" if we were successfully to develop our case that it represented, in fact, religion and not science. Hence the necessity of perusing these documents carefully in order to uncover the logic of the creationists' position, the leading ideas they proposed, and what sorts of arguments they presented. What I discovered in those documents forms the substance of this chapter. At the same time, my discoveries give the reader a necessary introduction to the issues at stake in the trial.

The statement of creation science in the law, being brief, was at many points full of ambiguities. "Creation-Science," so the law stated, means "the scientific evidences for creation and inferences from those scientific evidences." Then it defined this "scientific model" to include: (1) sudden creation of the universe, energy, and life from nothing; (2) the insufficiency of evolutionary theory to explain the development of life and of "kinds of things"; (3) changes only within fixed limits of originally created "kinds"; (4) separate ancestry for man [sic] and apes; (5) the explanation of geological history by catastrophes, including a worldwide flood;

and (6) the relatively recent inception of the earth. Here, obviously, was an idea or theory that sought to present itself formally as science ("scientific evidences and inferences from them") and yet whose *content* as specified in all points except (2) entailed what was clearly a "religious" notion, the creation of the world by a divine being. So, thoroughly intrigued, I went to these background documents to see where they came from, who had written them, and what sort of notion or theory this really was.

Most of these documents had one major source in California, a source that had been formed by a series of "begettings."[1] The original group was the Christian Research Society (1963), which in 1970 formed the Creation-Science Research Center in San Diego. Subsequently, the Institute for Christian Research (1972) was established as an affiliate of a Christian Heritage College, an unaccredited Baptist college linked with the Moral Majority. Interestingly, each of these three interrelated societies (CRS, C-SRC, and ICR) seeks to be "purely scientific" and professional. As one example, according to its own membership rules, the voting member of CRS (693 in 1980) must hold a Master's or Doctor's degree in science. All the major texts but one have been published by the Creation Life Publishing Company in San Diego, a concern obviously sponsored by these same societies. These texts include three by Henry M. Morris, Ph.D.: *Scientific Creationism* (henceforth SC), in two editions, one general one, replete with Biblical sources, and one for public schools with these "religious" sources deleted, *The Scientific Case for Creation* (SCC), and *The Bible Has the Answer* (BHA); *Origins: Two Models*, by Richard B. Bliss and *Origin of Life: Evolution-Creation* (OL), by Bliss and Gary E. Parker; *Evolution: The Fossils Say No!* (again in two different editions), by Duane Gish, Ph.D.; *Handy-Dandy Evolution Refuter*, by Robert E. Kofahl; and *The Creation Explanation* (CE), by Kofahl and Kelly G. Seagraves (this latter volume published by Harold Shaw, Wheaton, Ill.).

When we turn from the sources of these creationist documents to their authors, we find a most surprising situation. I say "surprising" because the persons who have formulated, elaborated, and defended creation science are not "preachers" ignorant of modern science and its implications—as most of the media and certainly the established academic and scientific communities have assumed. Rather, these are "scientists" by any normal, useful, or descriptive definition of that word.[2] That is, most of them have gone through a scientific training of the highest order, and numbers of them have been, or are at present, functioning as professors or instructors of science in recognized universities.

Since this fact is frequently questioned ("They're all engineers and not real scientists!"), a few relevant statistics are in order. If one counts the explicit and public supporters and formulators of creation science and adds to this the witnesses who agreed to testify against evolution science and in favor of creation science the total is *twenty-four* Ph.D.'s in the natural or theoretical sciences, including physics, astronomy, chemistry and biochemistry, geology, biology, physiology, botany, and zoology. Their doctorates have come from institutions including UCLA, Berkeley, Harvard, Columbia, Stanford, the University of Southern California, the Universities of Illinois (four), Penn State, Michigan, Ohio State, Iowa, North Carolina, and Western Ontario. Presently, members of this sizeable group (and creation science claims many score more) have professorial or instructional positions in the natural or engineering sciences at Iowa State, the University of Texas at El Paso (two), Purdue, Penn State, Auburn, North Carolina State, the University of Louisville Medical School, Michigan State, and the Universities of Wyoming and of Illinois.[3] The Director of the Midwest Center for Creation Research, located in Naperville, Illinois, has a doctorate in physics from Massachusetts Institute of Technology; the dean of the Science Faculties at Liberty Baptist College in Lynchburg, Virginia, has a doctorate in biology from Ohio State. Both represented creation science in debates with this author; each identified himself on these occasions as speaking "as a scientist" while I was identified as "only a theologian."

By any useful descriptive standard of science or of scientists—except possibly agreement with the established elite of science—these men and women represent the world of science. No remotely comparable list of representative theologians or Biblical scholars supporting creationism could be found. In fact, there is *not one* advanced theological or Biblical degree from an accredited institution (with the not-surprising exception of a doctorate from Edinburgh!) among their proponents—compared with more than two score of reputable scientific doctorates. If one says, "Oh, well, they can't be scientists because they're not recognized by the community of scientists, and they're not members of the AAAS," it could be pointed out that their writers on religion are not recognized by the professional communities of theologians and of Biblical scholars, nor are they remotely members of the American Academy of Religion, the American Theological Society, the Society of Biblical Literature, or the National Council of Churches. Strangely, they are *more* representative of the community of scientists than of the community of theologians, and fully as much at war with "established" forms of religion in American life (as the list of plaintiffs shows) as with American science. Creation science is as much an example of the warfare of scientists with American religion as of the opposition of American religion to science. In fact, the case cannot be understood at all in terms of the myth of a "perennial warfare" of clear-headed scientists with benighted clergymen and theologians.

More important by far, however, than the professional status of the leading creationists is the character of the ideas or concepts represented in creation science. For the question, Is this "theory" or "model" science, or is it religion? represented the central issue of the case;

and a very complex question it was. It was interesting, therefore, though not surprising, that in their more reflective texts the representatives of creation science themselves were not completely clear on its answer. Or at least in their explanatory texts they seemed to present two diverse views of the status of their model or theory. On the one hand, they claimed creation science as "a scientific model" (Act 590, Section V) or a "scientific alternative" to "evolution science." It is, they said, "origins treated solely on a scientific basis" (CS 4). And they promised "to bring together the facts from science" to support this alternative (CE 11), "to gather scientific data in favor of the Creation model" (OL 10), to show that "the Creation model of origins and history may be used to correlate the facts of science at least as effectively as the evolution model" (CS 4).

Thus beyond a doubt the assertion is continuously made that creationism is a legitimate scientific model or theory, one to be questioned and tested fully as much as are other major, all-encompassing scientific models or theories. This assertion was, of course, necessary for the legality of the requirement to give balanced treatment to creation science in biology classes throughout Arkansas. As the Findings of Facts (the final brief of the State of Arkansas) stated: "Creation-Science and evolution science . . . are the only scientific explanations of the origin of the universe" (#19).

On the other hand, most of the writers for creation science recognized that in some measure, at least, creation science is something else than or more than an "ordinary" theory in science. They said this in multiple ways: "Creation is not observable—it is not possibly a part of science" (CS 5); "Creation is *not* a scientific explanation" (CE 112); "Views of origins are 'faith'" (CS 4, CE 12) and "lie outside the scientific enterprise" (CE 160)—and thus all we can learn about creation processes "must come by revelation from the Creator Himself," that is, in the Bible (BHA 64; see also 21, 82). The reason given for this "transcendence" of ordinary science by the concept of creation is that all strictly scientific hypotheses are said to be testable by observation. Thus, since creation can not be a repeatable and therefore an observable event in present experience, a theory about it is not capable of being tested and cannot be scientific.[4]

Far from regarding this as a damaging admission, however, creationists simply applied the same stipulation—and on much the same grounds—to "evolution science." The agelong formation of the earth's surface, not to mention that of the solar system, and the so-called development of one species into another are, said they, processes "not observable today and so [they] too, [are] outside the realm of empirical science" (CS 5). Thus, theories of origins, even those uttered by a conventional scientist as "science," are in reality metaphysical and not scientific (CE 113). As a consequence, *both* of the models, evolution and creationism, are to be seen as "transcending" science, as being in fact expansions of a religious viewpoint, the one materialistic, humanistic, and atheistic, and the other spiritual, theistic, and Biblical: "Materialism traces all reality and being to the properties and processes of eternal matter. Theism traces all reality and being to infinite-personal Spirit. Neither view can be established by science. They are both belief systems" (CE 12-13). Thus the two models are equally unprovable (CS 4-5), equally "faith," equally "dogma"—and as the Findings of Fact minimally stated this point: "Creation-science is at least as non-religious as evolution science" (36).

These two models, then, are each seen by creationists as expressing an ultimate religious or philosophical viewpoint, the one atheistic and the other Christian. Now, as any student of modern philosophy of religion and philosophy of science knows, this is by no means an unsophisticated nor a totally indefensible position. On certain levels and in certain contexts, there is much truth in it—as most contemporary apologists for religion realize. Many aspects of modern science manifest what can be called a "religious aura," and many spokes-persons for modern science are wont to declare that science has "disposed" of religion and shows religion's purported "knowledge of God" to be illusory, the result of wishful thinking. Thus the creationists are quite right when they maintain that many spokesmen and women within the scientific community in fact espouse and articulate views that are not simply tested conclusions of science but on the contrary represent total views of reality, views that are in their own way "religious positions," ones that can legitimately be called "secular, naturalistic or atheistic."

This religious penumbra surrounding much of modern science, what one might call its "naturalistic aura," means, however, neither that creationism represents a "scientific" alternative to evolution nor that "evolutionary science" is simply a religious rival to belief in creation. On the contrary, the creationist concept of creation, being essentially a *religious* concept, and the scientific interpretation of the development of the physical universe, being essentially a set of *scientific* theories, represent significantly different levels of ideas or forms of conceptuality—and it soon became clear that this was what we would have to establish in court. Perhaps the trickiest intellectual problem of the trial—far more subtle than just proving creation science wrong or even unscientific—would be to distinguish the scientific from the religious elements of *both* creationism and evolutionary science, so that while the truth of this point about the religious dimensions of much science could be admitted, the radical distinction *on the scientific level* between the two could be unequivocally asserted. In any case, it became at once clear to me as I studied the documents that creation science had misunderstood and confused its own religious speech or conceptuality with scientific speech or conceptuality, and that that represented one of the major problems of the case.

Continuing, then, with creation science: If creationism is, as they had just admitted, not a provable hypothesis and not "strictly scientific," on what basis could creationists claim it to be "as scientific as evolution"? If the ultimate source of each is admitted to be religious, or to be in faith (CS 4), what can be meant when the act states that both "shall be limited to scientific evidences for each model and inferences from these scientific evidences"? What, in short, is the understanding of *science* that permeates creation science, the documents representative of it, and Act 590 itself?

The first criterion of science (what makes science *science*), on which all creationist writers agree, is that a scientific model or theory "fits" the "facts of science." A scientific model, say they, "correlates" or "explains" (makes intelligible) the "scientific data" (CF 34, CE 12), "the observed facts of science" (CS 215). Consequently, when two theories are compared, the more valid scientific theory, the better and truer model, would be the one which "fits the facts better" (CS 10), "fits the data best" (OL 1, 47), "explains the facts of science better" (SCC 2). And on this point, "Creationists are convinced that when this procedure is carefully followed, the creation model will always fit the facts as well or better than will the evolution model" (CS 10).

In sum, science is here defined as a body or collection of facts, as composed of what are here termed "facts of science," the "data of science," that is, facts uncovered by scientific inquiry. Science is located in its factual content; inquiries of science are inquiries devoted to the discovery and collection of facts; and scientific knowledge advances when more facts are uncovered and correlated.[5] Scientific theories are, therefore, those explanations that "explain scientific facts best"; a scientific theory becomes *scientific* when it explains and correlates these scientific facts. In principle, then—and this is the crux of this definition—any sort of theory, whatever its logical status, can be called "science" if it explains or makes intelligible these "facts of science."

Reasonably enough, therefore, most of the arguments of the creationists take this path. That is, they rehearse what they regard as the "scientific facts" or the "data of science," and then they argue that the creation model fits these data better or explains them more intelligibly and satisfactorily than does the evolution model. Insofar as they have been successful, they argue that they have justified this model as a "scientific alternative" to evolution: "The essential scientific question related to origins has to do simply with whether the evolution model or the creation model provides the more effective vehicle for correlating and predicting scientific facts of observation" (CS 33). This is the ground on which they can make the surprising claim that the theory of the creation of the world by God out of nothing is a *scientific* theory, namely that it "explains" these "facts of science."

As the last quotation cited indicates, a less frequent, and certainly less persuasive, argument is from what is called prediction. The scientist must, they recognize, be able to predict on the basis of a given model; and the validity of the model will in part depend upon that power of prediction. Innumerable predictions are given in the documents (see especially CS 12-13, 26). As examples of this capacity of the creation model, we may cite the prediction of the two basic laws of physics, the first and second laws of thermodynamics (CS 37ff., SCC 11-13); the prediction that no fossils of transitional "species" or "kinds" will be found (SCC 29), nor that any new kinds will appear (SC 13); the prediction that stars are unchanging (SC 13); and five precise predictions implied by the hypothesis of a worldwide flood, predictions about geological formations (for example, their order of deposition), and so on (SCC 37). Five more predictions are given for the solar system (CS 30).

In every case, so the claim goes, these predictions are more than substantiated by the actual facts of science. Whether or not these examples are what the category of "prediction" in experimental science really means is (to this amateur) dubious. These represent predictions of principles or facts already generally known; genuine *scientific* prediction is always of an experimental result in the future, and thus of a fact or event distinctly not *yet* known. In any case, to creationists this power of prediction represents one aspect of what they term "the scientific evidences for creationism."

Certainly for the creationists the most pervasive and significant "scientific" argument is the argument from design, an argument that has had a long tradition in religious reflection. It is in connection with this argument that they list most of the "scientific data" to which they make appeal, and it is by its means that they show that the "creation explanation" best explains these data or "fits the facts" best. Long called the "teleological argument," this argument asserts that the universe of our experience manifests so many examples of astounding order, and is so suffused with evident purpose, that it requires an intelligible and purposive Creator if we are to give a reasonable or intelligible explanation of it.

Classical examples of this argument can be found in Greek and Roman thought, early and late medieval thought, and in Enlightenment philosophy (especially in Deism, in the writings of Bishop Butler, of Immanuel Kant, and of William Paley). It was sharply criticized by David Hume (*Dialogues on Natural Religion*, 1790), but it reappeared in arguments based on early nineteenth-century science (see *The Bridgewater Treatises*) and, ironically enough, in the late nineteenth and early twentieth centuries (e.g., F. R. Tennant's *Philosophical Theology*) in innumerable proofs of God's existence based on theories of evolutionary development. In all these cases, the argument was regarded as a philosophical and not a scientific argument. To be sure, it used facts uncovered and organized by science as well as data of ordinary or common experience. Nevertheless, since generally its conclusion "leaped" beyond the natural order to the divine source or cause of that order, the argument from design or from order was viewed as an example not of science but of "natural theology"—that is, the attempt to demonstrate the existence of God through the use of speculative reason applied to general experience. It is, therefore, something new that this argument is used in the creationist literature as one of the major evidences of the "scientific" character of the creationist model—that is, as a *scientific* argument for creationism. And clearly this new use is directly dependent on the creationists' understanding of science as a collection of facts, and of scientific theory as an intelligible explanation of these facts. Thus these arguments begin with a careful recitation of selected and relevant "scientific facts" or "scientific data"; and then they seek to demonstrate that their creationist model or explanation, as opposed to the evolutionary one, will interpret or correlate these facts or data better.

Prominent in these data appealed to—data uncovered by recent scientific inquiry in botany, zoology, anatomy, and contemporary ecological studies—are both familiar and unfamiliar instances of natural design, adaptation, and purpose (see CE, chapters 1 and 6, CS 34). Interestingly, these data usually also include the mental, moral, and "spiritual" powers and capacities of human life (CE chapter 5, CS 200-201)—although few laboratory inquiries would regard these as present in their data! To try to explain all these instances of purposive order as the consequence of the blind processes of nature is, say these writers, a hopeless endeavor; the probabilities against such an intricately and mutually adaptive result arising by chance are simply too great (OL 38-39): "Could an ape produce Shakespeare even in an infinite time?"

That these have throughout the Western philosophical tradition been persuasive arguments, there can be little doubt—though the ever-present experience of disorder and of evil tends, as Hume noted, to soften their impact. But that they represent *scientific* arguments with a legitimate place in a particular and specialized scientific discipline is another question, and on this issue there has been, to put it mildly, almost nothing but doubt! Again there appears to be in creation science evidence of confusion as to what science is. In the creationists' description of the concept of creation, we have already seen evidence that religious thinking and scientific thinking have been misunderstood and confused with each other; at the present point, it appears that scientific and theological arguments have been misconstrued and identified with each other. As I continued to read the literature, it became clear that we would have to sort out and distinguish these significantly different, although importantly interrelated, modes of thinking and of knowing.

According to creation science, then, scientific thinking proceeds (1) by organizing, correlating, and explaining what are called scientific facts, scientific evidences, or scientific data into consistent and persuasive theories, and (2) by "predicting" on the basis of these models other things already found out by related branches of scientific inquiry. If this be what science does, it follows that both evolution and creation can be termed "scientific models" concerned with origins and that, so defined, neither model represents "religion." As a consequence, both of these mutually exclusive theories can and should be taught in a public-school science course. This is the intellectual center of the creationist argument.

Although it is not difficult to show that this argument is at many points in error, nevertheless it is clear that it represents a carefully worked out and internally consistent position grounded on a wide familiarity with the results of many areas of modern scientific inquiry. Where, interestingly, it is fatally lacking is in its almost total ignorance of the issues discussed in the philosophy of science, in philosophy itself, and in the philosophy of religion and theology. It is precisely in those reflective disciplines that questions of the nature and methods of science, of the nature of philosophical reflection, of the character of religious thought and language, and the interrelations of these three to one another, are discussed. Who would have thought that *these* esoteric subjects would become relevant to—in fact, the heart of—a public debate?

One of the major claims of creation science, repeated over and over again, is that these two models, evolution and creation, are the *only* two models concerned with origins. Other "religious systems"—for example, those of India, China, and Japan—are, for creationists, merely "esoteric evolutionary systems" (CS 15), presupposing an evolutionary development out of blind matter eternally in motion (CS 15, 16, SC 3, 9, BHA 21, 82). This bizarre and utterly false assertion about the rest of humanity's religions is by no means insignificant to their argument. Certainly, first, it provides a basis for the important if implicit *religious* claim that "we alone speak of and so for God"—all others believe only in matter! To admit that a cosmology is "Biblical" or has its origin there (as is frequently stated in this literature) might seem at first glance to admit the particularity and even partiality of this view: It is only one among the many religions. But if there are only two models—one from God and representing "faith," and the other from unbelief and representing atheism—then there is nothing particularly partial or parochial about the first. It represents the only possible religious position and thus is, whatever anyone says, universal.

Secondly, the claim that these are the only two views of origins provides an obvious rationale for limiting "models" in the public schools to these two. If there are only two views of origins, it is surely both morally just and intellectually respectable to teach them both!

Finally, this claim also has important logical implications for the creationists. If, so they argue, there are only two models, then negative points against one of them immediately become positive arguments for the sole alternative model.[6] It is largely for this reason that creationist documents are filled not only with the positive arguments from design and the predictions mentioned above, but also with detailed critiques of various facets of what they call evolutionary science. Most of these critiques are lifted out of the literature of standard science; that is, they represent criticism that reputable scientists have made of one aspect or another of evolutionary theory. Every challenge within scientific circles to established theories, every accusation of interested "speculative tendencies" in opposing arguments, every heated controversy, even every reticent emphasis on the tentative character of one's own results or theories—in fact, every negative shout or even whisper from within the scientific community about its own hypotheses (and especially about those of rivals!)—is noted and used on the principle that all of these demonstrate "weaknesses" in the structure of evolutionary science, and that such weaknesses function logically as new support for the validity of creation science.

Whether it makes any intellectual sense to borrow and use arguments presupposing for their cogency principles or theorems one is setting out in one's own argument to repudiate is an interesting question. In reading these passages, I found myself picturing the creationist author as heedlessly sawing off the branch he or she was already straddling. In any case, this literature is replete with ad hoc quotes from scientific writings critical of a given theory in astronomy, geology, paleontology, and so on.

We have seen the foundation documents of creation science first of all admitting freely that each model about origins has a religious source and a religious purpose to it, a religious "aura," so to speak—for "no view of origins can be scientifically proved." Secondly, and somewhat paradoxically, we have seen them claiming that this fact does not compromise the scientific character of either model, since arguments "from the facts of science" can in principle be given for the intelligibility and the rationality of both, and (so they assert) more effectively for the creationist model. And it is, so they aver, those scientific facts and those "secular" arguments alone, and not its religious source in Biblical revelation, that will constitute the creation science that is to be taught in the schools.

Outside of school this source in revelation can be admitted, spelled out, and correlated with the scientific evidences and inferences from these evidences that make up creation science. But such a correlation with the Biblical source is not itself to be part of the teaching of this model in courses in science. This is the rationale behind the "two editions" common to this literature, one for school with no Biblical references and the other for general use replete with such references. Since for most Protestant fundamentalists the Bible is the only source of true religious ideas and thus the sacred locus of all true religion, Biblical quotes *represent* or *constitute* religion. If they are omitted, religion is omitted—and the ideas contained in them lose their religious character and can become "science" if they are correlated with "scientific data."[7]

Just as the source of creation science lies in Biblical revelation, so to the creationists the main source of evolutionary theory, and hence its central meaning for life, lies in atheism. To the creationists, therefore, evolution science—and all the astronomical, geological, paleontological, botanical, and biological theorems associated with it—is not merely science, not merely a set of tentative hypotheses dealing with a circumscribed, carefully delimited area or level of experience. It represents, on the contrary, a *total* explanation of the origins of all things, a view of the universe as a whole, a complete account of how all things came to be. Since evolution science is a total explanation of origins in terms of matter in motion, of blind chance, of purposeless flux, it is for them essentially atheistic, godless, and anti-religious in form.

Evolution science, therefore, represents the precise opposite, the adversary or competitor, to belief in divine creation, in the origin of all things by the purposive act of God; the two models are, therefore, mutually exclusive. "The evolution system attempts to explain the origin, development and meaning of all things in terms of natural laws and processes which operate today as they have in the past. No extraneous processes, requiring the special activity of an external agent, or creator, are permitted" (CS 10). "The evolution model presupposes that the universe can be completely explained, at least in principle, in terms of natural laws and processes, as a self-contained system, without the need of external, preternatural intervention" (CS 17). Thus appealing neither to God nor to a creative spiritual principle, evolution represents essentially and necessarily a materialistic, atheistic philosophy or religious viewpoint: "Neither one [evolution or creation science] therefore is a science. They are equally religious; the one is part of the religion of materialism, the other of theism. . . . Materialism traces all reality and being to the properties and processes of eternal matter. Theism traces all reality and being to infinite-personal Spirit. Neither view can be established by science. They are both belief systems" (CE 12-13).

Two points that will be important to our entire discussion should be noted in these quotes and in the view of evolution science as "essentially Godless" that they represent. (1) No distinction is made between the question of *proximate origins* (how did something arise out of something else: e.g., the solar system out of a general gaseous state, life out of non-life, one species out of preceding forms of life?—that is, "scientific" questions), and the question of *ultimate origins* (how did the *whole* system of the universe arise, what is its ultimate or final source, ground or principle?—that is, speculative, philosophical, or religious/theological questions of origins). Because they fail to make this important distinction, creation scientists regard *scientific* theories of origins as in fact *philosophical* or *religious* theories of origins, and therefore as theories which compete with and thereby exclude a theistic position. (2) As a result, no distinction is made between scientific theories on the one hand and philosophical or religious theories on the other, between scientific questions and the sorts of questions religious beliefs seek to answer. All are regarded as theories *on the same level*, dealing with the *same* sorts of truth. Thus again, the two models cancel each other out, the one representing a universal origin in a material, blind, random process void of deity, the other a purposive and meaningful origin through creation by the Christian God.

It is, therefore, no surprise that in their theological works, as opposed to their creation science writings, creationists regard evolution, and all other theories associated with it, as the intellectual source for and justification of everything that is to them evil and destructive in modern society. For them, all that is spiritually healthy and creative has been for a century or more under attack by "that most complex of godless movements spawned by the pervasive and powerful system of evolutionary uniformitarianism" (CS 255; see also BHA 80). "If the system of flood geology can be established on a sound scientific basis . . . then the entire evolutionary cosmology, at least in its present neo-Darwinian form, will collapse. This, in turn, would mean that every anti-Christian system and movement (communism, racism, humanism, libertarianism, behaviorism, and all the rest) would be deprived of their pseudo-intellectual foundation" (CS 252). "It [evolution] has served effectively as the pseudo-scientific basis of atheism, agnosticism, socialism, fascism, and numerous faulty and dangerous philosophies over the past century" (BHA 90).

In the sharpest contrast to this godless model which makes random, blind, amoral material processes ultimate, and which spawns immoral social and moral theories, is the creation model. Although for obvious reasons creationists did not wish—at least in the documents designated for use in school—to emphasize too heavily the religious, Christian, and Biblical dimensions of the creation model, still it is clear throughout that the main *point* of their argument with evolutionary theory is religious—that is, the defense of a "Biblical faith in Jesus as Lord" (see CE 14 and CE 15).

And this is, of course, the source of many of the problems of their case in court: that they too fervently agree—whatever they declare officially—that creation science represents what is to them a crucial religious position. Furthermore, try as they may, they cannot deny or hide this religious center of their model. For in each description of creation science, even as science in the sense already outlined, it is continually admitted that the creation model requires, in fact presupposes, a Creator, a "supernatural" being—that is, one who is omnipotent, eternal, intelligent, personal, and purposive, a being thus capable of creating the world from nothing, of ordering it with design and harmony, and peopling it with beings both material and spiritual (see CS 11, 17, 33, 59, 200-1; SCC 4; CD 11). It is, moreover, further admitted that without such a divine Creator the creation science model is incredible. "Only God can create in this sense [out of nothing], and in all the Bible no other subject appears for the verb 'create' than 'God'" (CS 207); and "Obviously, if no Creator exists, then special creation is incredible" (CS 8). And finally, "If the earth is only thousands of years old [as creationists maintain], intelligent purposeful creation is the only acceptable explanation" (CE 182).

As we pointed out in relation to Act 590, the creation model is defined in that Act as specifying creation out of nothing, separate creation of "kinds" at the beginning, and the recent creation of all things. As these quotes indicate, even the creationists admit that such a model necessitates a supernatural Creator, one who is omnipotent, eternal, intelligent, and purposive, if that model so defined is to make any sense. Clearly, "God," as God has been understood in the Judaic and the Christian traditions, forms the conceptual center in the creation model, for only God can do what this Act specifies was done at creation. To make this point clear, and to argue that such a set of concepts necessarily involves religion,[8] would obviously have to be the continual focus of the ACLU case at Little Rock, I soon realized.

We may conclude this introductory survey of the concepts that constitute creationism, or creation science, by pointing to its essentially paradoxical, in fact, its possibly self-contradictory, character. On the one hand, in order to remain within the terms set by the Constitution, it must represent itself as merely a scientific model. That is, as a theory to be taught in public schools, it must contain no religious teachings or doctrines. On the other hand, the driving motivation impelling its adherents to promote it in the school system was unquestionably religious: to defend what they took to be *the* Christian interpretation of our existence against what they understood to be an atheistic, immoral, un-Christian interpretation. It became clear to us that the intrinsic dilemma our opponents faced was to show the "secularity" of a concept whose significance for them was very unsecular indeed, to treat as merely an objective hypothesis a notion which constituted the center of their own religious existence.

This dilemma was of course by no means inescapable for religious persons. Countless Jews and Christians have believed wholeheartedly in the divine creation and have also accepted, in fact have helped to develop, the methods and conclusions of modern physical science. As the history of Jewish and Christian religious reflections shows, however, such a resolution of this dilemma has entailed not only an abandonment of the literalistic interpretation of Genesis but also a reinterpretation of many of the religious concepts or doctrines associated with the issue of origins, especially the doctrines of creation and the Fall. In effect, modern theology in various ways has created syntheses or unions of Biblical concepts with modern evolutionary science and a modern understanding of history; and in this process it has fashioned one form or another of evolutionary and historical theisms in order to understand in a modern way God's creative activity. And as their presence at the trial indicated, most of the major churches and synagogues have accepted and encouraged such a rethinking of their traditions.

All such forms of reinterpretation, however, the creationists have brusquely dismissed, on Biblical and theological grounds, as false or heretical religion. Such reinterpretations of the origins of things, even in terms of theistic concepts, they said, do not accord with a literal interpretation of Genesis and hence show no respect for Scripture or for the revelation enshrined within it. Further, since evolutionists deny the historicity of Adam, Eve, and their nearly fatal Fall, their views reject what is to the creationists the orthodox and irreformable view that death and suffering have followed as consequences of that historical Fall. To creationists, then, such theologies challenge the entire traditional understanding of Christ's atoning sacrifice redeeming us from the sin, suffering, and death initiated by Adam and Eve at the beginning of history (CS 218-220, 229-230, and BHA 92, 95, 110). In effect, for them the credibility and consistency of the entire Christian faith—and with it every vestige of true religion—depends upon fidelity to the literal interpretation of the creation story. For creationists, therefore, there was no escaping the necessity of challenging the teaching of evolution.

Clearly, in making our case against this Act establishing creationism in public-school instruction, and making our case not only in court but in the wider debate on this issue in the culture as a whole, we faced our own set of tricky conditions. For in our arguments we must show (a) that despite its claims to be science, creation science represents a *religious* set of theories, a *theological* and not a scientific model; thus it contravenes the First Amendment; (b) *that* it was not, and *why* it was not, a model within the limits of scientific inquiry and hence was not a legitimate subject for scientific instruction. But at the same time, if in countering creationism we were to support and not dissolve a positive religious position (and most of the plaintiffs wished to support positively a theistic view), then (c) we must also show that it was possible, both on scientific and on religious grounds, to understand evolution in such a way that that theory neither excluded nor denied the creation of all things by God. And we must in turn (d) understand the divine creation in such a way that it neither excluded nor rejected the theories about the beginning of things basic for all of modern science. Plainly, almost every element of recent reflection in philosophy of science, philosophy of religion, and theology would be needed to make this case accurately and coherently, saturated as it was with these complex theoretical issues. Yet we had to make our case so simple and coherent that it would be persuasive in an American court of law and to the wider audience of the interested public everywhere.

Despite the evident subtlety of the case we had to make, theirs clearly faced much vaster difficulties. Our brief survey of their major texts and of the ideas lying back of Act 590 has shown us four serious weaknesses in their interpretation, not only of religion but surprisingly (since they were trained in science) of science. Since calling attention to these weaknesses was to form the heart of the case we were to present in court, we only summarize them here.

(1) Their insistence that these two views (creation science and evolutionary science) represent the only two views of origins is patently false.

(2) Their understanding of science is in error. This is, as we shall see, a threefold error: (a) they center science in the facts it explains; (b) they, therefore, fail to center science in its *theories* explanatory of the facts; and (c) consequently they overlook the "canons" of science, those rules that specify what sorts of theories are science and what sorts are not.

(3) As a consequence, they fail to understand that scientific explanations have certain intrinsic limits, limits which differentiate them from religious theories or explanations—and hence they mistakenly regard their own religious concepts and theories as alternatives or rivals to scientific ones. They seem to hold that religious belief and scientific theory, insofar as each can be understood to be true, represent precisely the same sort of "truth"—a large confusion indeed.

(4) Finally, they do not understand what the word "observation" means in scientific inquiry and how it is possible to have a legitimate scientific explanation of a series of unique and unrepeatable past events.

In sum, a serious misunderstanding of scientific method and a literalization of religious beliefs have together led to these errors. In turn, these errors have presided over the birth of that changeling, creation science, half-misinterpreted religion and half-misinterpreted science. This changeling could have been born only in a scientific culture where religious understanding takes on the lineaments of scientific truth and where much of science in turn aspires to have the global ultimacy of religion.

After reading these documents, therefore, it was clear to me that creation science did not represent an anachronistic antique, something "out of place" in our modern technological scientific culture, nor did the trial represent a clash between this surviving remnant of traditional religion and the new enlightened forces of science. Rather, creation science represents a quite contemporary, even (alas) "up-to-date," synthesis of both modern science and contemporary religion, a synthesis to which each one had substantially contributed. As a consequence, it is a synthesis that is more a *product* of modern scientific culture than its antagonist. It is, in fact, one particular form—a most uncreative and unfortunate form—of the union of these two permanent and essential aspects of all cultural life, the cognitive and the religious.

Our present political life illustrates another unfortunate but also very modern form of union: that of contemporary right-wing economic and imperialist politics on the one hand, combined with old-time fundamentalist religion on the other, both seemingly intent on forming a "Christian, capitalist America." As fundamentalism has joined with science to form creation science, so the politics of the Moral Majority is dominated by a union of fundamentalism with modern conservative social theory—and, regrettably, neither one seems about to go away.

3
Deposition

As a consequence of my study of creation science documents, by early November I had almost completely
rewritten the original "tentative testimony" I had sent
to Tony. After he had received this revised version,
Tony called, expressed satisfaction with the new text,
and told me I would get from him by the end of the
week my first "witness sheet."

"What's that?" I asked.[1]

"Oh, that's your testimony so far, all the pages you
sent to us, turned around, translated or 'laundered' into
questions and answers: my questions and your
answers."

"What's that for?"

"That's your script at the trial, my friend. First of all,
you're to fill in the answers to some of the questions on
the sheet now left blank. And then you're to study and
restudy what's there till you can spit it right out as if
you'd just thought it up. We'll rewrite it all several times
and go over it together even more—but it's high time
you got started working its details over in your mind."

In the same conversation, he told me that soon he
would visit me to get me ready "to be deposed."

"To be *what*?" I said in mock horror. "You can't do
that, Tony—I've got tenure!"

He laughed and said, "Oh, we know we can't unseat
you academics! No, as a witness you have to give a
deposition to the lawyers for the State, answering any
legitimate questions they may have and giving them
some idea of what your testimony is likely to be. We call
it 'being deposed.'"

"Can't you use the noun form instead?" I asked. "The verb makes me a bit nervous."

"I see your point," said Tony—and gaily continued to speak from then on of "deposing" me. The lingo of lawyers is as permanent and unyielding as that of theologians!

"Can you be deposed the week after next, on Friday or Saturday, November 20 or 21? The Arkansas lawyers are doing some other depositions in the Midwest over that weekend."

Looking over my black book, I registered some hesitation: "No, I'm sorry, Tony—I've promised my wife to go with her to St. Louis for a weekend of Tantric Yoga—and I can't go back on that promise."

"Oh, that's all right," said Tony, "but let's just keep the reason you're going there a bit vague, okay? It'd seem queer in Little Rock for our chief theological witness to be away doing Yoga when the Arkansas lawyers came to call!"

"After this weekend, we'll have some friends in St. Louis," I suggested.

"That's fine," Tony said; "you just went there on a visit."

"Correct," I said.

"Anyway," Tony concluded, "as I said, I have to come to see you next week to get you ready for the deposition, whenever we set it up, and to go over our testimony for the first time together. Can I see you the afternoon of November 17? We'll need about two or three hours for the coaching; then we'll have dinner, and I can get my late plane to Minneapolis."

So we set that date, and Tony promised to arrange another deposition, sometime, somewhere, before the trial in early December.

Sharply at 4:00 on the 17th of November, as he had promised, Tony arrived at my office: wide-brimmed hat, trench coat, leather shoulder bags, three-piece suit, and all. For three hours he coached me, explaining what I was to do, how I was to behave, what it would be like, and, above all, what to avoid—as I sat there staring at him, wide-eyed, fascinated, and awestruck with everything he had to say. Suddenly I realized what a different, what an intensely serious, not to say fateful, world the law, and especially the courtroom, represent. As in standing alone before God (as Sören Kierkegaard reminds us), here everything counts; not even a murmur is inconsequential or trivial; nothing once said can be taken back; and any foolish or careless slip can be fatal. I wondered what I had gotten myself into.

"First of all," said Tony, looking me fixedly in the eye and hitching forward on his chair, "you're under oath, and you're there as an expert. That's the *only* reason you're there. So, to retain your credibility you must speak at all times *as* an expert—whatever you're talking about or saying. This means no guessing, no speculating, no thinking out loud, no wandering verbally, however charmingly or divertingly, off into what *might* be the case. A smart lawyer can close a steel trap on you after you've sailed off somewhere into facts you aren't sure of, or ideas you haven't tested—and even if what you're caught out on is quite unrelated to the subject of your actual testimony, your credibility as an expert is then mush. On the stand, *everything* you say must be the statement of an expert. Don't chatter!

"There's another good rule we tell witnesses: Don't start to answer a question as soon as you've heard it, or even worse, before the questioner has finished. Many professionals, especially professors, are eager to show they're savants, that they know everything—and so they start right out without thinking through their answer, organizing it, or weighing in their minds what they intend to say down the line—for its accuracy, its coherence, and its implications. They get started on a promising line and then suddenly find themselves headed for trouble. The opposing lawyers can smell this coming and will be there waiting for you.

"Above all, don't start before he finishes his question. A crafty lawyer can let you get your answer well started, lead you down a certain road, and then end his question —after you've spouted off a while—with a twist you hadn't expected. And you're left looking over-eager and a bit garrulous, anything but a careful, dependable, formidable expert. And if you start off running before you've thought out your answer, you'll have to stop in the middle, pause, and ho-hum a bit to check on what's going to come out next—and that will make you look as if you didn't know what to say next, what your point was, as if you were a bit lost at sea, even in your own subject. So, remember: Listen carefully; wait till he's quite finished; hold back your reply; and formulate your thoughts—you've got plenty of time—before you begin your answer; and then, once you've got going, speak steadily and deliberately."

("My God," I thought, "how chatty, rushing, foolish, and loose-tongued we all are most of the time. That's good advice anywhere—a kind of Ockham's razor for communication!")

"The worst thing is to speculate, to run on when you're not sure, to try to show you're an expert on the universe. Say only what you know. It's better to say, 'I don't know'—which shows that at least you're clear about your limits and those of your subject—than to try an answer on for size and get shown up as an empty fool. It's even better to say, 'That is not my area of expertise.'

"The other fatal thing to do is to try always to be seen as scrupulous and fair—a vast temptation for academic liberals. Then, when you do give a definitive answer— which is why you're there—you immediately see the other side. With each 'Yes, that is so,' you immediately qualify it with, 'But of course we *can* view it in this way, too.' You can be sure the lawyer will, on cross, throw that 'Yes-but' at you, accompanied and buttressed by some opposing theory on their side that *doesn't* see two sides to that question. Always remember, he can slap you down on cross—and he will—with any evasions,

hedging, stretching the truth, parading of your knowledge—anywhere he can, like a trap, catch you up." And
Tony cracked his hands together.

I thought to myself that after this Tony would be
lucky to get me to open my mouth, either at the deposition or at the trial!

"Now," said Tony, warming up to his task (I thought
"He isn't an athletic coach before a game; he's someone
preparing me for survival on a safari through the jun-
gle!"), "let me tell you about lawyers. At the deposition,
the lawyers always *look* very nice, and they'll be very
polite—oh, so polite. But remember: they're your
adversaries, and they want to get out of you stuff to use
against you on cross. They're going to use any sort of
trick—and they know a pile of them—to lure you, to
catch you out, to milk mistakes out of you. If the question is illegitimate, or difficult, or dangerous, I'll object.
But half of the time the witness gets himself into his
own trouble—and then I have to stop him or warn him
with signals. That's my role. Watch me the way a base
runner watches the coach on third: I'll signal—I'll even
kick you—when you talk too much, when it looks as if
he's leading you off a cliff, when he's about to set a trap.
Don't for God's sake, wonder, 'What's Tony doing
scratching his head that way?' And don't say, when I
stretch and suggest we stop to go the men's room, 'Oh, I
don't need to go yet—I'll finish my answer.' When I do
that, I mean, 'Stop your chatter. I want to talk with you
now!'

"You have to keep your eye on the other lawyer and
be aware of his tricks. He'll have a lot of them, a lot of
different methods and approaches, to lure you into mistakes. First, there may be what in the trade we call the
'Neanderthal Approach.' It's used a lot by New York
lawyers; Arkansas lawyers may be too nice to use this
one. Here, the lawyer sits near you, bumps you now
and then in getting up and down and doesn't apologize,
blows smoke in your face, gets a bit sarcastic and fresh a
couple of times, and raises his eyebrows or chuckles at

your testimony—as if to say, '*This* guy is an expert?' After half an hour of this barbaric treatment, your cool is gone, you're hot and furious, all you're thinking of is what a rude slob this guy is—and soon you're making all kinds of mistakes. I've seen lots of good witnesses, unused to being roughed up this way, become quite unravelled by this treatment.

"Another one—and this is probably what these lawyers from Arkansas will pull—is what we call the 'Aw, Shucks Approach.' Here, the lawyer in all he says and does signals"—and Tony began to act it out—"that he's 'just a little ol' uneducated country boy, Professor. Won't you educate me all about this fascinatin' subject that you-all are an expert in?'"

Tony went on. "Professors, who all dream of educating the whole world, fall for this one every time. They warm up to this poor little uneducated fellow, glow in the wonder of their own learning, their powers of articulation, tell him all they can think of on both sides of the case, all its nuances, its fascinating paradoxes and complexities—and load the smart bastard up with innumerable contradictions to their own testimony! Then later, when the professor gets to court, and on the stand makes one or two direct and unequivocal assertions, on cross this little ol' country boy says to him: 'But Professor, didn't you-all tell me in your deposition that. . . . ?'"

Tony and I both laughed heartily at this picture of the collapse of professorial grandeur—but I must say that I hardly thought this was either the funniest or, unfortunately, the most unlikely scene I had ever imagined! Afterward, at our very pleasant and relaxed dinner together at Orly's in Hyde Park, before Tony went off in a cab to his plane, I noted that Tony, feeling very expansive, did most of the talking, and that I sat there unusually subdued, even apprehensive.

*　　*　　*

-47-

On Tuesday night, the 24th of November, I caught the late Eastern flight to Atlanta and, well after midnight, met Tony at the airport. He smiled, even at that hour, when he saw me; I was, for once, clad in a fairly formal grey suit, tie (which I had borrowed from Joe Price, a graduate student friend), and I was bereft of the ring in my left ear. We spent the night in Atlanta's newest and most elegant hotel, the Omni, and had breakfast in time to be at the local ACLU office—where the deposition was to take place—at 9:30 A.M. Soon the lawyer for the State of Arkansas arrived—a very pleasant, neatly dressed, polite, intelligent young man. After setting in place and then winding up the two court reporters, their silent typewriters, their blank rolls of paper, and their even blander faces, and after completing the formalities of swearing in, we began.[2]

"Good morning, Professor Gilkey. My name is Rick Campbell. I am with the Arkansas Attorney General's office. Today I want to ask you just a few questions [it was to go on for five hours!] about your background, your interest in scientific creationism, and then about your prospective testimony at the trial. I am really here to learn about where you are coming from, and I think you will get a little vision about where I am coming from. If I refer to you as 'Dr. Gilkey' instead of 'Professor Gilkey,' will you please forgive me for that?"

Encouraged by this evident courtesy and this unexpected and welcome recognition of the difference in our perspectives, I smiled and murmured appreciatively that I would certainly forgive him—though I did, I said, prefer to be called "Professor" so as not to be taken for an internist. At once, Tony, looking at me apprehensively, said somewhat sternly, "Speak up, please. The reporter can't record either a nod or a mumble." Recalling Tony's nervousness about "Aw, shucks" lawyers, I unsmiled the smile and snapped to attention. Tony relaxed.

Rick's entrance into our subject matter was interesting and, I suppose, Southern. He asked me about my children and where they had been, or were going, to school. Then: "Do you know if in these classes the subject of origins is taught?"

Tony immediately demanded a definition, but I liked the question immensely and cut in: "I was going to say I could helpfully distinguish two different aspects of the question of origins, and then if, in the light of this distinction, Mr. Campbell will rephrase his question, I will be delighted to answer it."

"All right, sir," said Rick.

"Well, one question of origins we might call the question of *ultimate* origins: Where does it *all* come from; what is the source and ground of the entire universe and of its whole system of causes and effects? This is a question of interest to the speculative philosopher and the theologian, but especially the theologian—and not to the scientist as a scientist.

"The other question is the question of *proximate* origins, the origins of this or that entity or form of life *within* the entire system of nature: the earth, the planets, the rocks, the forms of life—how each of them arose out of something that came before, something already given—how concrete and measurable changes took place and take place *within* the system given and 'already there' of the universe. This is a scientific question and rightly so—and about this the speculative philosopher and the theologian don't have too much on their own to say. Now let's go back; you rephrase your question, and I'll know how to answer it."

"All right, sir. I appreciate that. Is the question of ultimate origins discussed in these schools?"

"No."

"Is there a discussion of origins of this or that form of life?"

"Oh, yes, indeed, yes. I understand from both my son and his teachers that in general-science classes some aspects of geology and evolutionary biology have been mentioned, and in social studies lots about early human life—cave man and woman, and so on—but nothing about the religious questions of ultimate origins."

"Is this the same as the distinction between primary and secondary causes that you wrote about in your book on science?"

"Yes—the two roughly correspond. The question of first causation, of primary causality, is the question of ultimate origins—if you will, of God's causality of the entire system. The question of secondary causality is the question of the finite natural causes that bring things about *within* the system of the universe. It is one of the most fundamental of the hypotheses of modern science that the forms we find around us in the finite world—forms of the stellar system, of the earth, of plant, animal, and human life on the earth—can be understood as arising through *secondary* causes, out of *earlier* forms of stellar gases, of earth, and of life.

"The argument in the case before us, put precisely, comes to whether *species* can be understood as arising from secondary causes, from developments by *natural* causes out of preceding forms of life, or whether they came to be only from the primary causality of God at the beginning of all developments. Theologically, this question is: Does or can the primary causality of God work *through* the secondary causes of nature and history (as I believe it does); or does God's causality work only alone and on its own, and only at the beginning, outside of, and before secondary or natural causes? as apparently the creationists believe.

"Anyway, the question of secondary causes, of the natural or historical causes that bring things into being, is the *scientific* question; the question of primary cause is the *religious* question—and they are quite different questions. One might put it that the scientific community agrees that science is confined to or 'stuck with' secondary causality alone. There is, therefore, a kind of roof over science, a limitation on what science can talk about. The theologians, on the whole, agree that what *they* talk about, insofar as they can, is the infinite, the primary causality of God, the divine activity which brings the entire universe into being, gives it form and purpose, and sustains and directs it over time. The two are clearly interrelated, but they *are* different sorts of questions."

"Would you go on with that and relate it to creation so I can get all this straight?"

"Certainly. Secondary causes are natural or historical, finite causes: water, air, molecules, genes, DNA, factors in the environment, mother and father. Primary causality is the power and wisdom of God. Obviously, in the Christian or Biblical doctrine of creation, where God is said to bring all else into being, there is *only* primary causality, only the power, wisdom, and activity of God. No other causes, no 'secular' or secondary causes, are at work there. For it is precisely they which are brought into existence or produced 'out of nothing.' That 'out of nothing' *means* that nothing else, no secondary cause, was there but God, that *all* things other than God were in this act produced. So science can't deal with that question. To speak somewhat carelessly, science can't operate until the system of secondary causes appears and gets itself going; and it can only explore the interrelations of causes and effects, the sequences of events, on that finite level of natural and historical influences. This is why science is testable and relatively certain; but also it is the basis for the sharp limitation of science—for its inability to deal with certain important questions."

"Dr. Gilkey—excuse me, Professor Gilkey—do you think that science is a threat to Christianity?"

"That is, like all interesting questions, a complicated one, one deserving both a 'Yes' and a 'No' answer. So again, let's distinguish a bit what we are talking about. Frequently in the past, science has, for many Christians, posed a threat to what they felt to be true Christianity. The Catholic church felt this to be true with Copernicus and Galileo; many Christians felt this with the universe of Newtonian physics, a universe run by necessary laws and thus one in which miracles seemed out of place. After 1790, many Protestants felt this when geology began to uncover a very ancient earth; many felt this with Darwin—and so on. In each case, Christian faith had been identified with a certain understanding of secondary causes, a certain interpretation of astronomy, of natural laws, of geology, of biology; thus the development of new scientific theories in these fields threatened a Christianity so defined. It was what we might call the 'Biblical astronomy, geology, and biology'—or what were taken to be that—which was threatened.

"None of these new theories touched, or challenged, the deeper religious understanding of God as primary cause working through second causes, however we may come to understand the latter through scientific inquiry. So understood, science is no threat to Christianity—but then religious theory is limited to *its* proper arena, namely, to talking about God in relation to nature, and not about the sequences of natural causes in and of themselves. There is theological discourse about God, but there is no theological astronomy, physics, geology, or biology.

"Science can also be a threat to Christianity when science, in turn, oversteps its limits; when it claims, or seems to promise, to answer all questions, even those of ultimate origins; and when it claims to resolve all our human problems—as it has done often in the last two hundred years. Then the advancing truths of science are seen as dissipating or dissolving religious ideas or beliefs as light chases away darkness; scientific authority, therefore, replaces religious beliefs, which are seen to represent anyway only pre-science, the ignorant speculations of men and women prior to science.

"Many scientists hold this view: that religion gives erroneous theories about secondary causality, about when and how it all began, and these errors science has now shown up. But that is because they see science as the only way to truth of *any* sort, scientific kinds of truth as the *only* kind, and thus religion as providing only a poor edition of that same sort of truth. They do not see science as perhaps our most reliable, and yet also a definitely circumscribed, way of knowing the physical world around us, and religion as providing a different level of understanding. If, then, the kinds of truth in science and in religion are distinguished, there is essentially no threat of religion to science or of science to religion."

"Dr. Gilkey, in some of your writings the phrase 'theological liberal' has come up. Are you a theological liberal?"

"I should say not. This is, after all, the twentieth century!"

"Excuse me, sir. Would you please explain that?"

"That *was* a misleading answer! What has been called Liberalism in theology began when, toward the end of the eighteenth and in the early nineteenth centuries, educated Christians found themselves living in a new physical and historical world, a natural world reshaped by the recent developments of science: of physics, astronomy, and later, geology, and a historical world beginning to be revised and extended backward by the new investigations of the distant human past. For example, no extinct species were known until about 1800, and ancient Egypt, especially its incredible age, was not guessed until Napoleon's time.

"This new world contradicted, or radically refashioned, the older picture of the physical universe and its recent past, as well as the older understanding of the beginnings of human history. We had inherited these views of the past from earlier cultural periods, in fact, from the Greco-Roman world and in part from the Biblical writings. These older views had pictured the universe as having recently come into being (six to seven thousand years before); it was, since its beginning, complete with all its present kinds of plants and animals and replete with the familiar hills and valleys of England, France, Germany, and the colonies. And it saw history as beginning simply with the Biblical stories in Genesis, continuing through the patriarchs, Moses, Joshua, the kings, the exile, and then on into the periods of the Greeks and Romans.

"Now, since the liberals accepted the new and radically different understanding of the physical and historical worlds developed by the new sciences and history, and yet since they knew that, despite these changes, their Christian faith remained *true*, they were intent on harmonizing these two, to *reinterpret* their doctrines or beliefs in the light of this new vision of secondary causes given them by science and by history. Many Jews, I might add, similarly reinterpreted historic Judaism into what is called Reformed Judaism. These were the 'liberals,' and I believe they were right in this effort: If we live in the world of modern science, fly in its planes and go to its surgeons, as we do, then we already *believe* in large part in its truths. And we mustn't kid ourselves that we do not so believe, for then we are not at all honest, even to ourselves.

"Thus in order to be a unity in ourselves, and in order to be honest, we have to understand that world in the light of our religious beliefs, and our religious beliefs in the light of that world. This is what theology always has done since the first centuries; this is what the liberals did—and what we must do in each age. The same, incidentally, is true of theories of democracy, of the common law, of a sociological or psychological tradition, and so on. They, too, must reinterpret their inherited tradition in the light of changes in their common experience and changes in their interpretations of nature, history, and the human self."

"Why, then, did you say you are *not* a liberal?"

"It has seemed to many in the twentieth century that in accommodating Christian thought to the scientific and historical understandings of the eighteenth and nineteenth centuries, the older liberals took over too much of that early modern culture, especially its optimism. I mean by that its sense of the perfectibility of human beings and of history, its confidence that each advance in science and technology, and in economics and political organization, represented a step in a steady march of humanity to a better world and ultimately toward a Utopian world. In effect, the liberals took over the 'religious' optimism of the modern world —its belief in itself and in progress—and they built their understanding of Christianity and of Judaism around that optimism.

"To many in our day, however, the twentieth century has shown us that this faith in historical progress— closer, let us say, to a real *faith* than to a scientific truth —was in large part error, a poor form of 'faith,' even of 'religion,' you might say. And thus they have rejected the liberal acceptance of this faith of the modern world. To them the classical Biblical and Christian understanding of human beings as in deep trouble, as characterized both by estrangement and by creativity—in other words, the sense of the ambiguity of history as well as its creativity—was closer to the real truth as we now see it than the liberal optimism had been.

"Thus they have distinguished themselves from the liberals, and they have sought again to reinterpret the Biblical and Christian symbols—only this time emphasizing Fall as well as creation, God's judgment as well as God's love, and divine revelation and incarnation as well as human wisdom, goodness, and growth. What they shared with the liberals was the effort to understand these traditional religious symbols in terms of the new world of science and of historical understanding.

"This was the group that interested me when I was a bit younger: They were then called 'neo-orthodox' or 'dialectical theologies'—not orthodox but *neo-*, and saying 'No' as well as 'Yes' to our modern experience of historical life. I think they were right about the earlier liberals; and thus they brought a needed sense of the tragic element of human life back into theology, a sense that modern experience and contemporary history could be as filled with sin and destruction as the experience in history of any other time had been, and thus that the fundamental message of Christian faith concerned with sin and death, with the divine judgment and the divine grace, is as relevant now in our modern age as it ever had been.

"So I *am* a liberal in agreeing we must rethink our religious symbols in terms of all we now know from science and history about secondary causes, and *not* a liberal in that I think the Biblical vision of our origin, of our troubles, and of our destiny is truer than the modern progressivist *or* the modern pessimistic visions, the naturalist or the humanist visions."

"This has meant—as I gather from your writings—a different view of *revelation* and a different understanding of *creation* than the orthodox views. Is this right? Can you explain these differences and tell me your personal views of these subjects?"

"All right. This is complicated, mind you. But I will try. The orthodox Christian (Catholic and Protestant) view always regarded revelation as centrally pointing (1) to God's Word to Israel through Moses and the prophets, and (2) to the event, the coming, life, death, and resurrection of Jesus who is the Christ. Here, first to Israel and then to the Gentiles, God had 'revealed himself.' God had manifested himself in ways that revealed the divine promises, purposes, will, and the destiny for men and women. Along with this basic meaning of revelation was another meaning: (3) God's *dictation* (and that's frequently their word) of the words of the Scriptures which reported, witnessed to, and interpreted these events. Thus the book itself, the Bible made up of Old and New Testaments, was a part or a product of revelation; and each word, sentence, and proposition in that volume was held to be infallible, literally and eternally true—much as conservative Catholics have believed that each official statement of the pope is infallibly true.

"Now, what has happened in nineteenth- and twentieth-century theology—due in part to the forces of science and historical studies already mentioned—has been that this latter part of the idea of revelation has been reinterpreted. Revelation still refers to the special revealing and healing presence of God in Hebrew life and in the person and destiny of Jesus; but the witness to it, in the prophetic and other Hebrew writings, and in the apostolic preaching and in their writing (i.e., in the Old and New Testaments), while certainly inspired, is regarded nevertheless as a *human* witness, a human witness to the decisive presence and activity of God in that sequence of special events. Thus the scriptural writings are viewed as being shaped (as on closer inspection they seem to be) by their cultural situation, the 'scientific,' the 'historical,' and the 'psychological' understandings of their time. Or, one could say, they reflect the astronomy, the view of the earth, the biology, botany, and history of the historical period in which they were written. Nevertheless, through that limited cultural vision, these writings witness and continue to witness, witness to *us*, to what transcends culture: the presence, the power, and the purposes of God

"It is, therefore, appropriate for us to reinterpret that witness into the terms of our culture, our science, our understandings of nature, history and human being. As many have said, this means that the words of the Bible are not literally God's words but human words; however, the Bible contains the Word of God *through* its own human words, for that human witness points to and defines the revelation of God in these events. Again one sees the conviction that God works *through* human writing, witness, and speaking—and this is the way God manifests and reveals himself to us."

"Thank you. And how do you understand creation if it is not to be understood as an act six thousand years ago, an act stretched out over six days of special divine activity?"

"Let me say first that from the very beginning, it was clear that the literal interpretation—that creation took place over six days of time—had to be reinterpreted. As St. Augustine realized in roughly 400, if at creation God was bringing time and space into being, the act of the creation *of* time could not be *in* time, and *of* space could not be *in* space. Thus he reasoned that the divine creative act must transcend time—that is, be at a 'moment' that 'precedes' every moment—for it is the act in which all moments come into being.

"In other words, from almost the start of Christianity, it was seen that a too-literalistic interpretation of Genesis distorted that act of creation and reduced the character of God, making that act one *within* the universe's space and time and not *of* that entire universe, and making God merely a being in the universe's space and time and not the Lord over both. The answer to the question of ultimate origins cannot be put into precisely the same sort of language and concepts as an answer to the question of proximate origins; this is the theological (not the scientific) error of the creationists.

"As to the meaning of the belief in creation—or, as I prefer to put it, the *symbol* of creation—this is the most fundamental conviction we can have about God, about ourselves, and about the universe and history in which we find ourselves. Creation as a religious symbol does not tell us matters of factual information: how old the world is, by what natural processes it came to be, what sorts of causes made this or that arise—and so on. What it *does* manifest to us is the ultimate divine source and ground of the world around us and of ourselves: that however it may have come to be, the universe is of God and not merely of blind chance; that it has a meaning and a purpose and is not void of either.

"Creation does not tell us the process by which *we* came to be, either as a race out of other forms of life or as individuals out of mother and father and their parents. It opens up to us that *we*, too, are here because of the power and the purpose of God, that we are, therefore, responsible, personal, as well as physical organic beings —responsible to one another and to that purpose for which we are created. The symbol of creation, because it resonates with and manifests the power and the goodness of God, stresses also the reality, the goodness, and possibility of meaning and value of our existence and of the existence of the universe and of the history in which we live.

"Correspondingly, faith in creation represents a fundamental trust in life itself, a confidence in a continuing and pervasive meaning and value to life, however tragic a given moment may be. The symbol of creation refers to the divine activity in continually bringing the world and ourselves into being, continually holding it there, and giving it powers, order, and potential purpose. Creation does *not* refer to *our* attitude of trust; it refers to God's activity; thus it evokes that trust. As a symbol expressing God's creation of our world, it is not so much the expression of our faith in life as the cause or ground of that faith.

"Furthermore, this positive attitude toward the world evoked by the symbol of creation has been by no means unimportant; in fact, it has been more important than any particular scientific information about the age or the extent of the world. On it has been based most of the confidence in order, the hope for meaning, and the energy that have characterized our Western cultural life. These have been the presuppositions of science and of the scientific community itself, and crucial for the appearance of each. Despite the fact that it is not itself scientific, this religious symbol is loaded with meaning, and with meaning for the development and continuation of science."

"Could you say something about how such an understanding of the symbol of creation is different from science, or is not science?"

"Certainly. In the first place, the model of creation contains God as the sole reality, the sole actor—only God's power and purposes are referred to. This is, as we said, because all other actors or powers are by this act said to be produced or brought into being. Thus here a supernatural force or power is referred to—and no scientific hypothesis or model can refer to such a factor.

"Secondly, both of the common analogies of coming to be that are found in ordinary experience are here negated: (1) coming to be by birth (as with a mother and her children), and (2) coming to be by 'making' (as with a carpenter and a cabinet). In the first, if it were applied to the divine creation of ourselves, we would be 'godlets' or divine offspring of God, and not creatures of God—which the Jewish, the Christian, and the Moslem traditions deny. And in the second, the material out of which the world is made would not be created by God (for no carpenter creates his wood)—which again these traditions deny. Thus all direct analogies from experience, all ordinary sequences of secondary causes, are here transcended, even negated, in the religious symbol expressing the origin in God of that whole experience and that whole system of causes. This *cannot* be a scientific model.

"Thirdly, since this event transcends all ordinary events—being that event from which all other events arise—it cannot in principle be controlled, repeated, or tested in any mode of human experience, nor can its constituent parts. This untestability is different in kind from that of astronomy, geology, or biological science. In their early development, the solar system, the earth, and present forms of life represent series of events that cannot now be repeated; but those processes follow from and illustrate principles of laws present and at work now in our world, and those principles and laws *can* be illustrated in present experience. The *origin* of those principles and laws, of the whole system which they govern, represents something qualitatively different, qualitatively transcendent—and thus again is beyond science.

-60-

"There is, therefore, a qualitative difference and a difference in language between a *scientific* interpretation of *proximate* origins and a *religious* interpretation of *ultimate* origins, between a scientific model and a religious symbol."

Since we had gone already for two hours, Tony suggested that we break for lunch and order in some Chinese food from a nearby restaurant. When we were washing up, Tony said he figured things were going along okay, that no fatal slips had been made. As he reminded me, "At the deposing, the point is not to win the case—after all, the judge is not here—but to avoid losing it!" Then he went on, "I must tell you that when Father Vawter [the scholar of Genesis] was being deposed in Chicago, the court reporter suddenly stopped him, after a long exposition of the meaning of Genesis, and said, 'Father, I must break in and tell you (I am a Catholic) that for goodness knows how long I have been bothered by some of these problems of interpreting the Book of Genesis. What you have just been saying has helped me immensely, and I want to thank you.' That," said Tony, "is the first time I have ever known of a legal reporter actually listening to what it was he or she was recording."

Recalling the utterly blank looks on our two reporters as I droned on, I prophesied somewhat ruefully that in the present case we would return to normal practice.

When we began again, Campbell veered off on quite another tack: "Professor Gilkey, do you think that alternative views should be taught in schools—and, if you do, why not alternative views of creation?"

"Of course alternative views in a discipline should be taught. If we are studying evolutionary biology, then alternative explanations of evolution in biology should be studied; if we are studying religious views of creation, then alternative religious beliefs and myths— Christian, Jewish, Hindu, Buddhist, American Indian views, and, if possible, both literalistic and liberal forms of each—should be discussed. It is important, however, that these be genuinely *alternatives* to one another—that is, comparable views. It is not useful, but confusing, to teach a Freudian interpretation of personality *as an alternative* to an interpretation in biochemistry; they represent different disciplines and so both can be true, and they do not exclude each other.

"In a somewhat similar manner, evolution and creation, as I understand the latter, are not alternatives, and so it is misleading and a misinterpretation of both to state that they are alternative views, or that they exclude each other. Further, alternatives should be taught if *all* the alternatives are mentioned; if they are not, and only two are brought up, that is itself misleading since it omits mention of other possible views of the subject. Not everything can, of course, be covered; but it should be clear that the two chosen are *not* all there are. On both these counts—that these two are not true alternatives, and that it is stated that these are the *only* two— Act 590 falsifies the situation and is misleading."

"Is it possible for creation science to be taught in school, in your view?"

"Of course, if it appears in the right place and under the right conditions. That place, in my view, is not in a class in science. This is, as I have said, a religious theory at base; it raises problems in religious reflection, in philosophy of religion, theology, and possibly philosophy of science. A teacher of science is ordinarily not trained to deal with these questions, namely, the relation of this view to scientific inquiry, to other religious views, to philosophy, and, above all, to Genesis and to Christian or Jewish theology.

"It should appear where it belongs, in a course on comparative world views or comparative religious views, along with other alternative religious views of ultimate origins: liberal Christian, Jewish, Islamic, Hindu, and so on. There, it can be discussed in its proper context, among *its* alternatives, in relation to its real sources in Scripture and in the Christian theological tradition. And then, quite possibly, each of these views from different religions could be compared with current scientific views and each could, if one wished, be 'tested' with regard to its correlation with scientific theories and scientific data. This would be a grand course in any good high school."

"Dr. Gilkey, tell me, if one is a believer in creation, must one, as a Christian, automatically be opposed to non-creation?"

Siano: "I object; the question is obscure and therefore impossible to answer. What on earth is 'non-creation,' and how can anyone be opposed to it? I will ask you to rephrase it."

Campbell (to me): "Do you understand the question?"

"I would be happy if you would rephrase it, though I can probably put it together into a question I can answer. I will try the question on, if I may, by first unpacking the word 'opposed' that you were using. Historically, what we can call the 'heavy' meaning of 'opposed' was: If you have a different view from ours, then we will cut off your head, burn you at the stake, put you in jail, or, at the very least, prevent you from speaking your mind or publishing your opinions. An alternative view in religion meant one could no longer remain a citizen of the community, or even a resident of the earth! Our joint tradition, Mr. Campbell—the Baptist—said this was not right; and from its view, and from other views, the separation of Church and State, the freeing of theological disagreements from civil prosecution, resulted.

"If one does not mean this heavy meaning of 'opposed,' then, one can mean 'intellectual opposition,' disagreement with another view in argument or debate while retaining personal charity and tolerance, and in the public sphere, the right to free expression. Such intellectual opposition, such fair and open argument, is, it seems to me, essential and healthy—and I do it all the time. To hold to and affirm one's convictions does not mean either to hate those who disagree or to try to silence them. To confuse these two has been the great sin, and tragedy, of Christian history; we have finally learned to honor and even to love those with whom we disagree—let us not unlearn it!—though I will say that with some notable exceptions, the arenas where this problem currently arises with really explosive force are in the political and economic, and not in the religious, realms."

"Is evolution an inherently impersonal concept?"

"This is a complicated matter. As a theory in science —and insofar as it remains that—evolution can only ask questions about preceding natural causes, the facts in the surrounding and preceding world, and in the forms of life themselves, that brought about changes in these forms. These would possibly be environmental factors, genetic factors, and so on—all of them secondary causes. In this sense, evolutionary theory is secular by definition, *a priori*, so to say, because, like medicine, history, or law, it can inquire only into the finite causes that brought something about. As I've said, on this level all scientific models, hypotheses, or theories are secular (and, as I've also said, this does not mean that the divine power is not at work there).

"Now, many people can take, and do take, this scientific account of origins through the long chain of natural causes as a *total* explanation of how things arose. Then the statements 'Things arise by natural causes' and 'We will try to trace these kinds of causes back' cease to be *rules* of scientific method, a *program* in inquiry (as they are in science itself), and change into a form of *metaphysical* understanding: 'All arises from natural process or from Nature,' which is an entirely different view. Here scientific method has been expanded in two directions: (1) scientific inquiry has become the *sole* relevant form of question and provides the *sole* legitimate answer to the questions 'What is real?' and 'How did things come to be?' As a result, (2) scientific conclusions are expanded into a naturalistic view of reality as a whole which finds the source and ground of present existence, and of our human existence, exclusively and entirely in deterministic and blind natural processes. This view is inherently anti-religious, if by the latter you mean anti-theistic; there is no place in it, obviously, for any sort of deity or divine ground.

"On the other hand, this view can be said to be itself 'religious,' or at least 'philosophical' (I would prefer to call it 'religious'), in the sense that it seeks to give a total explanation for all of reality, for our own place within reality; thus it provides the basis for our own self-understanding as humans of our possibilities and tasks in life. Here science has expanded from a method of inquiry into a full-scale philosophical/religious viewpoint and has produced in the process a religious myth (the naturalistic myth) among other religious myths. This is not at all reprehensible or evil of it (except as it pretends that it has not done this); nor is it surprising in a scientific culture. As a fishing culture produces religious myths built on the experiences associated with fishing, so a scientific culture produces myths based on the experience of and confidence in scientific inquiry. But despite the religious character of these ultimate or global myths in each case, fishing and science are, on their own and by themselves, secular activities."

"Is scientific theory generally set within a framework of presuppositions? If so, can a theory genuinely be falsified—that is, shown to be not true?"

I started to answer, but Tony immediately objected: "How is the word 'presupposition' to be defined in this context?" He went on to argue that I was not a scientific expert prepared to answer questions about the logic of science, and, further, had I not been asked a hypothetical question? And so on.

A long discussion ensued. Finally, seeing that Campbell had raised an interesting as well as important point, I offered (despite Tony's scowl) to answer, provided I could make some distinctions that seemed to me to clarify the essential points.

"Let me begin by saying that there is no contradiction, as Mr. Campbell has implied there is, between presuppositions and falsification, between already having theories and showing something else to be false. Clearly, he has in mind the apparent dilemma, contradiction, or paradox that, if the process of falsification *itself* depends upon presuppositions which can be questioned, then any specific falsification in turn depends upon assertions that are dubious—and so the falsification is itself questionable. This is an important point, because if this critique is valid, if there is an opposition between having presuppositions and being able to prove something false, then science itself—and so even creation science as it views itself—is impossible or self-contradictory.

"Let us begin by distinguishing two different sorts of presuppositions for the procedures of science. First, there are what we might call the metaphysical/epistemological beliefs that make science possible —that is, that make it a sensible or reasonable enterprise for humans to carry on. Without them, science as we know it would not have been something that historically could have arisen, nor would it be a sensible thing to be doing now.

"First, as a basis for the empirical side of science is the conviction—hard to establish but widely held—that the material reality we encounter through our senses is both real and intelligible or orderly; thus sensory experience provides the starting place for real knowledge. If experience represents to us a veil of illusion, empirical knowledge would not be worth much; no knowing would be gained by tracing out the sequences or contours of our experience of the material world around us. And, believe it or not, some cultures have thought it was precisely that.

"Secondly, there is the 'rational' presupposition that thinking is relevant to reality, that the structures of mind (our logical sequences) are in some way related to the structures of what we are seeking to know. Without this, the confidence in inquiry would flag. Thus the empirical and the rational components of scientific method presuppose certain metaphysical and epistemological assumptions (assumptions about what's real and how we can know it) that science depends on but cannot, for the same reason, itself prove by its own methods.

"Thirdly, there is the confidence that similar or identical material things remain steady over time and space —an obvious assumption, to be sure, but, considering the variety of cultures, not all *that* obvious. Because of this, measurements at the end of an experiment are relevant to those made at its beginning, and the yardstick I use today, or in Chicago, is relevant to making the same measurements in New York next week.

"Finally, one must add the assumptions that human subjects (scientists) have a similar set of experiencing and thinking processes, that communication among them is real, that arguments hold water, that minds can be persuaded by evidence of new truth, that our conviction that something is demonstrated is not a conviction determined only by physical causes but justified by logical grounds, and finally that truth is important.

"A host of these sorts of assumptions are presupposed for *any* process of falsification to take place. One could say: *If* we agree on all these things, *then* we can falsify by experiment. Needless to say, if someone said, 'Oh, no, the experiment did not work because the magic those "characters" wielded at Yale has transformed all our instruments and our data,' no falsification in the ordinary sense could be possible or make sense. Or if we agreed that sense experience was *maya* or illusion, then any falsification or verification of our hypothesis would take a very different form from what it does in laboratory experiments, possibly by checking it with experience at a 'higher level of consciousness.' In this sense, then, certain presuppositions make our modes of falsification possible or sensible. Granted other presuppositions, what we presently do to check out a statement would make no sense at all.

"These sorts of presuppositions—and I have loosely called them metaphysical/epistemological—are cultural and historical in form. That is, they have been and still are assumptions widely pervasive in modern culture; thus it is no accident that science has arisen in *this* culture. Ultimately, their roots trace back—as do any such general assumptions or beliefs—far beyond modern culture, in fact all the way to the Greek and to the Biblical cultures out of which the West was formed. Whether another cultural parentage could have formed a culture pervaded by these presuppositions, or whether empirical science could have arisen out of quite other presuppositions, are questions too speculative to settle easily. Anyway, when anyone from another cultural matrix 'falsifies' in our modern sense— and many do—this means that they have not only donned a Western white coat and bow tie, but also that they have, in one fashion or another, accepted these presuppositions as their own.

"One could perhaps say that it is one of the most important tasks of metaphysics, as done by a philosopher or a philosophical theologian, to uncover, explicate, interpret, criticize, and unify these most general presuppositions of all the special disciplines of a culture: the assumptions that lie back of its sciences, its art, its morals and customs—and its religion.[3] The reason this task is important is not only that it is interesting; it is important also because those sorts of presuppositions are usually unconscious, unarticulated, and consequently uncriticized. We are not aware we hold them until another viewpoint appears, and then we suddenly see that the 'world' we took for granted is not the objective world at all but our particular view of it.

"The second sort of presuppositions (in addition to the metaphysical/epistemological) is methodological—

that is, these presuppositions are the accepted 'rules of procedure' or 'rules of the road' of practicing sciences, its 'canons.' These are, plainly, dependent on the above sort. They are probably also more explicit in the minds of scientists as they proceed with their work—though they are by no means necessarily thought about, explicitly held, *as* they work. In fact, as we have noted—and as this trial makes plain—these rules of procedure are frequently not at all known, have never been reflected on, by many leading scientists. The actual consciousness of the scientist is, therefore, irrelevant here. When a scientist says, 'I have no need of these presuppositions in the laboratory; therefore they do not exist,' he or she is talking nonsense.

"Generally, only a few extremely reflective persons are aware of the assumptions on which a special society depends and by which it works. Most scientists absorb these in their training; gradually they practice *with* them rather than think *about* them—unless once in a while they break off and ask 'What are we *doing* in scientific method, and why?' That is precisely why they are called *pre*suppositions, thoughts or theories not thought but thought *with*, in whatever we do. These rules of procedure are the main subject matter not of science but of *philosophy* of *science*. Now clearly, these do not cancel out or nullify falsification, since they set the rules by which falsification is accomplished in modern empirical science."

"Last question. Is truth a legitimate goal of science?"

At this, Tony exploded in frustrated expostulation: "I don't know what sort of an opinion question *that* is. You're miles outside the witness's expertise. What's more, it's getting late, our plane goes soon, and it's the day before Thanksgiving. And you ask *that* sort of question?!"

"But, Mr. Siano, the witness has written volumes and volumes [a slight exaggeration!] on this theme!"

"I don't care what the witness has or has not written. But I will not direct the witness not to answer."

"I will be glad to take a shot at it. First of all, let us be clear: No good scientist thinks that he or she is going to arrive at *the* truth. In fact, the community of science, over the course of history, has effectively rearranged or reshaped for most of us the understanding of truth. This has been one of its most important creative achievements in Western culture as a whole: to make us realize that *any* human truth is always an *approximation* of the truth[4]—an approximation to be subsequently challenged, criticized, refashioned, and finally replaced.

"This understanding of all expressions of truth as human and historical—and of *this* time and place—and not as absolute, unchanging, and final, has had slow but gradual and cumulative effect on the religious communities of our culture. We now know that our theologies are neither absolute nor final, and that every expression of a doctrine is historically related to the community that expresses it and to the epoch in which it appears. It, too, is an approximation to the truth. I wish this sense had penetrated also into some of the social sciences, especially politics, economics, and psychology—but that is another matter.

"On the other hand, there is, I believe, nothing to science (as there is nothing to religion) if it is *not* directed at an approximation to the truth. Science is a cognitive endeavor; its whole meaning rests on its fidelity—and that 'moral' word is absolutely crucial—to the task of uncovering the truth, or approximating to that uncovering. No other consideration or aim can here take predominance, or science disappears without a trace. When we find a genuine scientist, this is all he or she really cares about. If scientists' efforts are directed instead at making money, becoming famous, winning a prize, or gaining power, then you can forget science—it will not appear, or, if it does, it will disappear soon enough. I would say the same about the legal profession. Without some concern for justice, the law will change its character radically—and cease to be *law*. This sounds sentimental, but it is true. If everyone in the court can be bought, the law is a facade.

"I merely want to insist that science is not the only way to get at the truth, that science does not, in that sense, possess *the* truth or the *sole* access to it. But this is the basic *eros* or aim of science. *Eros* is the only word to use: 'Desire' is not right, nor is 'motivation.' It is *eros*: the experience of being drawn by the truth to the truth, gathered in by it; truth here is an ultimate concern because of which all else is to me preliminary and expendable.

"A scientist who does not have an ultimate concern for the truth is not a scientist. Such 'scientists' will (if tempted enough, and those temptations arise all over the place and always will do so) fiddle with the evidence, and then you don't have science.[5] This *eros* is specifically enacted by commitment to the canons of the scientific community, by respect for its authorities and judgments, and by adherence to its norms and goals. It is a communal or shared ultimate concern, structured by common symbols and standards, and enacted by each in the name of all—it has, as you see, a 'religious' character, though I will not here stress that point. But the sacrality of truth, despite its continuing relativity, its approximate character, is the essence of science."

We then went over all the documents I had brought with me as materials for my testimony: creationist documents, anti-creationist articles and tracts, letters—and finally my witness sheet. The former were handed over to the opposing lawyers for copying. The latter Tony carefully excluded and kept in our hands as a "privileged document" because it was "part of the lawyer's working papers," or "trial preparation materials," and thus did not need to be shown to the opposition.

With that, we closed the deposition at 2:45, got our coats, and flagged a cab. Along with Tony and me in the cab were three others who had also just completed a deposition in the offices of the ACLU. I assumed that they were a part of the Skadden team, and so I started to talk with an interesting-looking Italian geologist who sat next to me about how it had gone. I had hardly gotten two sentences out when Tony said firmly, "Langdon, please note that Arkansas hat placed between me and the cab driver; he's friendly enough, but he's an adversary, and he's craning to hear everything you say." I shut up in a hurry!

When I asked Tony later whether the Italian geologist next to me would appear as a witness of ours in Arkansas, he said, no. "He was just there to help with a deposition. We were taking a deposition of one of their scientific witnesses."

"How could he help?" I said.

"Oh, that's part of our game plan," said Tony. "Whenever we depose a witness of theirs who's a scientist, we ask a couple of well-known scientists in their own field to join us at the deposition. They don't ask questions, of course; the lawyer does that. All they do is look sharply at the witness every time he starts to speak, take careful notes, shake their heads grimly at his answers, whisper at length in the ear of the lawyer, and then nod their heads. This makes the witness nervous enough to make mistakes—I've heard them say they don't enjoy these depositions at all!"

My opinion of the formidable character of Skadden, Arps, Slate, Maegher, and Flom was rising. It overflowed later when Tony, in another expansive mood, told me that the Skadden offices ran two full shifts, the second one from 7 P.M. until 1 A.M. every night. He said that when they had a tough case, they liked to take the adversary lawyers out to dinner and then, along about 11 P.M., say, "Oh, I hope you don't mind if we stop by the office—I left a document there I should look at tonight." They proceed to the company offices in a darkened building, their innocent companion expecting to enter an impressive but unlit empty space. When the door is opened, the whole office is brilliantly lit, teeming with workers, all in high gear. Tony assured me that every time this happened, it had its effect! I remember thinking: How could we at the Divinity School try out this one on Yale and Harvard?

4
The Trial:
Religious and Historical
Backgrounds

After the deposition in Atlanta on November 17, a number of things still had to be done before the trial, set for the first week in December. The witness sheet had to be carefully reworked twice more in the light of the long discussions at the deposition and still more reading of creationist documents. And Tony came once more to Chicago, this time to coach me on the nature of courtroom witness, as opposed to depositions.

"In the courtroom," he said, "the stakes are increased, the psychological ante is vastly raised, and so the whole atmosphere is much less relaxed." (In some fear and trembling, I recalled courtroom scenes from Perry Mason in which that diabolically clever cross-examiner dismembered an expert witness, piece by piece.) "Be careful *not* to pause too much and hesitate; a steady, deliberate, slow rate of speaking is much to be preferred. Give a full answer; that's what you're there for. Start with the main point, the center, and then gradually fill it out.

"Remember, above all, be calm and unruffled; don't be rude or flip. If there's a signal in my question, catch it and follow it—this time I can't call for a break and whisk us out of the room for a talk. Speak directly to the judge: No one else—lawyers, courtroom officials, reporters, audience—is in the slightest degree important. In a case like this, the judge alone decides, and that decision is all that matters. Even more than at the deposition, make your case clearly, strongly, and definitely. At the deposition it was important not to lose the case; now it's important to win it—which means that positive arguments for our interpretation, rather than defensive evasions, are of the essence. You're teaching and you're selling—if he asks you a question, that's all-important. Stop, think, and instruct him carefully on your point; that's what he wants you to do now.

"On cross-examination, the lawyer will be doing his best to chip out small holes in your testimony, to discredit you as a witness by finding little points you have to retract, and small limitations and qualifications about your conclusions, or in your work. Too much self-denigration on your part, or constant qualification, is a great danger; up there, you're not a nincompoop but an expert. Say 'As far as I know, it is x'; 'This is what I recall.' In your answers, use your own words, verbs and characterizations, not the ones the lawyer uses in his question; they may well be loaded. Don't be helpful to him; don't try to educate him. And remember, you're under oath, and you're in Arkansas."

Tony left me with a copy of my own deposition and that of the man who was, I guess, my opposite number in the case, "their" theologian, one Norman Geisler of Dallas Theological Seminary. Pointing to Geisler's deposition, Tony said, "Read this over by tomorrow. If you have any ideas about fruitful cross-examination, call me at once in New York. I'd like to know where this man's testimony as an expert is vulnerable."

The next day I began reading his deposition with some sympathy for Professor Geisler.[1] Having just that morning read the transcript of my own deposition and seen what a total literary disaster it was, I vowed to give him the benefit of the doubt whenever vagueness, apparent omissions, misstatements, and so on, arose. And I had to admit that a lot of what he said presented creditable arguments and reflected both a wide acquaintance with a good deal of philosophical and theological literature and a consistent determination to construct a coherent and reasonable argument for his views. Nevertheless, I noticed some strange things. Despite the large number of volumes he had produced on philosophy and its history, he seemed unaware of some central elements of its usual "lore": for example, that Aristotle had first stated the rule that "nothing can come from nothing," and that this was a forerunner of the later Leibnitzian principle of sufficient reason and not of the law of non-contradiction.

But it was when he got going on his own views that my eyes widened as I read. First, in one of the strangest marriages of literalism and modern science I had encountered, he admitted under questioning that he did not regard Noah's "flood" as representing a sea of water, but as, in fact, the appearance of a universal ice age—a view sharply disputed by most, if not all, of his creationist colleagues. Most entrancing of all, however, were his views on UFOs. Through something he had said, Tony (who was taking the deposition) was led to ask him if he believed in a personal devil.

"Oh, yes," said Geisler.

"Are there, sir, any other evidences for that belief besides certain passages of Scripture?"

"Oh, yes," said Geisler. "I have known personally at least twelve persons who were clearly possessed by the devil." (I thought to myself with a chuckle: a quite normal experience on a large theological faculty.)

"And then," continued Geisler, "there are the UFOs."

"The UFOs?" said Tony. "Why are they relevant to the existence of the devil?"

"Well, you see, they represent the Devil's major, in fact, final, attack on the earth."

"Oh," said Tony. "And sir, may I ask you how you know, as you seem to, that there *are* UFOs?"

"I read it in *The Reader's Digest*."

At that, I hooted with delight, sprang to the phone, and when I got Tony on the line, said to him, "The Lord has delivered him into our hands! Go after that whole sequence on the UFOs, the Devil, and *The Reader's Digest* as if your life depended on it. When he states on the stand his dependence on that most unimpeachable of all sources of American folk wisdom, his status as an expert will have dissolved completely away!"

Needless to say, I was elated later when, unable to hear Geisler's testimony at the trial, I read in *The New York Times* of December 12: "Dr. Geisler acknowledged under cross-examination that he believed in unidentified flying objects as 'Satanic manifestations for the purposes of deception.' He said, amid courtroom laughter, that an article in *The Reader's Digest* had confirmed their existence."

When I left Swift Hall (the home of the Divinity School) the Friday before the trial began, one of the students called out to me, "Good luck! We students are with you. After all, that's the *big* oral exam, Daddy!"

*   *   *

Sunday afternoon, December 6, I took the flight—along with Father Bruce Vawter of De Paul—from Chicago to Memphis and from there to Little Rock. To our surprise, we were royally met by two Little Rock ladies representing the Arkansas ACLU: They could hardly have been either more helpful or more charming—and the local ACLU maintained that high standard throughout the week. I guess at that point all of us had pretty moist palms; certainly none of us wanted to blow the case, and each was fearful of doing so. But they made us feel like visiting heroes, strong and capable warriors, tested by larger battles in the great world, and come briefly to their town to settle this local skirmish quickly and efficiently on their behalf. Although this heroic image hardly fitted my own nervous self-estimation at the moment, it felt very good indeed—and I suppose we soon enough got to believe in it, at least a little.

We were taken to the Sam Peck Downtown Motor Inn, directly across the street from the imposing-looking Federal Building that housed the courtroom.

That afternoon I repeatedly went over the witness sheet of my testimony for the next day, trying to get all its points clearly implanted in my mind. At dinner we met for the first time the entire "team" (though the witnesses who were scientists would arrive later in the week): the large group of lawyers from both New York and Little Rock, other witnesses for the plaintiffs, the leaders of the local ACLU, and some representatives of the National Association of Biology Teachers. We were a large and diverse group.

Although we shared a most important common cause, nevertheless, as in so many political alliances, our deeper attitudes toward that cause, and our reasons for espousing it, were significantly different. Many were there to defend science against the ignorant, backward, and malevolent forces of religion; some of us were there to defend reasonable, self-critical, and liberal religion against its irrational, intolerant, and absolutist varieties.

Inevitably, therefore, these real differences began to surface as we discussed the case. Whenever a scientist would refer too frequently to the tyrannical excesses, blindness, or fanaticism of religion, I would find myself pointing to the fact that many scientists were responsible for communicating a philosophical naturalism as well as scientific theories of evolution when they "taught" science, or I would recite the long list of "scientists" among the leaders of creation science. I am sure that, as they went off to their rooms that night, many of the scientists present wondered whether I—or any of the "religious" witnesses on their side—could actually be trustworthy, or whether we were really duplicitous advocates of the opposing cause! And they clearly had no idea what we, as religionists, could contribute to our common effort, the cause of science; why we were there at all was a mystery to them. I certainly felt anything but at home among their self-confident, and in many ways self-righteous, forces of scientific light arrayed in Little Rock against the dying legions of religious darkness. I remember comforting myself with a couple of somewhat frustrated and irritated thoughts: first, that none of the lawyers I had worked with felt that way—they were glad of our help. And secondly, that of all the cultural forces represented at the trial, this sort of buoyant secular rationalism, happy about its own openness, tolerance, and progressiveness in an illiterate and prejudiced world, was probably the viewpoint most clearly on the wane, even in the West, in the latter half of the twentieth century.

At breakfast the next morning (Monday), the sun shone, the air outside was warm, and I felt relaxed. This was not because of some spiritual victory over my nervousness, but because the lawyers had assured me that there would be a lot of preliminary bickering about what evidence would be admissible and what would not, with the result that I would not be called until Tuesday morning. So I enjoyed reading the local papers filled with news and views of the trial, pictures of the local principals, stories of scores of dedicated "Christians" trundled up in a fleet of buses from southern Arkansas to support the State's defense of the Act, and rumor of the crowd of reporters in town from London, the European continent, and even distant New York. We were part of a large event, and—so long as I didn't have to go on the stand today—that was exhilarating indeed.

The federal courthouse across the street was teeming with people: visitors who had arrived in the buses, reporters with notebooks and satchels, TV camera crews, troopers, lawyers, federal officials, office workers, and pols—and nervous witnesses. When we finally found room on one of the crowded elevators, we rose to the fourth floor and were disgorged into a blinding sea of light. Through the glare, we could see across the corridor a phalanx of TV cameras hoisted unsteadily aloft on shoulders, a battery of klieg lights, and, interspersed among them, snapping cameras—one presumed there were also humans among these aggressive lenses. When it was discovered that no one of much worth had emerged from the elevator, the lights went out and the lenses lowered. But even the unimportant ones had to charge the phalanx and fight their way through to the corridor leading to the courtroom.

Once one was admitted inside the courtroom by a large, bland, uniformed St. Peter at the doorway, the atmosphere radically changed. The room was lofty, spacious, and well lit, with high windows, sober paneling, and heavy, carved furniture; it seemed immense, restful, and dignified after the crowded, cramped, and feverish corridor. High in the center of the front wall was the large bench; lower to its left, but still raised above all else, was the witness stand, and in front of that two large tables for the opposing lawyers. On the right-hand wall, seated, so to speak, in the choir stalls, were the score or more of reporters and court artists, and opposite them along the other wall the officials and servants of the court. Behind the plaintiff's table sat a number of the plaintiffs themselves (mostly the Little Rock clergy), and in the first two rows of seats the witnesses-to-be and their local ACLU supporters, nervously chatting together or rechecking their notes. Beyond a partition were the rows of spectator seats stretching back to the far wall at the rear, seats already crowded to overflowing with a sea of excited, babbling visitors. Again I thought, this *is* an event—and how strange not to have the slightest idea how it will come out!

Suddenly there was quiet. Looking up, we saw the bailiff standing under the high bench and saying, in that strange, laconic, toneless, unaccented voice people use when performing something (rather than communicating) through their speech, that all must rise, be silent and respectful—that the court will come to order.

Then the door behind the bench opened, a huddle of lawyers poured out, and the judge, robed and impressive, walked solemnly up to his seat behind the high bench. Clearly an alert, intelligent man, Judge Overton immediately dominated the room—one could not but feel immense confidence in any proceedings under this capable figure's control.

The trial began at once. First came the chief lawyer representing the plaintiffs and the ACLU, Robert Cearley of Little Rock, presenting a summary of our case.[2]

"We make in this case no challenge to any religious belief," he emphasized, "especially to belief in God the Creator however that is understood, even in the most fundamentalistic or literalistic manner. We are concerned here only to challenge this law as unconstitutional, as contrary to the First Amendment since it represents in fact the teaching of a religious doctrine in the guise of science. We will seek to prove that creation science, far from being science, is actually a religious apologetic, that it is an effort by a particular religious group to teach its own particular belief. Thus the Act represents the establishment of a particular religious point of view, the preference of one religion over another in the public schools, and the inevitable involvement as a consequence of the State in the affairs of religion.

"The scientists will, moreover, show that creation science as specified in the Act is not science, that its theory does not, and could not from the nature of both its form and content, exist in the world of science, and does not use the scientific method. Finally, we will argue that the Act is educationally impossible either to enact or to monitor. Creation science cannot be taught intelligibly without reference to the Bible, and yet no references to religion are to be made—how can this possibly be determined in each one of Arkansas's classrooms? There is no possible way of knowing what a 'balanced treatment,' which the Act demands, means in the concrete—

and yet the job security of each teacher depends on this. The Act, therefore, makes each teacher infinitely vulnerable to attack on the emotional and controversial topic of religion, and it gives him or her little resource for defense. Liberty of religion has been given to us all; this Act violates these fundamental principles of our common life."

Next the young, energetic attorney-general rose—a man, I decided, actually more intelligent than his blond, all-American looks might at first indicate. There was no question he was doing his best with a difficult case. "The only question before us," he argued,[3] "is the constitutionality or unconstitutionality of Act 590, of its specific and particular wording—not of any ideas, theories, or documents purportedly lying back of that Act. The fact that some of the implications of the Act are parallel with, or consistent with, so-called 'religious doctrines' in Genesis or in fundamentalist documents, is quite irrelevant; if its actual wording is free of such matters, they are not contained in the Act. The purpose of the Act is definitely not religious. On the contrary, it has a secular purpose, namely to broaden the discussion of origins to more than one exclusive model. Thus, far from restricting teaching, the law broadens the search for truth and furthers academic freedom. The issue is not whether creation science is science or not; neither model qualifies strictly as science, as we will show. We will also show that creation science is at least as scientific as is evolutionary science, and so at least as nonreligious as the latter.

"Since, moreover, these two are the only 'scientific explanations' of origins, the Act is neutral and immensely educational, and it does not advance the cause of one religious viewpoint. In this context, the word 'creator' and the idea of creation are neither religious nor supernatural; creation science presupposes the existence of a creator no more and no less than evolutionary science presupposes that there is *no* creator. Each is, therefore, equally scientific and equally nonreligious, and the relation to fundamentalism is merely coincidental. Does the law not specifically prohibit religious instruction? How can it, therefore, encourage it? The motivation for its introduction into the legislature, the manner of its passage through the legislature, the reasons for the governor's signing of the Act, are of no interest whatsoever to this court. Solely relevant is the question of its constitutionality, and that it is clearly, as it says itself, free of any religious entanglements."

Rather impressed with this presentation, I thought to myself that the attorney-general should be given an *A* for effort.

The first witness called was the Methodist bishop of Arkansas, the Reverend Kenneth W. Hicks. Clearly an articulate and charming man, as well as a significant ecclesiastical figure, Bishop Hicks had been selected to represent the plaintiffs in Arkansas who had objected to the law. Whether or not it was relevant that two of the three lawyers for the State were his parishioners, only the ACLU strategists could reveal. In any case, he was cross-examined briefly and with the utmost courtesy.

His testimony was eloquent and crucial for our case.[4] He stated how important it was to the churches of Arkansas, and to his own large denomination (eight hundred churches in Arkansas), that the separation of the authority of the State from the life and affairs of the churches be maintained, especially in the public schools. The Methodist denomination, and many of those other denominations for which he was privileged to speak, had been established on the principle of freedom of religion from State control, and they would struggle long to maintain that freedom. For the State to represent, through its civil power and its programs of education, one religious view among others threatened the free activity of every other religious group in the State.

Part of the reason for this concern in this case, he went on, was that the alternative to evolution science in the law under consideration, namely, so-called creation science, portrayed belief in God's creation in totally different terms from what his own denomination did. Thus, were the law enacted, his parishioners—and he looked sharply at the Arkansas bench—would be excluded from either alternative provided by the law: from those called "godless evolutionists" and "secular humanists" on the one hand, and from those asserting a literal, recent, and six-day creation on the other. By this exclusion, the law thus abridged the religious rights of his people, of his church—and of all those churches with whom he joined in this action. It also denied the alternative represented by all of the church groups for whom he had the honor to speak: an interpretation of God's creation which was nevertheless quite consistent with the findings of modern astronomical, geological, and biological science.

On cross-examination, the assistant attorney-general was excessively gentle; clearly, he wished to draw no blood. He did, however, begin an interesting line of questioning that they were to repeat with all of us. First, David Williams asked the bishop whether he did not consider divergent views helpful in good teaching, and so why did not this law represent good pedagogical method? Secondly, he sought to establish that the bishop had, for most of his adult life, been a student of Scripture and of religious doctrines; was it not the case, Williams then asked, that repeatedly, in fact, exclusively, he had encountered the idea of creation as a religious doctrine, as a belief of a religious community —rather than as an aspect of a scientific hypothesis? Was not this association with religion, so important for the plaintiff's case, thus really the accidental consequence of the bishop's training and life as a minister, rather than an essential aspect of the idea in itself? And finally, if it were the case that there were solid "scientific evidences" for the position of creation science, would not the bishop have a problem with *excluding* creation science from the scientific classroom?

These were difficult questions if encountered for the first time; the bishop gave both thoughtful and honest answers to them. In noting down his answers, I noted down also that obviously it would be necessary between then and my own testimony the next day to work out in my mind definitive replies to each. These questions were sure to return in some form or another; and, if not squarely dealt with, they would divert and soften the force of our argument.

*   *   *

The next witness to be called was Father Bruce Vawter of De Paul University in Chicago.[5] As Tony's questioning made abundantly clear, Vawter, after forty years of study of the Hebrew texts, qualified as an expert on the Book of Genesis. Vawter explained the various ways the text was "scientifically" studied in present scholarship, and the many different disciplines which went into that understanding: philology, linguistic science, calligraphy, archaeology, history, literary critical methods, comparative religions. He went on to say that Genesis was basically a religious document, a narrative expressing the religious convictions of the Hebrews about human origins and the world, and, as a consequence, about the duties, obligations, and possibilities of human life. Since the narrative included certain factual elements, a sort of view of the cosmos and of its beginning was implicit there. But since this was not the main purpose or impact of Genesis, it was misleading and almost impossible to extract a "science" from this document.

At that point there was an objection: Religious questions about Genesis are irrelevant, since creation science refers neither to Genesis nor to religious matters. In reply, Tony said they were going to establish the relevance of Genesis to the Act. The judge then overruled the objection. He was, he said, prepared to admit a very wide range of evidence; and then, in going over it, he would proceed to determine its relevance to the issues in the case—which was certainly good news for us.

After Vawter described in detail the wide varieties of interpretation of Genesis characteristic of different religious groups, and some of the diversity in even the literary accounts of Genesis, Tony brought the discussion to Act 590.

"In its description of creation science," said Vawter, "Act 590 has as its unmentioned reference book the first eleven chapters of Genesis. The major ideas of creation science are rephrasings, often with the same words, of central concepts or events in these chapters of Scripture."

"Can you specify these ideas?"

"Certainly: (1) creation from nothing; (2) the use of the phrase 'all living kinds'; (3) fixity of kinds or of species, stretching back to the first beginnings; (4) separate creation of kinds of things and as a consequence separate ancestry of each kind of thing; (5) the Noachic flood (only in Genesis is the flood story set in juxtaposition to creation); and (6) a relatively recent creation— for the dating in all creationist documents depends, explicitly or implicitly, on Genesis.

"There are in other cultures," said Vawter, "a number of creation accounts and even other accounts of a flood that have roughly parallel elements in them, especially accounts stemming from Sumeria and Babylonia. But at certain important points, these are quite different, especially vis-à-vis the role of God, the relation of God to humankind, and the role of men and women in creation, so that Act 590 clearly stems from Genesis and not from these others."

In the cross-examination Campbell again pressed the point that probably a long religious education—beginning early in a Catholic school and lasting for forty years of religious scholarship—had convinced Vawter that creation was a religious matter. Then he asked, Where in Genesis does it refer to the insufficiency of evolution, to fixed species or separate ancestry, catastrophic geology, or even the recent character of creation—the main elements of the Act? "How can you say these come from Genesis?"

Vawter patiently explained the difference in language between an original document and the later explication of its ideas, that in fact the Genesis narrative *did* describe separate acts of creation of present fixed species, and so on. Thus the concepts making up the material in Act 590 were rooted in the Genesis narrative. Finally, when he was asked if he thought that evolution, as defined in the Act, was compatible with Genesis, Vawter said he found evolution, if it were defined differently from what it was in the Act itself, to be quite compatible both with a religious and an educated interpretation of Genesis—and that, on the stand, he was not prepared to go warrant for the definition of evolution found in the Act. On re-cross, Tony listed again the six elements of the Genesis account relevant to the case. ex nihilo, the use of the phrase "all living kinds," fixity of species, separate ancestry, the Noachic flood, and recent creation.

"Are these in Genesis?"

"Yes."

"Are they in Act 590?"

"Yes."

"Are there any other views of origins that contain these elements, or these elements together in this way?"

"No, there are none."

*　　*　　*

The next witness formed an interesting contrast. A good deal younger, with a full beard, quiet, very relaxed and assured, George Marsden introduced himself as a professor of American Religious History at Calvin College in Michigan—an institution which, he admitted modestly at a later point, could be said to represent "an extremely conservative evangelical Christian viewpoint." When asked what his area of expertise was, he cited his large volume, *Fundamentalism and American Culture* (1980), recognized, he smilingly admitted, as the definitive account of the rise and development of fundamentalism up to 1930. Immediately, Rick Campbell rose in objection and said, in effect:

"This man, from his own testimony, and statements in the deposition, can qualify as an expert on the history of fundamentalism obviously only up to the year 1930. Yet our case concerns legislation in Arkansas fifty years later. How can he claim to be an expert on any matters relevant to this case?"

Marsden, sitting as relaxed as if he were in his own office, smiled:

"The finished manuscript for a companion book to that historical volume up to 1930, namely, a relatively complete account of fundamentalism up to and including 1980, is on my desk in Grand Rapids. I expect to send it to the publisher shortly. In my profession, Mr. Assistant Attorney-General, we do not call ourselves 'experts' until our works have been published!"

The objector drooped, and his objection collapsed before it reached the bench.[6]

In his testimony, Marsden described the rise of fundamentalism since the second half of the last century, when, as he said, "evangelical religion enjoyed a dominant position in all public schools, and Protestant principles and Biblical narratives pervaded all textbooks. Most public schools were in fact extensions of Protestant Sunday schools." After 1880, this clear dominance was challenged by an increasingly heavy series of "shocks": immigration, growth of the cities, increasing pluralism—and, on the intellectual level, historical relativism, a critical interpretation of Scripture, humanism, and Darwinism. As a result of this series of blows, "fundamentalism" appeared; it represented an appeal by a very diverse number of groups to certain "fundamentals" of the older evangelical faith. Although at the close of the nineteenth century the issue of evolution had by no means been central, with World War I antagonism to evolution became one of the main features of this group: Evolution was blamed for the excesses of the Kaiser's Germany as it is now blamed for the "barbarity" of communism. In the 1920s, the anti-evolution movement appealed exclusively to the Biblical doctrine; since only God, said they, was there as a witness to that great event, the Bible contains our only reliable report of the beginning of things. Very few, one or two, sought to marshal scientific evidence for the creationist position. Since then, and especially because of the Scopes trial, anti-evolution has been a major emphasis of fundamentalist movements.

Marsden then testified that the creation science, or creationist, movement—which lay back of Act 590—was itself an outgrowth of the historical fundamentalism he had studied and described. The ideas, even the words, were identical. The five elements of creation science defined in the Act had had a long history in fundamentalist arguments: The antipathy of creation to evolution, and the tendency to see the one as the obverse of the other, were the same. The insistence, moreover, that there are only *two* models or views of origins—one of them of God, the other of the Devil—was typically fundamentalist. Marsden here quoted several passages from creationist literature, especially the works of Henry Morris,[7] to show this identification of evolutionary theory with the Devil. For example, "evolutionary philosophy is the foundation of the rebellion of Satan himself and of every evil system which he has devised since that time to oppose the sovereignty and grace of God in this universe." And he showed by more quotes from Morris and Gish that creation scientists themselves asserted that the source of the ideas of creation science is, and only can be, the Bible.[8]

At this, the Arkansas lawyers registered a loud objection, one for which we had been waiting, since it represented a fundamental point in the procedures of the case.

"Quotations from these works, are, Your Honor, irrelevant. The Arkansas legislature passed this Act, not these gentlemen. The fact that 'someone out there' writes similar ideas as are represented in the Act is immaterial."

At that, Siano replied that these documents represented the logical basis for the creation science model as stated in the Act; as a consequence, it is to them alone that one must turn if one wishes to understand the precise meaning of the model and to assess its character and value. Finally, it is these works that must be used as texts and taught if there is to be any instruction in this model, as the law clearly requires. As the available literature makes plain, it is these same two men quoted a moment ago as fearful of the Devil and appealing to Genesis who are the authors of the works designed for public-school instruction in creation science. "And, Your Honor, I might point out that the defense cites both of these authors as 'experts' in creation science at their deposition. It is, therefore, quite legitimate to appeal to all their works in relation to the creation-science model."

In response to these arguments from the two sides, Judge Overton expanded a very significant earlier statement of his. First of all, he said, his policy in this case was to accept a wide range of evidence in order to develop the fullest possible perspective on the case, and then later to decide what weight to give to each sort of evidence. "These authors here in question have," he said, "produced the works that lie back of the law, the suggested textbooks of creation science. Thus their works are certainly relevant to the important question of the status of the model cited in the law. For that model merely refers to a so-called theory, and argues for it; it does not present either the theory itself or the arguments warranting it. If," continued Judge Overton, "these same authors also write works that emphasize the religious character of creationism, that is itself a relevant point as to the character of creation science in the understanding of those who have devised and who support the theory.

"They cannot wear two hats," Judge Overton said. "The writers can't call it religion for one purpose and science for another" (*Arkansas Gazette,* December 8, page 4).[9] This judgment, opening up our capacity to appeal to the written documents of creation science, delighted us all. It was also a very good omen that the judge, as indicated by his "two-hat" analogy, saw clearly the ambiguous role and status of creation science in the minds of its creators and supporters: on the one hand as "Biblical religion" for the loyal troops, and on the other as "nonreligious science" for the public schools.

When Marsden finished his testimony, it was almost 1 P.M., more than time for lunch. I realized with a gulp that the trial had moved much more rapidly than the lawyers had originally promised. They had expected a great deal of legal bickering about admissible evidence and documents, even some serious challenge to this opening battery of religious witnesses—all on the grounds that since the Act excluded the teaching of religion, discussion of its religious character and appeal to such issues might require long and careful argument. To their surprise—as our notes have indicated—from the very start the judge opened up the case to all the ramifications of Act 590, specifically to questions of its religious grounds and implications and, later, to questions of its scientific adequacy.

Moreover, the cross-examinations in each had been perfunctory at best, namely, touching and retouching on the value of alternative views in teaching, the bias of religious witnesses toward regarding this matter as religious, and the need for an open mind with regard to new scientific hypotheses. As a consequence—as far as my own schedule was concerned—it was now evident that my testimony would come up later that first after-noon, rather than on Tuesday morning. This meant that the last-minute preparations that Tony and I had to do must take place during lunch and during the testimony of the next witness, rather than tonight as we had planned.

Needless to say, I was sorry to miss Dorothy Nelkin's testimony. Professor Nelkin is a sociologist from Cornell who has concentrated on the roles of science and technology in the wider society, especially the ways other "lay" groups use science and technology to advance their particular causes and purposes. In the process of those inquiries she has made a detailed study of recent fundamentalist and right-wing religious groups, and their relation to ("use of") science, including, of course, the creation-science movement. The point of her testimony was to give a graphic picture based on her own research of the scientific creationist groups that developed the ideas lying behind Act 590, where these ideas came from, what sorts of people were involved with those groups, and so on.

Among the points she brought out was the "oath" or creed to which members of the Creation Research Society—all of whom must *also* have a degree in some recognized area of science—must subscribe on entering the society. This "confession" included an affirmation of the Bible as the "written Word of God," its infallibility on all historical and scientific issues (including origins), the separate creation of all "kinds," the Great Flood, the Fall, and the universal salvation through Jesus Christ. Thus to the account of the sources of the Act in Genesis and its bases in historic American fundamentalism was now added the recent history of its origination and espousal in fundamentalist groups in southern California, Texas, and South Carolina.

I did hear one last portion of Dorothy's cross-examination when I returned to the courtroom after my final coaching session with Tony. The Arkansas lawyer, on cross-examination, was asking her:[10]

"Professor Nelkin, do you believe in a personal God?"

"No, I do not," answered Mrs. Nelkin—at which point three spectators in the back, sitting just ahead and to the left of where I was standing, rose from their seats, stepped quickly into the broad aisle, and sank to their knees to begin very audible prayers for the skeptical professor.

Chapter 5
The Trial:
Theological and
Philosophical Issues

After a hurried sandwich for lunch, Tony and I slipped out to prepare for my testimony, sure to come up later that afternoon. We found one of the "lawyers' rooms" in the rear of the courtroom open and available, and we sat down to get to work. Tony said we had two things to do: first, to go over, one last time, the main body of my testimony. Not only was this important for the clarity of my memory, but also he wanted to be sure he had questions ready in relation to each section, concept, or point we wished to make—in case I forgot something. I had to some extent memorized an outline of almost four pages of my full testimony, which itself ran to some twenty or twenty-five pages; but it is easy to leave something out, and I wanted to get immediate help from Tony if I seemed to falter or to forget something.

Secondly, I was to read over quickly a document called "Defendants' Proposed Findings of Fact and Conclusions of Law."[1] The first part—Findings of Fact—contained nineteen legal-sized pages, outlining the main arguments or claims on their side of the case (some fifty-eight separate theses), establishing, as they saw it, the constitutionality of Act 590 over against the plaintiffs' stated case. (Its title "Findings of Fact," was, I thought, another interesting example of the worship of "facts" in our culture.) The second part ("Conclusions of Law") included detailed appeals to legal precedents backing up these claims and consequent legal demonstrations or arguments establishing the constitutionality of the law.

"I'm interested," said Tony, "in your reading carefully (we still have almost an hour before you go on) those first fifty-eight theses or claims, and letting me know which ones, if any, you think make important points against our case. If you locate such, then tell me, for God's sake; your testimony, and that of the scientists to follow, will have to be redesigned to plug those holes. Also, I want you to tell me points where *their* case is vulnerable, where their facts are wrong or their interpretations and conclusions weak. If we get them clearly located, then we can go after those points and nail them down."

"Okay," I said, and began.

Continually during the next hour as I read over their case, courthouse cops and officials poked their heads into our room to see who was there, and the sounds of the reconvening of the court floated along the corridor outside.

Most of the points made in the brief had been part of their case all along, as recorded in their depositions and in the opening statement. A few new points, however, with which we would have to deal in our testimony had emerged. Most of them, I told Tony, were for the scientists, but our dialogue, while I was on the stand, could engage some of them as well. These latter points concerned, for example, the familiar definition of scientific method as requiring evidence that is directly "observable" and "repeatable"; as a result, they argued that neither creation science nor evolution, being theories about events in the distant past (nor *any* theory about the past in astronomy, geophysics, geology, or biology), could truly be called "scientific theories" (#10, p. 3). The scientists, I said, would have to explain the logic of science when it dealt with singular, past, and unrepeatable events; how were theories about such events brought under the canons of scientific inquiry? Secondly, #17 stated that the defense "credits the expert testimony of defendants' witnesses" (all Ph.D.'s in one branch of science of another) that "much scientific data or evidence . . . supports the creation-science model and is contrary to the evolution-science model" (p. 4).

"This reiterates," I said, "their error that scientific method is concerned solely with 'scientific facts'; we can deal with this too."

The claim, repeated throughout the literature, that creation science and evolution represented the only two models concerned with origins, was here (clearly in response to our deposition) changed to "the only two scientific explanations of origins" (#19, p. 4). Thus they also asserted the point that Act 590, besides not mentioning "religious writings or doctrines," "does not refer to God"—clearly in response to our central claim that it is religion.

"We must," I said, "make really clear that the creationist model *essentially* refers to God as the sole actor capable of creation as they define it. Such reference, whether explicit or not, must be there else the model represents a void, an empty, meaningless concept—and that such reference is inescapably religious."

"That's right," said Tony.

Interestingly—showing they had done some theological homework—the document defined religion as "ultimate concern." It went on, correctly, to note that humanism, without a Creator, could thus be said to be "a religion," and that as a consequence, evolution, a major element of modern humanism, could thus "be a tenet of a humanistic religion" (#24-28).

"Tony, there's no question they're right about that, and I've said as much in print a hundred times. So we must bring this matter up and show how the use of science *as religion* is significantly different from the method and conclusions of science *as inquiry*. If we can do that, this point will be no problem. Anyway, I'm quite prepared to say on the stand that I agree with the creationists' complaint that science is often taught as a religion, as answering religious questions. In fact, to bring that up will give us a good chance to go on to say it's just as wrong and misleading for scientists to introduce their humanistic religious views *as science* as it is for the creationists to do the same—and that's why I object to the law, just as I'd object to a law that specified a scientific theory as religion."

"That's fine. Let's do that," said Tony.

When I had read on a little further to #35 (p. 5), where they admitted that "creation-science does presuppose the existence of a creator, to the same degree that evolution-science presupposed the existence of no creator," I got more interested.

"This is false," I told Tony, "and we can show it. Creation science presupposes the existence and activity of the Creator essentially and substantially—there can be no act of creation, no creationist model, without God. On the other hand, scientific inquiry excludes the creator *methodologically*, as a limitation set by the character of its method. Science *cannot* talk about God; thus no assertion is being made at all about God's reality or unreality when God is not included in a scientific theory. That distinction is crucial to our case, as this false distinction is to theirs. Let's make sure we clarify this point, for the scientists will never even have thought about it and probably wouldn't understand it."

Then, four sentences further (p. 6), I sat up straight in my chair and whistled.

"What is it?" said Tony, sitting up as well.

"The Lord has again delivered them into our hand," I said. "Tony, they've opened the way for us to accuse them—oh, my God in heaven—of heresy!"

"What on earth are you talking about?" said Tony, now greatly excited but not yet aware why.

"Well, simply this. In order to keep themselves clear from our accusation in the deposition that creation science is religious because the creator they presuppose—and cannot well deny—is 'God,' they're here, in these sentences, claiming that the creator they speak about is not necessarily 'God'—and, by so doing, they're backing, without knowing it of course, into a very old heresy! Tony, make a note. When we're on the section on ex nihilo—right?—ask me if the creator ex nihilo is necessarily 'God,' and if, in this case, I have anywhere run into an apparent *denial* that the creator is God. Then I'll take it from there. Got it?"

"Okay," said Tony, clear about what he had to do, but not too clear why.

At that point word came that the testimony of Dorothy Nelkin was drawing to a close, so we gathered up our papers and hurried into the courtroom just in time to see the three spectators in the back of the room sink to their knees right next to us to pray for Professor Nelkin.

*   *   *

After a brief intermission—it was now about 2:30— the court was declared to be again in session, and I was called by our chief lawyer to the stand as plaintiff's fifth witness.[2] Under the guidance of Tony's questioning, I identified myself in those ways relevant to my role in the case: I said where I had taught and presently teach, what sorts of courses I had given over the years, what books I had written or was about to write, and so on. At the end, Tony declared me to be an "expert" in the philosophy of religion and in theology—about what sorts of things religious ideas were and were not—and on the relations of religious ideas and religious thought to science and to theories in science. Since there were no objections to this stipulation, our pas de deux commenced in earnest.

"Professor Gilkey, can you begin by giving me a definition of religion?"

"Surely. Religions are so diverse, and can be viewed in so many ways, that it is difficult to provide a definition that is either precise or generally accepted. Still, it is, I think, accurate to say that anything we would call a religion, or a movement or community we would call religious, involves these three elements:

"(1) A view of the nature of reality, and especially of 'ultimate reality,' or reality as a whole (for example, God or Brahman). In religion, this view of reality and of ultimate reality centers its attention on the relation of reality so understood (for example, God) to the deepest problems besetting men and women (for example, sin, injustice, death, rebirth)—in other words, to the question of meaning in existence. Finally, each religion is established on the basis of an answer to these deepest problems, and that answer is enshrined or expressed in myths, teachings, scriptures, doctrines, dogmas, and so on, in the 'truth' borne, cherished, and preserved by that religion.

"(2) Each religion has a way of life, a way or rules of behavior that are an important part of being a believer or a participant—that is, a way of life that people in the religion agree to follow. This way of life is thought to bring, or help to bring, rescue, rebirth, release; it is an essential aspect of the religion. As a part of this new way of life is some mode of relating oneself—alone or with others—to ultimate reality as defined above, in prayer, in worship, through the sacraments, meditation, yogic exercises, chanting, dance, or some other form of ritual or ceremony.

"(3) Finally, there is a community of persons participating in that way of life, assenting to that truth or truths, that view of reality, of our problems and their answer, and uniting in that mode of worship or ritual. This community will have a definite structure (for example, a church, as in Christianity, the *sangha* in Buddhism, or the *Khalsa* in Sikhism), with clear lines of authority and a definite tradition or rule of coming together in specified places, times, and ways. To me, whatever has these characteristics is a religion, and what does not is not a religion."

"Could you describe, then, the nature or character of religion in our Western culture, in America?"

"Religion in our culture has been shaped by the Jewish and the Christian traditions, especially the latter. These are *monotheistic* traditions, which is their central and dominant characteristic. That means that all religion centers on God, and God alone. In the terms of our definition of religion, God is the principle of ultimate reality, the source of all other reality, and the resolver (redeemer) of our fundamental problems; God is the source and basis for the way of life (the law) and the object of all worship, prayer, or meditation; and God establishes and gives final authority to the community. The meaning of the First Commandment, obligatory in both religions, is that God alone is to be worshipped, adored, and obeyed unreservedly. In these traditions, everything that is religious is related directly or indirectly to God—this is the functional meaning of monotheism.

"Correspondingly, in these traditions whatever is related to God is religious: God is the center of religion; whatever has to do with God has to do with religion. Put in terms of language, all religious assertions in our tradition have to do with God, and, correspondingly, all references to God and his acts are religious. Not all religions, to be sure, worship or speak of God; they have other views of ultimate reality. But where God is the center—as the ultimate reality that creates, redeems, and saves—ideas about God are religious ideas, and reference to God is a religious statement. Language about God is not a *necessary* aspect of all religious language, but it is a *sufficient* aspect."

"Does the religious character of ideas about God apply to creation as well as to other doctrines?" "Yes, indeed. As I said, a view of reality and of ultimate reality is an essential aspect of religion. In our monotheistic religions, God is the *creator* of all else; thus God is clearly the principle of ultimate reality, the source of the being or existence of all else. This activity of creation and preservation on God's part is as much an important concept in our *religious* ideas about God, of the religious 'truths' about him, as are revelation, incarnation, redemption, the Last Judgment, and any of the other ideas or symbols in the religions of Judaism or Christianity.

"Thus, quite appropriately, God's creation of the universe is expressed in the first chapters of the sacred scriptures of Judaism and Christianity, in the Bible; and it is reasserted in the first article of the oldest Christian creed, the so-called Apostles' Creed: 'I believe in God the Father Almighty, Maker of heaven and earth.' In all those religions which have gods, creators are always deities or gods as much as are redeemers or rescuers. Originating or creating the universe is a prerogative of the divine whenever it appears—and what has to do with God is religious or a part of religion."

"Can you explain further, or in more detail, this point: Why is an idea or a proposition about God religious?"

"I have said that, with us, God and religion are correlated: What has to do with the one, with God, has to do with the other, religion. In monotheism, where there is one God who creates or originates the universe, God *transcends* ordinary things and the relations to one another of ordinary things—of mountains, seas, animals, men and women, molecules, or atoms—because God is the *source* of all of them. As the origin of the system of nature, God is not a mere *part* of that system: It came from him; he 'preceded' it—he is not a moment or an entity within it.

"Thus, the way we speak of what God does and is, is different from the way we speak of ordinary events and people. Wherever, for example, *we* 'create,' we create either out of some material, wood or stone, or we bear children, out of ourselves, so to speak. Neither one is

-101-

true of the divine creation: It is said to be 'out of nothing'—since here God created all the wood or stone, and all the mothers and fathers, grandmothers and grandfathers. It is a *different* sort of act, an act beyond nature and human acts, an act beyond the system of nature because it founds that system as a whole. This is why the divine act of creation cannot be a part of science, for science inquires only *within* the system of nature and cannot go beyond it, as religion, monotheistic religion, essentially does—but we'll get to that later. This also is why, in both the Jewish and the Christian traditions— and you can add the Islamic—knowledge of creation, of God's act in creating the world, is *religious* knowledge— that is, something given and known only by revelation: through the Scriptures, through the religious tradition, and through religious experience, and not by ordinary, profane ways of knowing.

"The creationist documents admit this freely: We know, say they, creation *only* through the Bible in which God has revealed himself. As a matter of fact, this has always been the case in the history of religions: Everywhere myths of origins, accounts of what happened at the very beginning of time, are revealed, sacred knowledge or wisdom communicated to us by the gods and by special, sacred traditions, and not part of secular, ordinary knowledge compiled in the present and merely by men and women."

"God's act of creation in our tradition is part of religion, you say; why is creation ex nihilo in particular a religious idea or proposition?"

"Creation is a divine act, and creators are gods, as I said. Also this is, in our religious tradition—in both Scripture and creed—the first important thing said about God: God creates. It is the first foundation of Jewish and Christian religion. But in itself—and this is the important point for this case—creation *out of nothing*, the idea back of Act 590, represents what one can call the 'essence' of a religious idea or presupposition. We have agreed that language about God is religious language—for a monotheistic tradition to speak of God is, by definition, to use religious language. Now, in the concept of creation out of nothing God *alone* is there and acts. Nothing else is yet there, no other forces, powers, actors; for the precise meaning of this concept is that in and through this act, *they* all come to be, as did everything else we might talk about. Thus in this act no other entity is present, only God. Only God acts; only God is talked about in this idea or model. It is, therefore, a *purely* religious idea, one quite unmixed with any other elements. Or let me put it this way, it is even more religious than Christmas!"

(A gasp went up from the spectators.)

"More religious than Christmas? You can't mean that!" said Tony in surprise, playing his assignment to the hilt. "Why is that?"

"Well, at least at Christmas, whatever your theology, Mary was also there! Here, at creation, *only* God is present. And, let us note, only *God* could be present, all alone like that: underived, eternal, necessary, self-sufficient. Above all, only *God's* power and intelligence are capable of bringing all things into being where nothing at all was, and giving them the order and the reality to last. Only God can create out of nothing. Therefore, the idea of creation, as stated in the Act, *must* speak of God, or else it speaks of nothing, it makes no sense at all. It is a religious statement, or it is not statement at all."

I could feel from the vibrations in the large room (and even from some murmurs of assent from the crowded rows in the back) that this point was getting through—and that it might well be the time to let out a few more stops. So I winked at Tony, and he winked back.

"Professor Gilkey, the creator, you say, is necessarily *God*, can only be God—the God of the Bible, the God who loves us and saves us. Is there any point in these proceedings where you have seen this denied?"

I could see the lawyers for the State look up at this question in puzzled worry, knowing well that something fairly horrible was afoot.

"Oh, yes. Now mind you, I do not wish to accuse the State of Arkansas, or its excellent lawyers, of anything culpable, and I am sure they have done this innocently, not knowing what their words mean. But the *fact* is,"— and here I let my voice become a good deal more forceful—"they have in their presentation of the case come very close, yes, very close indeed, to the *first, and worst, Christian heresy!*"

The three Arkansas lawyers visibly jumped at these words, stared at me in horror, and in some real helplessness—they didn't have the slightest idea what I was accusing them of, but they didn't like it at all.

"My gracious," said Tony, his bright eyes snapping, "that's awful! What do you mean, Professor?"

"I mean that to prove that the creator presupposed in the Act—and they admit this—is *not* 'religious,' they try to separate him from God, from the personal God who reveals himself, who loves the world, who comes in the Covenant with Israel and later in Jesus Christ. Now this was precisely the early heresy of Marcion and the Gnostics (about 150 to 200 A.D.), who said that there were in fact two Gods, one a blind, cruel, but powerful God of creation (the God of the Old Testament), and the other a good, loving God of redemption (the God of the New Testament)—and thus that the creator God was *not* the same as the redeemer God. I don't think the creationists have this idea in mind, of course, but *if* they say the creator they presuppose is not *God*, nor is 'religious'— they are willy-nilly saying precisely this.

"This heresy was, of course, condemned at once by all the churches; it denied monotheism, it blasphemed the Old Testament and the God of Genesis, and it reduced in power and glory the God of Jesus Christ to the status and role of a second God. It was because of this controversy in about 150 that the first article of the Creed was written as it was: "I believe in God the Father Almighty,

Maker of heaven and earth, and in His only Son, Jesus Christ our Lord"—God is one, creator and redeemer, the only true God. This is said beautifully and forcefully in Isaiah 40, and repeated in Chapter 1 of the Gospel according to John: The Lord who creates is also the Lord who redeems. Without that main article about God, Christianity, as well as Judaism, is quite empty and meaningless. This concept of creation by God is not only religious; it is very near to the center of the Christian and Jewish religions."

As is evident, I had become downright evangelical in saying all of this, all of which I thoroughly believed, and which I could, therefore, with no trouble, sing out forcefully and clearly.

As these words came forth, there were clear and fervent responses from the back benches. I could hear a good deal of muttered agreement and even an "Amen!" or two. At the level of *feeling* in that courtroom, it was clear that at least one witness could have a very transcendent, even "orthodox," view of God and yet believe in evolution—which was what I intended to communicate.

The judge brought me to my senses with his first question:

"Professor Gilkey, for the sake of my notes, how do you spell the names of those heretics you mentioned, Marcion and the Gnostics?" (See *Judgment*, fn. 18, pp. 18 and 19.)

Grateful that he had so clearly gotten the point, I spelled each for him and turned back to Tony.

"Have you read Act 590, Doctor Gilkey?"

"Yes."

"Can you tell me specifically in what way this Act, mandating that creation science be taught along with evolution, represents the establishment of religion?"

"Yes. First, looking at the description of creation science in the Act, we can see that the structure of the model and the main elements of the theory reflect the scriptural narrative point by point: sudden creation out of nothing, creation of permanent or fixed species or 'kinds' at the beginning, separate ancestry or separate creation of animals and of human kind, a worldwide flood as *the* catastrophe, and all this 'recently'—the six- to twenty-thousand-year dating being Biblical. Above all, the concept intrinsic and necessary to the model, the concept of a creative act of God originating all this out of nothing, has its origin in Scripture, its main expression in the creeds of the Church, and is, as I have said, conceptually religious through and through.

"Let me underline this point. It has been said in this court that the religious character of this notion of creation is accidental, a matter of the education and the ways of thought of the plaintiff's religious witnesses. This is quite wrong. The religious character to the notion is intrinsic: It is intrinsic because 'God' is a religious concept, and activity by God is a religious assertion; take that activity out of this model, and there *is* no model. The concept is then completely void, telling us nothing and explaining nothing. The explanatory power of the model is that '*God* did it'; if God is gone, you have only unexplained 'facts': unexplained instances of order, recent appearance of the earth, and so on. And with unexplained 'facts' alone, you do not yet have science or a scientific model. The reason for the absolute central- ity of the concept of God is that, by the very nature of the idea of creation, God is the only principle of expla- nation there, the only actor, cause, or force on the scene. So if this is a theory or a model at all, it is religious; if it is not religious—and God is not a part of it—it repre- sents no theory."

"Granted, then, Professor Gilkey, that this is a reli- gious concept or idea, does it represent a particular reli- gious tradition, or does it represent the way all religions view the question of origins?"

"There is absolutely no question that the concept of creation enshrined in Act 590 represents a particular religious view of origins, and not that of all religions or of religion in general. Here let me say that the creation-science literature, and the Act itself, have again flatly stated an error—are clearly wrong. Repeatedly, they maintain that there are only two models of creation. This is false. There are literally hundreds of different views of creation, views represented in a wide variety of religious myths and doctrines or 'truths.' Nor are any of those 'esoteric evolutionary systems,' as creationist literature states. On the contrary, they are *religious* theories representing the world as arising from a divine and spiritual source.

"The main point is, however, that they differ markedly from one another. Major religious traditions of our present—Christianity, Judaism, Islam, Hinduism, Buddhism, Sikhism, Confucianism, Taoism, and Shinto, to name only a few major ones—vary widely and significantly in their interpretations of creation. Only the first three, the religions stemming from Hebrew religion, speak of creation out of nothing, or of an absolute beginning of things. Only those, therefore, contain either an idea of creation such as this or the particular concept of Creator implied in it. Other views are significantly different: Our world emanates from the divine as an appearance of God; our world is *maya*, an illusion, a dream; our world arises out of two independent and equally ultimate principles: matter and form, one divine and the other not; our world is the work of several gods competing with one another—and so on indefinitely.

"To establish the creationist teaching as mandatory would, therefore, establish the doctrine of one particular religion (Christianity) over all the others and would directly contravene the First Amendment. Let me add that it would establish only one interpretation of the Christian doctrine over other Christian interpretations, namely the literalistic or fundamentalist interpretation. Thus it would exclude not only other religions but also the interpretations held by most of the Christian churches of our nation, and by all of the Jewish temples and synagogues. If creationism were taught as stated in the Act, the civil law itself would imply that only those who were literal creationists believed in God, affirmed a divine creation, or revered Genesis—for the Act holds that there are only two models, creationism and atheistic evolution."

"You have said that religious speech or religious ideas concern God, and that, therefore, they point beyond the ordinary causes and entities of our common experience. . . ."

(A good summary, Tony, I thought.)

" . . . Your statement seems to draw a sharp distinction between religious ideas or religious theories and scientific ideas or theories. Would you agree with that? If so, would you tell us your view—as a theologian—on the differences between scientific and religious propositions or theories?"[3]

"This is a complex matter; I will try to be brief and yet clear. I think, though I am not sure, that what I say about science will be acceptable to philosophers of science." (Many scientists, I noted silently to myself, don't really know too much about the question of what science is or is not!) "All theories—scientific, philosophical, and religious—seek to explain or make intelligible the varied stuff of experience; thus, all theories—and here we are concentrating on scientific and religious theories—have certain general characteristics in common: (1) all seek to explain experiences, and appeal to certain types of 'facts'; (2) all ask certain specific sorts or kinds of questions; (3) all are responsible to certain sorts of authorities; and, as a consequence, (4) all theories have certain specific kinds of character and obey certain definite rules or 'canons.' While both are theories in this sense, still scientific and religious theories differ markedly in each of these areas.

"First, then, science seeks to explain sensory experience, facts that can be shared by everyone anywhere or any place, facts available to anyone by 'looking' or observing—that is to say, objective, sharable, external, and repeatable facts or experiences, what we ordinarily call 'sense data.' Religion is interested in a different level of experiences and in different sorts of facts: experiences of the world as a whole, its order or beauty, its meaning or lack of meaning. And religion concentrates on facts of inner life: responsibility, conscience, right and wrong, guilt, anxiety, meaninglessness, despair on the one hand, or trust, new life, release, wholeness, centeredness, forgiveness, peace—even ecstasy—on the other. Thus, science moves entirely in the sphere of objective, public experience; religion is more apt to point to special, inward, unusual, shattering, or healing experiences.

"Correspondingly, science asks objective questions, questions directed at knowledge in its strictest sense. What sorts of things are there here, or in the world? What causes what? What sorts of invariable relations are there between events—what laws govern existence? If we do (a), then does (b) follow? Does it always follow? And if so, how can we explain that? Science asks *how* questions, questions about the character and processes of change. It seeks after laws of change, and thus it concentrates on material, universal, and necessary or automatic causes, structures, laws, and habits.

"Religion asks different sorts of questions, questions about meaning. Thus religious myths, symbols, doctrines, or teachings answer these sorts of questions. Why is there anything at all, and why are things as they are? Why am I here, and who am I? Who put me here and for what purpose? What is wrong with everything, and with me? And what can set it right again? What is of real worth? Is there any basis for hope? What ought I to be and do? And where are we all going?

"These are important questions, important for life because basic to life's meaning, direction, and purpose. If not answered in terms of a traditional religion, they must still be answered. Wherever they are answered, the theories or views answering them will turn out to be examples of religious speech. These are questions of ultimate origins, of the why of things, of good and evil, of the promise of healing and reunion, questions of hope. Reality is questioned with regard to purposes, to salvation—with regard to its meaning, not primarily its structures, with regard to its spiritual dimension, not its material causes—though in the end, the two cannot be completely separated. This is what all the great religions, and certain central aspects of all the great philosophers, talk about. Wherever you have these questions addressed, you have religious speech."

There was a noticeable pause while I tried to remember where I was. I looked at Tony, and fortunately he broke right in.

"Do both science and religion recognize some sort of authority, and are these authorities different?"

"Yes, in science, the authority—the basic criterion of science—is represented by logical coherence and experimental adequacy. And by experimental adequacy is meant that a theory has not yet been falsified by experiment and that insofar as that is the case in repeated experiments, it is confirmed—that it is characterized by coherence with other established theories, fruitfulness for further questions, and simplicity or elegance. In practice, this means the authority of the consensus of working scientists in that field. This consensus of the scientific community alone determines what proposed theories conform to the requirements of logic, of experimental adequacy, and of coherence and fruitfulness. This authority among the scientists is an *earned* authority, through training, experience, and excellence in the common work of the community.

"In religion, or at least in monotheistic religion, the final authority is God, or the point where our relation with God appears, and is recognized. This point is often called revelation, or its equivalent—some special touch with the divine where enlightenment occurs and insight is given (as, for example, in the Word of God given in the Israelite Covenant, in Jesus Christ and in the Scriptures or in the 'higher consciousness' of Yoga or of Buddhism). Secondarily, authority lies with those who have received or receive revelation: prophets and apostles, holy men and women, teachers; in their writings and in those who can interpret their writings; or, in other traditions, in a holy person, a yogin, or one who has had a special experience or special authority.

"Such authority resident in special persons is not necessarily solely external to the rest of us. Usually it is also subsequently validated in some way in *my own* experience wherein I, too, make relation with the divine, through prayer or hearing the Word, through sacrament, meditation, ritual, or obedient action. But in all of these, the authority is special, and the experience of illumination is special and not ordinary or 'public' in the usual sense of that word. In each case, the authority is of a special sort; it is *given*, not earned—and is usually regarded as given by the divine. Of course, the authority in a religion may be supplemented and buttressed by rational argument—as in much theology or apologetics; but that is generally a supplemental and not an originating authority, and it is rarely the basis for the acceptance of the truth of what is there asserted."

"You said that as a consequence of these differences, the theories of science and of religion—the characteristics of these theories—were significantly different. How is that so?"

"The creation-science documents, although written by trained scientists, misunderstood science. That is, they locate science in its facts, what they call its scientific evidences—and they regard any theory that 'explains these facts,' whatever the logical character of that theory, and however it explains the facts, as science. Thus a theory about the action of God that 'explains' certain so-called 'facts of science' is regarded as a scientific model. It is not. What has been forgotten is that science is located in its theories, in its theoretical structure, not in its facts.

"Thus it is the *theories*, not the facts involved in scientific inquiry, that make it science. And only certain *kinds* of theories are scientific theories. A scientific theory, therefore, has to have a certain characteristic logical form, and it has to explain in a certain way—otherwise you don't have science, a scientific explanation, or a scientific model. We have already seen how creation science is religion; now, in discussing what scientific theories are like and how they function, we will see why it is not science and cannot be science, however many so-called 'facts' it may seek to explain. Explaining facts is not what makes science, for every sort of theory seeks to explain what are regarded as facts. It is the *way* a theory explains the facts that establishes it as science."

"Can you, then, Doctor Gilkey, describe for us briefly what sorts of characteristics you find scientific theories to have?"

"First of all, a scientific theory seeks to explain the facts of experience by means of laws—that is, universal patterns of behavior which are necessary (always happen), which are automatic and blind (not knowing or planning what they do). Or, as is often said, scientific laws are sets of invariable relations between events; if *p*, then *q*, and *always* if *p*, then *q*.

"Secondly, these laws can appeal to, or point to, only *natural* or *human* causes or powers, forces within the creaturely world, within the system of nature and of history. No supernatural force or cause from outside the system can be a part of a scientific explanation.

"Thirdly, the basic forces or factors referred to in a scientific explanation are quantitative, not qualitative, in character, and thus are they measurable, objective, and sharable. As a consequence, no scientific theory explains by means of purposes or intentions. None answers a 'why' question, except when in asking 'Why did this event happen,' we mean merely 'What were the proximate causes of that event?'

"Finally, a scientific theory or explanation starts with concrete, objective, sharable observations or data, and it is tested by them. A quite definite outcome is predicted that anyone can observe, a datum whose non-appearance would *falsify* the explanation. A scientific theory is not tested merely by seeming to 'make sense' or to provide an adequate and coherent explanation, but by a quite definite, observable experiment. Thus the language of science is quantitative, mathematical, precise; its referent is to quite universal patterns of behavior; it is limited to describing the impersonal system of relations between the things or entities around us."

"And religious speech or theories, what are they like?"

"In the West, religious language refers to God, an intelligent, purposive being or reality, one who is transcendent, that is, who is *not* part of the system of creaturely things but precisely their source and ground. Thus language about God, 'religious explanations' or theories, is personal and purposive ('God willed it' or 'intended it'), not necessary or determined; in referring to a transcendent being, this language is symbolic or analogical, not precise and univocal.

"Religious theories explain by speaking of God's actions or purposes, not of finite causes. Whenever finite things or persons are related to God, there is religious discourse or theories about them; wherever they are related merely to one another, one has 'secular' discourse, not religious discourse. Thus when we ask, How did *a* arise out of *b*? we are not asking a religious question of origins but a scientific question. When we ask how the whole system arose, and we give God as its origin, then we are *not* providing a scientific explanation but a religious one.

"The basic words here are qualitative, not quantitative; they have to do with purposes, God's purposes— with order and disorder, good and evil; religious explanations have to do with the meaning of things, the *why* of them, not the structure or the *how*. And, as we have seen, religious explanations are based on special sorts of experience, special insights or revelations, not objective, observable, sharable experiences. Religious theories or beliefs cannot, therefore, be falsified by evidence or by new evidence. When Paul said, 'Whether we live or die, we are the Lord's,' he was making a powerful religious statement: *Whatever* happens, God is there— and my faith in God holds.

"Religion, in other words, tends to answer—or to try to answer—our *ultimate* questions: questions of ultimate origins (where did it *all* come from?), of ultimate worth (what is the point or meaning, the *why* of life?), of ultimate destiny (where are we all going?). Religious answers thus provide confidence, hope, trust; they offer guidance and direction, the promise of healing, reconciliation, and fulfillment. They form the basis for our style of life, for our norms, for the shared beliefs that create community. Religious models are imprecise, untestable, often fuzzy, but they express immensely important issues, *the* important issues for our individual and communal existence.

"Science asks what happened, what made it happen, what universal habits are there in things—it seeks that sort of understanding, *how*, not *why*, understanding. It is precise, measurable, testable; thus it is relatively certain and reliable knowledge. But by the same token, science is *limited*; it asks only certain kinds of questions; it is limited to physical explanations, to objective issues, to understanding natural relations.

"As is plain, science and religion present to us very different forms of speaking or thinking, very different sorts of models or theories. To ask whether there is scientific evidence establishing or demonstrating scientifically a religious theory, for a theory or model speaking of God's creative action, is therefore an empty question. There *can* be evidence for a religious view, of course; but any amount of 'scientific evidence' (whatever that means) for a religious theory about God cannot make the theory scientific. It remains a religious theory or model for all the reasons we have stated, primarily because it speaks of God, God's power, God's intentions, and God's deeds.

"Science is, in short, *secular;* it deals with the worldly world: with nature and its forces, with human bodies, and—by extension into the social and psychological sciences—with social, historical, and possibly psychological forces. It cannot go beyond this 'secular' level because then it leaves the observable, sharable, quantitative, measurable, the natural or finite, level. Thus it leaves out a lot: my intentions, decisions, values, and commitments, as well as God's; it omits the human and the divine *person.*

"Thus, scientific discussions of origins are significantly different from religious discussions of origins. The first trace out the finite processes by which things arose and came to be; the second witnesses to the ultimate origin and purpose of these processes. Scientific accounts of development in astronomy, geology, and biology, are, therefore, not at all incompatible with religious views, even though they do not speak of God. The fact that science omits God is a result of the *limitation* of science, not of its atheism: Science is limited to finite causes and *cannot* speak of God without making God into a finite cause.

"Let me point out that this 'methodological non theism' of science is not confined to natural science—or to evolutionary theory. It is characteristic of all modern academic disciplines. If I write a history of World War II for the History Department at the University of Chicago, I will discuss the historical causes: political, economic, psychological, and social causes, and the historical actions by men and women, that seem to me to have brought about that war. I will *not* say, as a historian, that God's judgment on Europe caused the war.

"When, however, I write a *theological* account of modern history, I will—and I have done so in my own works —speak not only of all these factors but also of our common sin and of God's judgment; and, I must add, I do not think the event of that war can be understood until this theological dimension is included. For those theological factors, hidden though they be to the inquiries of secular historians, are, I believe, really there and vitally effective in the march of events. And the task of philosophical theology is precisely to unify in some coherent way those two diverse and yet valid ways of speaking of the war. Nevertheless, that latter represents a *theological* interpretation, not an example of inquiries recognized by most historians as 'historical.' The same is true of the law. If I am a lawyer defending a client from the charge of the murder of John Doe, I cannot offer—even in this court in Arkansas—an 'explanation' of the murder that holds that God, and not my client, struck John Doe dead."

(I noticed that Judge Overton was by now intensely interested and was looking sharply at me, and so I enlarged on this theme.)

"That would not be an explanation or theory recognized by the court; our law in this sense is 'secular' in principle. Legal procedures are limited to explaining an event by natural, historical, or personal causes, and can only develop theories that explain by means of such causes. That limitation does not mean that judges, prosecutors, and defending lawyers do not believe in God; nor that God is not at work in our society or in Arkansas society; nor that the divine hand might not have been at work in and through this event; nor that there may be, as I believe there is, a divine foundation to any 'secular' law that is just. Nevertheless, again, despite these 'religious dimensions' to the law, God is not recognized as an *agent* in a legitimate *legal* explanation of events, anymore than God can be an agent in a scientific or an historical explanation of events."

(I was relieved to hear the judge at this point mutter an almost inaudible grunt of agreement, so I continued.)

"To say that evolution 'excludes God' is, therefore, merely to say that it is a theory within natural science.

It is not to say that this theory is essentially atheistic or represents atheism. It is because science is limited to a certain level of explanation that scientific and religious theories can exist side by side without excluding one another, that one person can hold both to the scientific accounts of origins and to a religious account, to the creation of all things by God—which accommodation this law definitely excludes."

Figuring I had by now made my point as clearly as it could be made, I stopped and subsided back into my chair.

"Professor Gilkey, would you define for us what is meant in theology by the word 'apologetics'?"

"Apologetics traditionally has been regarded as one of the branches of theology, namely, that one which seeks to win over or persuade those outside a given religious community. It is, therefore, an enterprise engaged in by spokespersons for a religious group with the purpose of convincing 'unbelievers' by argument. For this reason apologetics does not appeal to the religious authorities recognized by its own group (e.g., Scripture) but must establish a common ground with outsiders, a ground usually found by invoking universal principles of reason and pointing to some aspects or aspects of common experience. In former ages, apologetics generally utilized philosophical arguments to make its case; in modern times, it has frequently appealed to the conclusions of science and arguments from them. Apologetics, therefore, takes what might be called a 'secular' form, but what it seeks to establish is a particular religious doctrine or belief."

"Can you give us examples of apologetics?"

"Yes, of course. The most famous by far was St. Thomas Aquinas, the great Catholic philosopher/theologian of the thirteenth century. His arguments *Against the Gentiles* for the existence of God, arguments to all intents and purposes based purely on common experience and universal reason, are classical examples of apologetics. One can also cite William

Paley of the late eighteenth century, whose books Darwin read carefully. Paley argued that the universally experienced harmony and adaptation of all the elements of creation pointed to the necessity of a divine Creator. In the twentieth century, the English philosopher F. R. Tennant and the French Jesuit Teilhard de Chardin are further examples, interesting in the present connection because both appealed to what they regarded as the certainties of modern evolutionary science to make their case for the work of deity in the creative process."

"Would you, as an expert in theory and in theological apologetics, say that creation science is an example of Christian apologetics?"

"I would indeed. Let me say at once, however, that by so naming it, I do not mean at all to say that there is anything wrong or underhanded in doing apologetics. I have done a good deal of it in my own lifetime, and St. Thomas, who outranks us all, was certainly no shady character. It depends on whether the goal of the argument is made clear or not—that is, whether one, as Judge Overton has said, clearly exhibits both of the hats that one is wearing, that of rational argument and that of a particular religious conclusion. The fact that an argument leads to a religious conclusion does not mean that it is a sneaky or invalid argument. It does mean, however, that, since it leads to a religious conclusion, to a conclusion about the existence or work of God, it is not in itself a scientific argument but a philosophical or theological argument. But we have been over this ground already."

"Can you tell us in more detail why you say that creation science, as we find it in this bill, is an example of theological or religious apologetics?"

"Certainly. In the first place, it is an argument aimed at reaching a religious conclusion, as we have already seen; namely, it argues for the divine creative activity as the sole rational explanation for the entire visible world as we experience it. Moreover, creation science, like all apologetics, claims to base its arguments not on any special religious authority (of Scripture, tradition, or religious experience), but on 'scientific fact,' on those common facts relevant to the question of origins to which creationists appeal. As did the whole tradition of apologetics that I have cited, creationists point to certain elements of shared experience—the so-called 'scientific facts'—and argue that only the divine creative activity can explain those facts. This is apologetics: an argument based on common experience, one carried on by a participant in a particular religious tradition, and finally, one seeking to establish the rationality of the religious beliefs of that tradition—in this case, the creation of the world by God.

"This is apologetics also in the sense that it represents arguments for a particular religious theory or belief, namely, a Christian and Jewish theory, and, moreover, one interpreted in a very particular or special way. Other large Christian groups and most of the Jewish community deny this particular interpretation of the common and fundamental Christian and Jewish belief in creation. That is why I am here, and why the plaintiffs in this case, representing most of the area's churches and certain main Jewish associations, are also here. In effect, creation science is not an argument for *our* religious beliefs, but precisely an argument against them—for in principle it excludes the possibility of a faith in creation that accepts the scientific understanding concerning the age and the processes of development of the natural world.

"Although the books cited by the defendants wrongfully deny this, other religions in fact propose quite different religious theories, doctrines, or myths of origins than this one. There are innumerable models from past and present religious communities that contrast both with the creationist model and with evolutionary theory. If this law is enacted, a religious doctrine representing only one among many religious options will be established by a State government."

With that word, Tony thanked me, declared the direct testimony to be ended, and sat down. He was replaced almost immediately by Rick Campbell, who greeted me politely and began his cross-examination. It did not seem to me very probable that Rick (despite the good beginning on philosophy and theology he had recently made) could ask any really devastating questions or make my testimony appear foolish or contradictory—as, might, say, an A. J. Ayer, an Anthony Flew, an intelligent Barthian, or a Buddhist philosopher like Nishitani. But still, not knowing what to expect, I was quite apprehensive. I certainly did *not* expect the question with which he opened.

"Professor Gilkey, can you explain the difference between primary and secondary causality and how that distinction enters into this case and into your testimony?"

I was astounded. After our long dialogue in Atlanta on primary and secondary causality, I thought that it was perfectly clear to Rick that this old scholastic distinction was made to order for our case and not his. Moreover, all during my own testimony to date, I had had the uneasy feeling of omitting something, of leaving some pivotal point out; and toward the end, even as I talked of other things, I realized what it was: a clear statement of the difference between the religious or philosophical questions of *ultimate* origins and those scientific questions of *proximate* origins. Now Rick had given me the opportunity to go over that ground as clearly as it was possible to do. I was greatly relieved, and said with marked sincerity:

"I am so glad you asked me that question." When the courtroom burst into laughter at this, I realized that I had made Rick look a bit like a fool, which I had not meant to do. But I decided it was not all that bad for our case, and Rick could recover, so I went ahead with my point.

"Primary causality in scholastic philosophy refers to the creative activity of God in bringing any creature—

-120-

any thing or person—into existence; secondary causality refers to the finite causes that have brought something or someone into being, for example, one's mother and father. This distinction illustrates very clearly the important difference between religious questions of ultimate origins, which ask about primary causality, about the *ultimate* origins of all the finite causes of the world, and scientific questions of *proximate* origins, which ask how something came to be out of the host of finite causes that preceded and effected it, or helped to do so.

"One may, for example, affirm that God created each one of us—that is primary causality—and still not deny that our mothers and fathers, and their mothers and fathers, were *also* responsible—along with a multitude of other secondary causes—for our being here. In this sense, in Christian belief, the religious symbol of creation refers to the *primary* causality of God in bringing the whole world system, and all things within it, into being out of nothing.

"The scientific evolutionary hypothesis refers to the *secondary* causality, the finite, worldly, 'secular' causes through which that primary causality worked; and so it refers, on the worldly level, to those causes by which you and I came into being in space and time. Just as there is no conflict between primary and secondary causality, each referring to a different level of causation, so there is no conflict between the religious idea of creation and the scientific theory of evolution, *provided* each is aware of representing a different level of discourse and hence a different level of truth."

"You have made a good deal of the distinction between *how* questions, which you said are characteristic of science, and *why* questions, which are characteristic of religion. This distinction is not clear to me at all. Can you give us some examples, some home-grown examples, so to speak, of this distinction?"

For a moment or more I paused, recalling Tony's admonition not to begin running before you know the road down which you are heading. I had not thought out any examples beforehand of this familiar distinction—and I realized, as I sat there, that you could easily get yourself into real trouble down the line if, without thought, you happily embarked on a pair of examples that might turn out fuzzy, or even contradictory, once you had explicated them. But fortunately, Bultmann's famous example of rain came to mind: "It is not easy to pray for rain after listening to a weather forecast on the wireless," and so I embarked on rain, not really knowing where I would find myself at the end of my spiel.

"Let us take the example of a rain shower, even a storm. A 'how' question about that storm would call as its answer for a meteorological explication, the kind of thing we are all familiar with on TV weather forecasts. Here we ask, 'How did it come about that there was a rainstorm?'—and we are answered by a description of the process, interpreted by a variety of so-called natural laws, by which a cold front enters our region and produces showers."

"I see that," said Rick, "but what is the *why* question you spoke to us about? Is there any such question, as distinct from the *how* question?"

"There certainly is," I said, being granted a sudden inspiration, I have no idea where from, "and it represents a most important personal question about rain showers. It is 'Why did it have to happen on this, my wedding day?'"

Since fortunately the courtroom, and even the judge, burst into laughter at this example, the difficult line of questioning that might have followed (for example, "Why, Professor Gilkey, *did* it have to rain on your wedding day?") never got started.

"In your writings on religion and science, you have referred to the work of Thomas Kuhn, and you have made a great deal—with him—about 'breakthroughs' in the history of science where new, unexpected, and often ridiculed ideas or theories have come to the fore, ideas quite opposed to what the consensus of the established scientific community held at that point. Is this not the case?"

"Yes, of course." I knew where he was going with this, and rather admired this tack as his best line of cross-questioning.

"Well, why then is there this adamant refusal on the part of the scientific community to respect an unpopular idea? Why this arrogant dismissal of a competing theory, this insistence on established orthodoxy, whenever creation science is introduced? Is not science *essentially* the story of once-unacceptable laws becoming accepted or the revolutionary victory of theories that were formerly repudiated? Can science appeal to an orthodoxy and remain science?"

"These are excellent questions," I said admiringly, "and they raise real issues. The answer is that breakthroughs in science, however radical, remain within the arena of science. While it is true, and I have myself emphasized this often, that religious, philosophical, social, and psychological ideas have had vast influence on scientific inquiry, still, what 'breaks through' in a new scientific development is not a philosophical, a religious, or a social concept, but a scientific one. Relevant scientific theories—even those presently rejected which later may become orthodoxy—obey the canons of scientific inquiry.

"Breakthroughs are thus of scientific concepts, not of concepts within another range of discourse and submitted to other sorts of criteria. There are, for example, many vividly divergent theories current in the scientific community about the origins of life on earth; those that are relevant to science, however bizarre they may seem, still postulate a set of *natural* causes, not the introduction of a divine or supernatural cause."

"Are you saying, then, Professor Gilkey, that because in your view creation science is not science, that therefore it cannot be taught at all in school, that you would prevent such teaching or discussion of it?"

"Not at all. I have stipulated only that, first, it cannot be *mandated* by State law as a theory to be taught, and that, second, it cannot be mandated as a *science*—since it is a religious notion. I see no harm, and, in fact, I envision a great deal of benefit, if such religious concepts, models, or theories are taught in the right context, namely, in a course on Comparative World Views, or Comparative Religious and Philosophical Interpretations of Origins. In such a course, which could, I suppose, be an elective, creationism would legitimately be taught and discussed alongside of other, parallel views. For example, along with a conservative, 'creationist' view, one could study the views of origins held by a liberal interpretation of Christianity, the views of orthodox and reformed Judaism, of Buddhism, Hinduism, Sikhism, and Islam—as well as contemporary Naturalistic Humanism, and so on. And each view could well also be compared with whatever 'scientific data' one felt to be relevant.

"Thus the central issues of this trial, the nature of science, its differences from and similarities to religion, and the relations of religions to one another, to the Scriptures of each religion, and of all of these to Naturalistic Humanism, could be discussed openly in the classroom. That is already done widely in state colleges and universities; it could well be done in high schools."

"But you have said, have you not, that in a science class, a teacher, even if he or she is a creationist, must not teach creation science?"

"No, I have not said that. I have said that I think it is against the Constitution, and against the interests of religion and science alike, for creation science to be mandated by law as one of two theories to be taught in all scientific courses—an entirely different issue. If a teacher considers this theory to be the best theory in geology and biology (even though I would think she or he wrong in that view), of course he or she should say so to the class and say why; this is the first rule of academic freedom. Still, as teachers of science, that is, as professionals representing in part the community of scientists, they are, I believe, responsible to teach also—and fairly—what *that* community considers to be the content of their discipline, what geologists consider legitimate geology and biologists scientific biology. Certainly, they are free to disagree with the consensus of these communities—as I am free to disagree with the theological community and to teach a view I find more adequate and coherent.

"To sum up, my point is not to silence fundamentalists or creationists, even in the classroom. My point is solely to witness against the State, or any arm of the government, mandating the teaching of a religious doctrine in the public schools."

"Thank you. The cross-examination is over."

And with that, it now being after 5 P.M., the session of the court was declared to be closed for the day.

*　　*　　*

I stepped down from the stand, vastly relieved that my stint as witness was over, and rather elated that apparently things had gone adequately with my testimony. The lawyers, plaintiffs, and other witnesses on our side came up to congratulate me, slapping my back and saying that our case was now really on the move; and even some of those who had felt some doubt the evening before about "religious witnesses" said they were very glad I had testified. One of my colleagues, from the "scientific team" of witnesses, came up and shook my hand warmly and said, "I never thought I'd have occasion to congratulate a theologian, but really, you did awfully well."

Such forms of sweet-and-sour, of half-insulting/half-complimentary flattery, always irritate me; they lure one into both treason and snobbery—as when a European may say, "I'm so glad to have met you, for I've never run into a really intelligent (or 'sensitive,' 'cultured,' 'charming,' 'courteous,' etc.) American before, and so it is exceedingly gratifying to do so." In accepting their compliments to oneself, one accepts as well the judgment that one's fellows—be they theologians or Americans—are dolts, barbarians, or knaves, and one assents to the assumption that one's new colleagues are a quite superior lot. An appropriate reply was, therefore, on the tip of my tongue:

"I, too, am grateful that we met. I've never before encountered a positivist who was actually intelligent." But feeling in my viscera that my colleague was trying, however difficult it was for him, to be cordial and warm to a theologian, I knew that a hostile reply on my part, however tempting, would be gratuitous and, in fact, undeserved. And so I only said, "Thanks a lot."

The prize response to my testimony came, however, at the back of the courtroom. Just before I reached the crowded door of the courtroom, one of the ACLU lawyers came running up to me and, cracked up with laughter, managed to get out the following:

"When you stepped down from the stand, a tall, middle-aged spectator next to me in the back stood up, stretched, and, snapping his galluses, said, 'Well, that was sure cotton-pickin' bullshit now, warn't it?' I guess that's the roughest review you've had yet, eh, Professor?"

Even more delighted with that authentic Southern summing up (in Chicago, it would have been simply "Bullshit") than with the way the trial had gone so far, I stepped out into the corridor with Tony and Dorothy Nelkin and was greeted by burst after burst of flash bulbs and the bizarre sight of stilted TV cameras, all in full retreat before us as we hurried, full of excitement, down the corridors to the elevators.

6
The Trial:
The Overwhelming Weight
of Scientific Evidence

The trial commenced again the next morning at nine. This time there were noticeably fewer TV lights and cameras in the corridor, and a diminished crowd of spectators in the courtroom. Clearly, the loaded buses from elsewhere in Arkansas had not returned. Whether this was from disappointment at the lack of spectacle in the courtroom, disapproval of the liberal mood that prevailed there, or lack of interest in the scientific testimony to come, there is no telling. Still, some two to three hundred people were there. From their dress and manner, they seemed to be mostly supporters of the ACLU case, representatives of the liberal church and intellectual community of Little Rock, and students from local science classes, rather than fundamentalist defenders of the inerrancy of Scripture.

The first witness to take the stand for the plaintiffs was Michael Ruse, the British philosopher of science from Guelph University in Canada.[1] A handsome man with a fine red beard, he gave us a very clear and enlightening discourse on the distinction between science and evolution as a part of science, on the one hand, and creation science on the other. I was immensely relieved that his professional description jibed sufficiently with my own to save me from embarrassment—although I presume that had there been any obvious discrepancy, the lawyers would have warned us of it.

Ruse stressed that the essence of science lay in its theoretical structure: what made it science was not the facts or data out of which a given theory grew or through which it was tested; it was, rather, the *theories* of science and the special *relation* of these theories to data that constituted it *as science.*[2] These theories were, he said, *explanations* of data; in fact, they represent a special sort of explanation, not just any sort of explanation. First of all, they explain by natural laws, by invariable rules that apply universally and necessarily (automatically) whenever similar conditions are set. We understand "scientifically" when we understand certain data —for example, the way a baseball thrown from the outfield drops finally to the ground—as functions, consequences, or effects of universal and necessary laws. In turn our "theory" is a statement of that explanatory law.

Secondly, scientific theories or explanations, in order to count as science, must both in principle and in fact be checked out in relation to "the real world." (Note the presupposition that the world known through the senses *is* the real world! See Chapter 3, p. 66.) It is not because they "make sense" or "seem reasonable" that we hold them as scientific; they can be said to be scientifically valid because they have been seen in fact to express the way things actually work. This means that any theory that can be called science must be tested experimentally. Such testing is carried out by predicting what observable event or events will occur if the law we propose to test is valid, and then seeing in concrete experiment whether or not that predicted event does take place. If that event does take place, the law can then be regarded as probable (there might be some *other* explanation of that event). If it does not take place, then usually the hypothesis (the proposed law) is regarded as falsified (proven false). (In science, a model or hypothesis does not predict a general law or general pattern or behavior of nature—as the creationists claim that divine creation "predicted" the first and second laws of thermodynamics. Rather, by means of a scientific theory, the scientist predicts a concrete experimental result, a particular sort of measurable event, as the test by which a hypothesis is to be judged.)

Next, Ruse made crystal clear the important distinction between the *happening* of the evolutionary process (the theory *that* all forms of life are interrelated and have evolved from simpler forms) and the *explanation* of this assumed process (the theory *how* this process of development took place).

Thirdly, a scientific theory is held tentatively. As Ruse effectively said, "At some point, every scientist has got to be prepared to say about his or her own hypothesis or theory: 'Well, enough is enough. The counterevidence is piling up too heavily. I've got to give up this principle.'" And finally, the evidence for a hypothesis, and the experience from which it originates and in which it is tested, must be objective and hence public, sharable, and repeatable. "Without these four characteristics, a theory or a model is simply not science."

Ruse then showed very deftly how, according to the criteria of science he had mentioned, the biological theory of evolution (in *both* its senses)—despite the many scientific questions biologists have raised about Darwin's original formulation—was in fact a scientific theory. Correspondingly, he showed that the same criteria demonstrated clearly that the creation science model was not science: It appealed to a supernatural cause; it failed to use any natural law as its fundamental principle of explanation; and its theory was, both in principle and in fact, in the way it was held by its proponents, not falsifiable.

As Ruse explained, in creationist literature, facts were not sought so much to test the hypotheses of creation science as to vindicate them. To illustrate the sharp distinction between science as he had described it and creation science as its supporters formulate it, Ruse quoted, with great effect, from Dr. Duane Gish (Ph.D. in biochemistry, University of California at Berkeley), a leading writer and spokesman for creation science:

"'We do not know how God created, what processes he used, *for He used processes which are not now operating anywhere in the natural universe.* This is why we refer to divine creation as special creation. We cannot discover by scientific investigation anything about the creative processes used by the Creator'" (Duane Gish, *Evolution: The Fossils Say No,* p. 40; his italics).

Ruse quoted this and then said, "Whatever else this may be, it is certainly not a prescription for science. It is an explanation, but not a scientific explanation. It appeals to a supernatural cause; it denies the presence or effective working of present natural laws; and it is in no way falsifiable nor is it tentative."[3] And Ruse cited the oath taken by creation scientists in the San Diego society to the effect that they hold to the inerrancy of the scriptural account and will defend it. It was, needless to say, very effective testimony.

Because in an article Ruse had made the point that scientific criticism of evolution was widespread and even growing, he was asked on cross-examination how he could square this with his present defense of evolution as science. Ruse answered by making once again the important distinction, one subsequently repeated by a number of the scientific witnesses who followed, between evolution on the one hand as a *fact*, as the actuality of the development of the forms of life over eons of time out of earlier forms to the present forms, and evolution on the other hand as a *theory*, namely, as the attempt by scientists to explain by theory that development. Over the *theory* explaining evolution, there has always been and always will be real disagreement and frequent changes. All such theories are tentative, subject to challenge and continual criticism and testing, and inevitably destined to be changed and reformulated. The *fact* of evolution, on the other hand, he said, has been established beyond any reasonable doubt, and "no reputable scientist in his right mind denies that organic evolution actually occurred." For obvious reasons, creation scientists confuse these two quite different issues and—"though they know better"—regard the frequent critiques of present formulations of evolutionary theory as challenges to the *fact* of evolution, which they certainly are not.

Much like the muddled questions of "origins," which my own earlier testimony had insisted had referred to two quite clearly distinguishable questions—how the entire system arose, and how certain things within the system arose out of other things—a muddled "theory of evolution" could refer to two quite different matters: on the one hand, the fact that a process of development had happened, and on the other, theories about how it had happened. Much of what persuasive power the creationist case was able to muster depended on these two sets of confusions.

In their literature, the creationists had made a good deal of the obvious fact that past historical developments, such as the formation of the galaxies and the solar system, the geological history of the earth, and the development of the forms of life—not to mention the Big Bang itself—being unique and past events or sequences of events, could not be repeated under present experimental conditions, and thus could not be "observed." How, then, creationists asked, could evolution be called scientific? Ruse was therefore asked why it was that the requirement that scientific theory or law be "tested by observation" did not exclude these theories about unrepeatable, and therefore unobservable, past developments. How is it that a description and explanation of a past and unrepeatable "story" can be a legitimate part of scientific theory? The answer Ruse gave was interesting and persuasive.

Scientific testing does not mean, said Ruse, observing all the forces or events referred to in a theory. In important theory, most of these are, in fact, unobservable. (As Ayala was later to say, "Nothing important in science is observable; you can't observe the intellectual construct

—and *that* is science.") What is observed is implications of the theory in the observable present. A scientist simulates in the laboratory conditions similar to conditions held to be the case in that past situation and looks for concrete, measurable data implied by the theory were it true. Or one tests a theory about a past event by means of a model erected in the lab. Knowledge of the unobservable past is possible, therefore, on the assumption that the same natural laws that brought that past event about are operative in our present experience—an assumption that makes possible knowledge of the distant stars in space and of the earth's distant beginnings in time.

Clearly, the use of natural laws as principles of explanation was not only the primary *characteristic* of all scientific explanation, as Ruse had already said. It was also obvious from this discussion that the assumption that there was a pervasive and stable *order* of natural laws, extending throughout the entire spatio-temporal scope of the universe, represents the basic *presupposition* that makes scientific inquiry possible. On this assumption, inquiry is enabled to move outward into space and backward in time, far beyond the scope of direct observation. Without the presupposition of this pervasive order, science, even the limited science the creationists accepted, made no sense whatever. This philosophical, yes, even "religious," presupposition of all science, including their own, the creationists, with their naive empiricist emphasis on direct observation and on facts as constituting science, had overlooked and ignored—as, ironically, do many of their most hearty antagonists, the positivists!

The final subject matter of Ruse's important testimony, wrung out of him, so to speak, on cross-examination, proved potentially embarrassing. Although, as he admitted under questioning, he had once been a kind of "sturdy positivist," discounting the role of fundamental beliefs and values in science ("Science tells you what is what, and that is all there is to it"), recently Ruse had become interested in how the convictions of scientists about society, politics, and history might influence even their scientific ideas.[4] And in public print, he had cited the example of Stephen Jay Gould (who was scheduled to be a witness for "our side" the following day!) as one whose "Marxist social beliefs" probably strengthened, if they did not suggest, his new hypothesis of punctuated equilibria (the view that evolution proceeds not in gradual, steady development but in sudden leaps and jerks). A slight gasp went around the courtroom when an upcoming witness was labeled, and by a witness on the same side, a "Marxist"; and all on our team wondered what sort of feast the defense might not seek to stage for themselves, especially since the creationist literature made so much of the linkage between evolution, atheism, and Marxism!

At the moment, however, the defense had other fish to fry. If Ruse thought Gould's Marxism had influenced his view of evolution, did that not imply, in parallel fashion, that *any* hypothesis in evolutionary theory had similarly been determined by the political, the social, or possibly the humanistic, bias of the scientists? Was Ruse not admitting here that creation science was not all *that* biased, irresponsible, and naive in its suggestion that evolution had an atheistic background which it sought to conceal? Above all, if all these were true even of evolutionary science, why were the creation scientists suffering such castigation for the religious beliefs and motives that they freely admitted lay back of their theory? Were they, in short, any different from the evolutionists? And if not, why were not the two models essentially similar in character? Were not the Christian motives of the creation scientists more than balanced by the atheistic motives of secular scientists?

One could see from Ruse's face that he knew well that he had dug a pretty deep hole for himself here, and that he had just then been very effectively toppled into it by the delighted, and now-triumphant, Assistant Attorney-General, David Williams. I had no doubt that our case was solid and well-structured enough not to be lost by one knockdown; still, it was evident that this was a tricky corner and that Ruse would have to get out of it somehow. Williams was in truth on to something, and this was the first (and last) time it would surface seriously at the trial (though it had arisen and been addressed in my deposition).

While Ruse was trying to clarify his thoughts, I too was pondering the problem. All thought *is* "theory-laden," even scientific thought; it is shaped and molded by the most fundamental presuppositions, attitudes, and convictions of its social world, including the philosophical and religious symbols that give any society its character. For many in the scientific community the metaphysical presuppositions of science, the world view which science implied to them, were alike those of Naturalistic Humanism. The "real" world was for them one with solely "natural" origins, and the only purposes or "meanings" in that real world were confined to the human beings who held them. To them, science, and particularly evolutionary science, bore indeed a "religious" message: that outside of the human sphere the universe was merely matter in motion, void of wider purpose or meaning.

This theory-laden character of all thought, in this case much scientific thought, and the secularistic bias of much of science, have been widely recognized, and most of us had written countless lines on this subject— though Ruse apparently had just recently run into it. But if all scientific thought has undemonstrated presuppositions, and if every form of thinking, therefore, bears with it a "religious aura," does this not give point to the creation-scientist critique that evolutionary science represents in fact a secularistic "faith," not an "objective theory," even that it is an instrument of atheistic and humanistic religion? Can the plaintiffs still deny that science, and especially evolutionary science, is as much "religion" as is creation science?

As this small drama was unfolding, my own mind kept racing on. How could this heavy barrage be answered? How would I reply if I were on the stand? Several points came to me.

1. All thought, including so-called objective thought, has unexpungeable presuppositions or conditions. These make scientific inquiry possible; they do not subvert it.

2. These presuppositions may be naturalistic or secular; but other presuppositions for modern science can also be—and were historically—"religious," in fact, Judeo-Christian. The choice of a naturalistic philosophical interpretation of science (i.e., an atheistic one) is thus an option, not a necessity; there is a perfectly legitimate and coherent theistic interpretation of science The division between the two is a religious/theological or philosophical, not a scientific division, a difference in philosophical/theological, not in scientific viewpoints, since one is here dealing with the metaphysical or theological presuppositions of science, not with science itself, and that is a very different level of thought, of discourse, and of truth.

3. The religious character of creation science is not derived from its motives nor from the large belief system in which it functions. It is derived from the fact that *the theory itself* is an example of religious discourse —in fact, a main element itself of that background religious viewpoint. Thus, as I had already argued, it was not science but theology. As opposed to this, evolution as a scientific hypothesis could be—and must be—distinguished from its naturalistic philosophical presuppositions and from its possible secularistic implications.

It was at this point in my hurrying thoughts that I realized that the scientific as well as the religious community had a grave responsibility if the confusions represented by this case were to be avoided in the future. The *limits* of science, the kinds of questions it asks and those it does and can *not* ask, must become clearer to the members of the scientific community than they have

been. Otherwise, in teaching science they too (consciously or unconsciously) will be bearing witness to a
secular "religious" viewpoint related to, but not identical with, the science they teach. And inevitably, in wit-
nessing to their own secular religiosity, they will breed
creationists as fast as they encourage humanists. I was
just beginning to imagine further points than these in
my own fantasized argument when Ruse began to
answer—and a very effective, if by no means final,
argument came forth.

Like any good philosopher, Ruse began with a clarifying distinction. We can, he said, speak of the "context
of discovery," and we can also speak of the "context of
justification"—and these two are very different indeed.
(Though—I thought to myself—they do share the same
presuppositions that make inquiry as a whole possible.)
In the context of the *discovery* of a theory, he explained,
many things are important which are not at all relevant
to the question of the *validity* of the theory. For example, parallel notions or ideas in other fields (paradigms,
as Thomas Kuhn has called them) can frequently support or suggest analogous models in the realm of
inquiry in question (e.g., computer programming and
DNA programming).[5] Also significant are the motives
inspiring both interest in the subject at hand and concern for the particular interpretation of that subject.
And finally there are all the normal and (often) abnor-
mal psychological and social factors that make a rare
insight possible but do not bear on the *truth* or the
insight. These other factors are, said Ruse, relevant to
understanding as discovery. They do, however, have
little to do with the question whether the resulting
theory is false or true, improbable or probable.[6]

For that question, whether a given scientific theory is
true or not, the criteria of the scientific method are
determinative. These are its success in explaining the
phenomenon (according to the stated canons of scientific explanation) and its capacity to predict subsequent
and quite specific empirical facts. Whatever Gould may

think about society and history, therefore, and whatever view other scientists may have of the universe as a whole, while these may be significant for the *development* of their hypotheses, they are irrelevant to their *testing*. On the contrary, their hypotheses are to be considered as valid instances of science solely on the grounds of their adequacy to the aforementioned criteria of science. As for the theories of creation science, they cannot claim to be science, but not because their proponents are religious or religiously inspired. On the contrary, it is because their theories or models fail to accord with the canons of science, because they cannot be tested in experience, and because they cannot usefully predict.

Even if this whole matter were much more complicated than the distinction between the contexts of discovery and that of justification might imply, still through that distinction Ruse had clarified the issue of the religious dimensions of evolutionary science. While both models might be correctly said to contain religious assumptions and implications, still scientific theory, *if* its proper self-limits were kept in mind, remains secular science, and hence different logically and conceptually from the theological theorems of creation science.

*   *   *

After Michael left the stand, the second wave, so to speak, of the plaintiffs' attack began in earnest. The first wave had been the argument that creation science was not a scientific model at all but, in fact, a particular religious doctrine, so that Act 590 represented the establishment of religion. Clearly, this argument constituted the main support of the plaintiffs' central complaint: that the Act contravened the First Amendment.[7]

The second wave had a significantly different emphasis. While continuing to argue the thesis that creation science could make no claim to represent science, it sought to show that the relevant theories of contemporary science (in geology, biophysics, biology, and paleontology) did, in fact, represent science. Thus the stipulation of Act 590 that creation science was a legitimate scientific model, or "at least as scientific as evolution science," was shown to be an unsupportable claim, as were the repeated allegations that evolutionary theory could be disproved by new "scientific evidence," or that it was itself merely a doctrine of atheistic religion.

While this second wave by itself could by no means have established our case with regard to the First Amendment (to say creation science is *not* science and that evolutionary theory *is* science is not yet to prove that the former represents the establishment of religion), still it was necessary in order to defend the teaching of evolutionary theories in scientific classes and to justify the refusal to mandate creation science as a legitimate alternative in biological theory. The scientists who presented this argument were, to those of us who heard them, unbelievably impressive, not to say awesome, in their command of their own realm of knowledge and in the intellectual authority with which they each made their case. My comments on what they said will be relatively brief, not because their testimony was either irrelevant or uninteresting, but because my lay mind frequently found itself completely at sea whenever any one of them really got down to work on the details of his own field.

The first scientific witness was Professor Francisco Ayala of the University of California at Davis.[8] A world-renowned geneticist, Ayala was graced with fully as much charm as intelligence; as a consequence, it was a continuous delight to listen to his impassioned as well as his very informative testimony. At one point in his recitation, the court reporter interrupted him:

"Professor Ayala, could you please slow down just a little bit?"

Ayala turned to her with great courtesy and said, "Madam, I do apologize for my fearful Spanish accent, which must be very difficult to interpret."

"Oh, sir," said the lady, demurely, "I think your accent is perfectly lovely—it is your speed I refer to."

Ayala's face beamed: "Ah, yes, I lived for ten years in New York City, and my speech has never regained a human tempo!"

"In that case, it is, I guess, hopeless," said the reporter, with a laugh, "so, sir, you-all just get on with it and I'll try to keep up."

It was a dialogue that delighted the courtroom and did as much credit to the Arkansas court reporter as to the courtly European intellectual on the stand.

Since Professor Ayala had at one time been a Dominican priest, he had had theological and philosophical training. Unlike the other witnesses from science, therefore, he was very aware of the reasons why creation science was an example of religious, and not scientific, discourse. Creation science, he said, appeals to a supernatural cause, and not to a universal natural law, for its principle of explanation. As a consequence, it is not a testable hypothesis (no one can test a divine act); nor, as an aspect of faith in God's activity, is it held tentatively. He went on to say that the phrase "kinds of things" used in Act 590 was a category from the Book of Genesis and not from contemporary science, where it had literally no meaning. In modern science, he said, "species" is a population able to interbreed. These populations over time do, in fact, change, and after enough time they are frequently no longer able to interbreed—that is to say, a *new* species has now appeared. Contrary to the claim of the creation scientists, moreover, species-change of this sort is observable: With bacteria it happens rather rapidly.

"And with my fruit flies in my laboratory, it can be observed and checked after not so long a time—after all, in two years there are twenty-five generations!"

And, turning to the courtroom, Professor Ayala invited those listening to him "to come to Davis and look at my families of fruit flies and see for yourself how genes combine, recombine, and even mutate, to form new interbreeding populations." Suddenly, those of us lay people who were listening realized that "observing evolution" did not mean the unreal claim to have watched an early form of primate change into a hominid some three to four million years ago. It meant (as Ruse had said) observing and checking similar, if not identical, changes illustrating the same principles in a current laboratory situation; and it meant making predictions according to these same principles that could be checked in our own future experience. Thus could empirical science in the present "know" a sequence of past events, a story of nature's development that had occurred eons ago.

Certainly the most dramatic moment I witnessed in the trial came toward the end of Ayala's direct testimony. Jack Novik, the ACLU lawyer who was, with impressive scientific know-how, feeding questions to the scientific witness, asked, "Professor Ayala, do you know of any other case when the State has sought to prevent, limit, or regulate the teaching of evolution?"

"Of course," said Ayala, in a hushed voice, his hands raised in the air. The whole courtroom waited with baited breath.

"Where was that?" asked the lawyer.

Then Ayala thundered out in a stentorian voice: "Joseph Stalin's Soviet Russia!"

With that, there was a sharp intake of breath on every side. The Arkansas lawyers jumped as if they had been shot. The day before, they had been accused of heresy; now—far worse—they were being labeled, albeit with some irony, unwitting but effective clones, or, perhaps, even accomplices of Soviet tyranny.

"And what was the result of that State interference?"

"Disaster for Soviet science. Russian geneticists are still coming to my laboratories in the vain effort to catch up—and it is hopeless; they are too far behind us."

The seriousness of the probable consequences of Arkansas's law dawned for the first time on the minds of many in the room, and a new solemnity dominated the proceedings from then on.

Cross-examining a renowned scientist on his or her own field of expertise, if one is only at best a beginner in science, is a futile and probably also a treacherous business, like tackling a large bear with one's hands. This the Arkansas lawyers knew all too well. As a result, questions were scattered and haphazard—random shots hoping to find a chink in the massive armor of knowledge confronting them. At one point, Williams had the misfortune to mention the "only two models (creation science and evolution science) dealing with origins." Ayala looked at him as if he were someone in the fifth grade.

"Son," he said, "in science it is impossible ever to say there are only two models or theories. Everything is always open; new ideas, new vistas, new perspectives, new forms of inquiry, are always appearing. No one of these is closed if it makes sense—and never are there only two possibilities."

Shortly thereafter Williams again made the mistake of referring to criticisms of evolutionary theory as representing positive arguments for creation science. Ayala regarded him with evident pity.

"My dear young man, negative criticisms of evolutionary theory, even if they carried some weight, are utterly irrelevant to the question of the validity or legitimacy of creation science. Surely you realize that *not* being Mr. Williams in no way entails *being* Mr. Ayala!"

With that, the young lawyer gave up and said there were no more questions.

The next scientific witness called was G. Brent Dalrymple, assistant chief geologist of the United States Geological Service, West.[9] He it was—so the lawyer intoned—who had been one of those placed in charge of the NASA team that first investigated moon rocks; his articles and books on geochronology list one hundred titles.

"We submit, Your Honor, that Dr. Dalrymple is an expert on rocks and on the dating of the earth."

"No objection," said the Attorney-General.

Dalrymple was a very neat, clean-shaven, modest, and courteous man, not at all extraordinary in appearance. But he possessed what was obviously an awesome intelligence; in fact I think his was the most precise and organized mind I have ever encountered. When he spoke, there was immense authority in his manner; he knew thoroughly whereof he spoke, and he knew he knew it.

"What, sir, is your interest in creation science?"

"Creationists maintain in the literature of theirs that I have read—and I have read most of it—that the earth is somewhere between six and twenty thousand years old, and that is very relevant indeed to my own geological work. There is, let me say, no evidence whatsoever for this view, none at all. There are not even the slightest data that the earth is less than ten million years old, and much excellent evidence that it is much, much older. Without evidence, a scientific theory does not exist; without evidence, a theory cannot be taught. Creation science is neither science, nor can it be taught."[10]

"Is there any evidence that the earth is older than they maintain?"

"Yes. The age of the earth is subject to testing in many ways. These methods of dating themselves have been validated over and over again. They show by a number of different routes that the theory of a recent creation is simply false; that the earth is, in fact, billions of years old—4.5 billion, to be precise. Thus their theory, such as it is, has been proven wrong over and over again. Its status is precisely similar to that of the theory that the earth is flat, or that the sun goes around the earth. It is not consistent with the scientific method to hold to a hypothesis that has been repeatedly falsified."[11]

Dalrymple then launched into an extended lecture on how the dating of the earth was accomplished. First he explained the major method: radiometric dating, or the rate of radioactive decay of isotopes. Then he moved on to the several reasons why this was a reliable indicator, and the several grounds for certainty that in this case the rate of decay did not vary, whatever the conditions of the samples. At each step of this complex process he would stop and explain the objections which creationists often cite to each of these arguments; frequently there were three or four of them to each argument. In turn, with each new objection, he would outline the double, triple, or even quadruple replies to that objection.

After about twenty minutes of his recital, all without notes and with hardly a pause, his testimony had become unbelievably complex, like some awesome fugue or vast family tree of a royal house. At the end of each one of these complex steps through which he led us—citing positive arguments, objections, and replies to such objections—as in some rich geological *Summa*, he would always return precisely to the next argument in line. Even though I am a remarkably careful note-taker, I soon found I had completely lost my place on my own page when we reached the fourth rebuttal to the third objection to the fifth step of the second method of dating! So I just sat back and listened, awed at the precision and order of this mind that could pick its way, without a note, through that maze of arguments and counterarguments.

In the end, everyone in the room *knew* that he knew what he was talking about—and knew as well that he, at least, knew, and *really* knew, how old the earth actually was. Scientific knowledge may, in logical structure, be only tentative and hypothetical, but when it reaches this high level, it bears along with it an extraordinarily rare mass of certainty—a knowledge that knowledge has been obtained—which I thought to myself, is fortunate, since daily, even hourly (and certainly when we board a plane or submit to surgery), we each place our life in its hands.

After this enthralling lecture on the dating of the earth, Dalrymple was asked to comment about several of the better-known "proofs" which the creationists continually cite to show the recent origin of the earth. It was clear that he was familiar with each of these arguments, for he quickly and expertly dismissed each in turn by showing where its facts were wrong or where a principle had been misunderstood, misapplied, or—as he frequently showed—misstated.

I recall one of these that concerned meteoric dust.[12] Applying a large body of seemingly valid data, the creationists had maintained that this dust should be about 185 feet thick *if* the earth and its moon were, in fact, as old as Dalrymple and his colleagues maintained. How, then, could he explain the fact that this prediction was so obviously false? Explaining first why the prediction of 185 feet was a grievous error in principle, Dalrymple went on to reply that the best data on meteoric dust was that gathered by NASA, where he had recently spent some time. According to their predictions there should be, in five billion years, a layer of twelve centimeters on the moon. When the astronauts landed, he concluded, they found ("to our satisfaction," he said), that the layer there was precisely ten centimeters—"about right for 4.5 billion years."

When the direct questioning was over, the defense counsel rose to say, "I have very few questions, Your Honor."

The next witness for the plaintiffs was Harold Morowitz, professor of biochemistry and biophysics at Yale.[13] By no means as dramatic a figure as Ayala nor as superhumanly articulate as Dalrymple, the more reticent Morowitz nevertheless made some telling points. One of the main arguments of the creationists concerned the second law of thermodynamics. Since, said they, the second law states that "over time the total supply of energy tends to dissipate and become increasingly unavailable," this law was a confirmation of the creation thesis and a disproof of evolution. If all matter and energy had been produced at once at the beginning, it makes sense that the supply of energy should from that time on decrease steadily. Further, if matter tends inexorably to degenerate towards a maximum degree of molecular disorder, this shows that life, which is a highly structured state, could not have arisen by natural principles from inorganic matter.

Asked about these two arguments, Morowitz replied that they were both based on a total misunderstanding of the second law. This law, said he, specifically refers to the dissipation of the amount of energy and of the molecular order *in an isolated or closed system*. In such systems, the dissipation and disorder referred to do take place. However, the surface of the earth is by no means an isolated or closed system: It receives new energy continuously from surrounding space. Thus, far from illustrating the second law, it exemplifies a precisely opposite development, namely, an increase of energy and of order. Morowitz concluded that "any responsible beginner in scientific knowledge knows all of this full well." This was by no means the first time during the testimony of the scientists that arguments of the creationists (who were, after all, trained in science) were shown to exhibit a surprising misunderstanding of contemporary science, a misunderstanding so gross, in fact, that it bordered on a misuse, even a deliberate misuse, of scientific principles.

Asked why he, as a microphysicist and microbiologist, was concerned with the question of the origin of life—was that not a matter for evolutionary theory in biology?—Morowitz replied that one of the major errors in creation science—and of the description in Act 590 of "evolutionary science"—was that creationists regarded the question of the origin of life as an aspect of evolutionary theory and hence as a part both of the Darwinian hypothesis and of the science of biology.

"Biology assumes the presence of life and then proceeds to investigate it," said Morowitz. "Correspondingly, evolutionary theory from Darwin on makes the same assumption; it presupposes that life of some sort is there, and then asks how the forms of life developed, and what laws or principles regulate that development. The question of the origin of life from non-life arises, therefore, in a quite different branch of science—the one I am involved in—than biology and the theory of evolution."

On cross-examination, Dallas Childs, the defense attorney, returned to this theme. He asked Professor Morowitz how long he had been involved in the inquiry into the origins of life.

"About twenty to twenty-five years," said Morowitz.

"Let me ask you, Professor—in all that time, have you yet found an answer to the question of the origin of life?"

"Not yet," said Morowitz, resignedly.

With this, the unfortunate Childs apparently thought he had an opening for a brilliant *coup*; if no answer had yet been found, did this not argue for a *divine* cause? With elaborate sarcasm, he moved in on Morowitz.

"Now, Professor, are you telling me that in those big laboratories in New Haven, Connecticut, with all that expensive equipment and all those bright Yale assistants, in over twenty-five years you have not uncovered the cause of life?"

"Yes," said Morowitz.

"Can you explain to me, Professor, *why* you have so obviously failed?"

Morowitz thought for a moment and then, smiling blandly, said, "Young man, it is a *very* difficult problem."

At this, the courtroom burst into laughter, and Childs' colleagues grimaced.

Childs was, however, no fool; and however distinguished a microbiologist he may have been, Morowitz, in turn, was neither a philosopher nor an historian of science. Childs therefore returned to the theme he had broached throughout his cross-examination of the scientific witnesses: How open, in fact, *was* the scientific community to new ideas? Was it not true, he asked, that science depended on novel, often revolutionary, theories? Yes, said an uneasy Morowitz. Was it not the case that the great scientists were innovators, radical innovators, whose ideas at first were laughed at, resisted, and disproved by "established science"? Yes, mumbled Morowitz. Was it not also the case that today the "establishment" that runs the scientific community resists, mocks, and scorns creation science; that creationists, despite their credentials, are not given leading positions; and that no article by a creationist has been "allowed" in the establishment journals nor in papers read at establishment meetings? Why was this case not a parallel to the disreputable, biased, and closed-minded rejection of new ideas in the history of science? Was not the whole polemic of "so-called science" against creationism really the effort of an established elite (in the East) to prevent novel but antagonistic hypotheses from gaining the hearing they deserve?

This was by no means an ineffective or invalid argument: As Childs was at pains to show, it bore the intellectual credentials of Thomas Kuhn and the sociology of science; it roused and appealed to all the resentments of the less affluent and egalitarian portions of the Southwest against the reputedly elite and privileged Eastern establishment; and it resonated again (as had the major points against Ruse) with the insight that the scientific community (like any "religious" community—though the scientists would shudder at the parallel!) was by no means as objective and open-minded as it might like to think itself or as it claimed to be.

Morowitz was effective and informed in defense of the policies and procedures of the main bodies of science against this charge. He listed the relevant scientific journals and societies; he demonstrated his thorough acquaintance with what they are about. And, having shown that he knew the facts of the matter, he asserted that the reason no articles had been published and no papers read was, far from being a biased exclusion, that none had been submitted.

"We can," he said, "hardly publish papers we have not received, or listen to addresses not yet written."

On the deeper issues of Childs' charge, however, Morowitz seemed at sea, a little beyond his depth. Creation science could not, he said, be compared to radical innovations in the history of science, because "it is religion and not science."

"And why is it not science?"

"Because the scientific community so judges it." This answer, which concluded Morowitz' testimony, resonated not only with the elitism at which Childs had hinted, but also reminded one of many all-too-familiar traditional reasons given for adherence to orthodoxy and resistance to unsettling innovations. In fact, it even appeared to be a secular echo of what the Roman Curia had recently said to Hans Küng when it rejected as "un-Catholic" his novel interpretation of Catholicism! All too apparently, Morowitz, like the other scientific witnesses with the exception of Ayala, found it hard to state conceptually the theoretical grounds (as Ruse and even I had done) *why* it was not science (i.e., the canons of scientific method); and it was even more probable that he would have been quite unable to articulate reflectively what he meant when he said he "knew" that it was religion. It was also plain that the scientific community only endangered itself when it ignored as useless or meaningless the reflective question of what science is, of what the relations of science are to other disciplines and forms of cultural life—and, like other established elites of history (for example, the established community of priests and theologians), contented itself with intramural discourse combined with fervent self-defense against any external change.

The last scientific witness was, by all odds, the most widely known of them all, both as a creative innovator and as an interpreter of evolutionary theory. He was Stephen Jay Gould, the paleontologist of Harvard. Like that of Ayala and of Dalrymple, his testimony represented both a positive and a negative movement. On the one hand, he showed how evidence from all sorts of investigations unequivocally established the "fact" of evolution, and he showed positively how this evidence supported his own reinterpreted theory (punctuated equilibria) of the character and dynamics of evolutionary development.

On the other hand, he used his wide grasp of the evidence to challenge the creationist explanation of the same phenomena. To creation science, the "geological column," the stratification of rocks and the fossils embedded in that stratification, is to be explained as one of the effects of Noah's flood, an event which to creationists occurred at the most some ten to fifteen thousand years ago. Most scientists, Gould said, take the fossils to represent a sequence over eons and eons of time of developing forms of life buried in strata representing different stages of the earth's long history. The same fossils are asserted by the creationists to represent *contemporaneous* species; thus their positions on the column are accounted for, not by the different ages in which those various life forms existed, but by their differing reactions to the flood, some (less mobile and intelligent) settling to the bottom, others escaping onto higher territory and being in the end found at the top of the column.

Gould showed that, on the contrary, the shells of many simpler forms of life were found on both the upper and the lower levels—"and clams could hardly be expected either to try to escape encroaching water or to succeed in doing so by climbing up mountains!" Again one realized that, however many gaps there were in current evolutionary theories, the alternative theories of the creationists bore almost no resemblance at all to the implications of the facts—and no wonder! Since those theories were developed out of other sources (a literal reading of Scripture) than the study of the evidence of rocks, shells, and bones, they could hardly be expected to correspond to these vast new ranges of evidence.

Gould's mind is exceptionally clear and systematic, a mind completely at home in the realm of theory. Thus, his explication of the fossil record and its relationship to the geological history of the earth's rocks ranged far across disciplinary borders, bringing in astronomy, geophysics, geology, paleontology, evolutionary biology, and even physical anthropology. As he spoke, therefore, it became even plainer that whatever the "gaps" between these different sciences—gaps of theory, of modes of inquiry, of categories and assumptions, even of fundamental language—still they were essentially and inextricably interwoven: astronomy, geophysics, and geology depending on physics and chemistry; paleontology, evolutionary biology, and anthropology depending on geology; geology depending on them in some respects (though, just as Dalrymple had said, not in all),[14] and so on. And the thesis or hypothesis, the most general theorem, that unites all of them, making legitimate their methods, directing their inquiries and dominating all their conclusions, is the thesis of a slowly changing universe, systematically interrelated, stretching back over eons of time and out into endless reaches of space, a universe producing along that nearly infinite course a vastly different and ever-changing sequence of forms: stellar forms, geological forms, life forms, historical forms.

Without this thesis of a universe in process over eons of time (what was referred to as the *fact* of evolution), there simply *is* no modern science: no astronomy,[15] no geophysics, no geology, biology, paleontology, botany, anthropology, agronomy, or meteorology. And it is precisely this general hypothesis (not the particular theory of poor, beleaguered Darwin!) that creation science challenges head-on, leaving nothing there in any of these sciences except bits and pieces whose methodological and theoretical foundations have already vanished. Creation science is not an alternative to so-called evolutionary science, a novel hypothesis to be integrated into an entire remaining structure of science; were it triumphant, it would represent the *end* of science as a tested and unified theoretical structure. It is, let us note, not only, or even primarily, the "religious aura" of modern science that conflicts with creation science, namely, science's implied humanism and/or atheism. Rather—and this makes creationism's conflict with science much less negotiable—it is the *scientific content*, the most general and fundamental theorems, of each of the major branches of natural science, that creation science rejects in the name of its view of creation.

* * *

During the course of the scientific testimony just described, there was a brief moment of what might be called comic relief. Sandwiched between the stunning performance of Dalrymple and that of Morowitz came what is called a "hostile witness," one called by our side but representing nevertheless the interests of the opposition. This was one James Holstead, the member of the Arkansas legislature who had introduced Act 590 and steered it through the Senate while someone else introduced it into the House. Holstead was the perfect foil to the disciplined and responsible intellectual brilliance that had preceded him. Tall, handsome, smiling, waving at everyone possible, touching people whenever he went by them, he represented the archetypal "pol," country-style (a Chicago pol would ethnically be very different). In any case, he seemed to this observer quite, quite vacant, unconscious of the various issues of constitutional law, religious truth, science, and education with which the court was so deeply involved.[16]

"Did you introduce the bill?"

"Yes."

"Who suggested it to you?"

"A Mr. Hunt, a constituent of mine."

"Did you know him well?"

"No, sir—he was introduced to me by a preacher friend."

"Did the Creation-Science Institute in San Diego write to you?"

"Yes, sir."

"Had you heard of them before?"

"No, sir."

"Did you inquire into who they were, or what they were about?"

"No, sir."

"Did you change it or amend it after you received it?"

"No, sir, but later I discovered it was drafted by Paul Ellwanger of South Carolina."

"Did you consult with the Attorney-General's office before you introduced it?"

"No, sir."

"Did you know that the South Carolina Attorney-General advised against a similar bill as being unconstitutional?"

"Yes."

"And you still did not seek the Attorney-General's opinion?"

"Yes, sir—I decided it was better to test the bill in court."

"Did you consult at all with anyone in the Department of Education before you introduced a bill that directly concerned them, and that would, if passed, almost totally re-form their curriculum? Did you consult with any individual science teacher or with any teacher organization?"

"No, sir."

"Why not?"

"I do not know, sir."

"Did you review any of the biological texts previously used by the State before seeking by legislation to change the biological curriculum?"

"Yes, I looked at the text used in North Little Rock and talked with a friend who sold textbooks about what was being taught around the State."

"When this bill was introduced on the floor of the Senate, had there been any committee meetings on it?"

"No, sir."

"Had there been any prior warning that it would be introduced?"

"No, sir. There were, however, plenty of questions from the floor, but I don't recall how many."

"Mr. Holstead, if you had made no effort to check this bill for its adequacy and usefulness, either with educators or with the Attorney-General's office, why did you introduce it? Were your own individual, deeply-held religious convictions a significant motivation?"

And the interrogator, pressing this point, claimed that in statements to the press, Senator Holstead had avowed that, as the lawyer put it, "God had spoken to you at the time and told you to sponsor the bill." At this, Senator Holstead claimed he had been misquoted.

"Did you say in your deposition that it favored one religious group?"

"I did say it favored the view of the Biblical literalists, of which I am one; and I said that the supporters of the bill are fundamentalists."

"Is it your view that this bill which presupposes the divine Creator complies with the First Amendment of the Constitution because it doesn't teach one particular view of religion or favor one religion over another?"

"Right."

"That is, Methodist over Baptist over Catholic over Jew?"

"Right. It doesn't mention any particular God."[17]

I remember thinking to myself as this dialogue unfolded that, since it is unhappily possible that in the course of political events legislators will appear who are seemingly as cavalier and uninformed as this one, and since apparently not a few legislators are eager to pass such nonsensical bills—as apparently in this instance had been the case—that it was fortunate indeed that bills already signed into law could be reviewed with some care in the courts!

*　*　*

With the conclusion of the testimony of the scientists, my own attendance at the trial unfortunately came to an end, since I had to return that evening (Wednesday) for my classes on Thursday. Thus I missed entirely both the testimony of those sturdy and responsible teachers in Arkansas who testified against the bill, and also of those witnesses—mostly scientists—who testified for the defense, that is, in favor of the bill. As has everyone else, I have read accounts of these matters in the papers and in subsequent articles. Because I was not there, however, I think it neither wise nor fair for me to comment on either one of these important aspects of the case. If, then, this account of the trial proceedings stops at this point, it is by no means because I think either that what preceded and is here described is more central, or that what followed and is omitted was more peripheral. It is simply because I was not there and so had no first-hand sense of what was afoot.

*　*　*

Although the outcome of the trial is well-known, it may be helpful briefly to summarize it here. After the plaintiffs had completed their case by calling some very courageous and thoughtful Arkansas teachers and educators to the stand the trial continued with the witnesses for the defendants. With the exception of theologian and philosopher Norman Geisler—referred to already in this text—these were mostly "scientists" (replete with doctorates in science and professional vocations in "science") who argued in various ways for the creationist cause. As noted, since the author was not present, comments on their testimony are hardly appropriate. Nine days after its beginning on December 7, the trial concluded.

I recall being surprised and somewhat disappointed that this trial would not, like most trials on TV or in the movies, end dramatically with the judge's ruling. "Oh, no," said one of the Little Rock lawyers; "rulings in trials like these come out when the judge has finally written them, possibly a month or a month and a half later. Overton is a bright and competent man; he does his homework and works like hell on his rulings. His will come out, I'm sure, within a month—and it'll be, I'll warrant, an excellent one."

Thus the case ended—as do all such civil cases before a judge—"not with a bang but a whimper," namely, with the testimony of the last witness and a summary statement by each of the head lawyers. Since these were neither reported in the national press nor is there any court record of what they contained, there is no public way of finding out what they were.

In any case, the Little Rock lawyer was quite right about Judge Overton. A month later, January 5, the judge announced his ruling, a verdict heavily in favor of the plaintiffs. In fact the judge's thirty-eight page ruling is itself an amazing intellectual document, summarizing with impressive comprehension and accuracy (as few of us could have done!) the entire complex testimony of the trial: of Biblical scholars, historians, theologians, philosophers, geneticists, geologists, paleontologists, and educationalists!

Practically restating the case marshalled by the ACLU, Overton ruled that creation science was, according to all the available criteria, not a scientific theory at all, but a "religious" doctrine or theory, its "model" being taken from Genesis, its proponents traditional fundamentalist groups, and its conceptuality that of a religious doctrine concerning the Biblical and the Christian "God."[18] Thus he concluded that Act 590, representing in fact the establishment of religion in the public-school system, inevitably involved the State in "entanglement with religion" and "the advancement of religion" and thus contravened the First Amendment of the Federal Constitution.

A month later on February 4, the State of Arkansas announced that it would not appeal this decision.[19] With this announcement, therefore, the case concerning Act 590 in Arkansas was permanently closed.

Meanwhile, in the State of Louisiana, a similar process had begun. On July 20, 1981, the Legislature, after several unsuccessful attempts, had passed Act 685, a parallel but (after the Arkansas debacle) significantly revamped "balanced treatment" law, and the governor signed it. Again the ACLU, accompanied this time by a law firm in New Orleans and a group of lawyers from Paul Weiss and Associates (one of whose partners, I noted with interest, was John McEnroe, Sr.), geared up for action and began to select witnesses, to take depositions, and to prepare its arguments for the trial to come in the fall of 1982 or the winter of 1983.

To our surprise, however, this whole process was delayed. First, the Louisiana Board of Education, troubled from the beginning about this law it would have been forced to implement, brought its own suit against the law in the federal court. Since, so its claim went, it was stated in the Constitution of Louisiana that school curricula are to be determined alone by the Board of Education and not by the Legislature, this new law, in which the Legislature had mandated subjects and theories to be taught in the schools, clearly infringed on the prerogatives of the Board of Education. Apparently the Federal District court agreed with this complaint, and on November 22, 1982, it ruled that Act 685 was unconstitutional in relation to the State Constitution. Although naturally I was exceedingly gratified that once again such an ultimately destructive public law had been defeated in the courts, I had to admit to myself that I was nonetheless somewhat saddened that we potential witnesses had lost our chance to enjoy a few days' fare in the restaurants of New Orleans!

With this "victory," however, the Louisiana case was by no means over. To our surprise, roughly a year later the Legislature brought suit against the Board of Education in the State courts. Its claim was that it, the Legislature, had in fact a perfect right to pass such a law governing school curricula. This claim was subsequently upheld; thus the original Louisiana law, Act 685, returned to life and to the statutes of the State. At this point, therefore, the ACLU and its partners in New Orleans took action again and reinstated their case as plaintiffs against the law.

The end of this case did not begin to appear until January 10, 1985. On that date (on a "Motion for Summary Judgment"—that is, without trial) Judge Duplantier of the United States District Court in New Orleans ruled that the Creationism Act (Act 685) was unconstitutional, and he therefore prohibited the State of Louisiana from implementing the law. Five days after this decision the State filed notice of its intention to appeal to the Fifth U.S. Circuit Court of Appeals. On July 8, 1985, the Court of Appeals upheld the lower court's decision, declaring, "The act's intended effect is to discredit evolution by counterbalancing its teaching at every turn with the teaching of creationism, a religious belief."

To our present knowledge, no other State legislatures are now seriously considering such bills, since defeat, as in the case of Arkansas, is not only somewhat damaging for the wider, national "image" of the State in question, but also drains the State's coffers. All observers agree, however, that these momentary victories in the courts will not prevent the creationist forces from continuing their pressure on the school systems of the land. Especially is this the case as the Religious Right gains, as it is unfortunately doing, more and more political support from the present administration. In all probability that pressure will now be more concentrated at the level of local school boards, where in numerous cases success may be easier to achieve. In turn, defense against these methods now requires *local vigilance*—vigilant action by the community's ministers, science teachers, educators, and parents—if the destructive consequences of such laws as Act 590 are to be prevented. This will, on the one hand, be a continuing and long-lasting siege. On the other hand, our defense—not, to be sure, against fundamentalism as such but against a fundamentalist manipulation and control of the public schools and of public education—is one that can be carried on successfully if it is prosecuted with dedication, patience, and informed intelligence.

PART II

Analysis and Reflection:
The Implications of Creation
Science
for Modern Society
and Modern Religion

7

Science and Religion
in an Advanced
Scientific Culture

Puzzles in the Data

The controversy that reached a momentary climax at Little Rock is perhaps most significant because of what it has revealed about the state of our current cultural life. Like a flash of lightning in the darkness, it has uncovered much that was obscure or hidden about that life, obscured by complexity but also hidden by conventional assumptions carried over from another age. As has been evident to any reflective reader, some of the "data" involved in this entire episode are (and were to me) surprising and unexpected; they seem to defy, even to outrage, our usual ways of understanding our cultural life. They seem pieces of a strange puzzle that will not fit. These data call, therefore, for *re*interpretation, for some explanation that breaks new ground.

For example, how is it that many fundamentalists intent on disputing most of modern science are themselves *scientists*? How is it that such a bizarrely antiscientific movement gains alarmingly wide support in a scientific society, not least among those who welcome military and industrial results quite dependent upon science? How is it that religion, and "primitivist" religion at that, is against all expectations gaining, not waning, in an increasingly scientific and techonological society? How is it that the mainline churches provided the preponderant legal bulwark against creationism? How is it that apparently—despite the vast numbers of their adherents—no one seemed to know that this was the case or why they fought creationism with such determination and courage? How is it that the established scientific community was, apparently, itself partly responsible for the controversy and was in fact "breeding creation science" because of the way it talked about, taught, and promoted science? How is it that this community, while intending merely "to do science," was accused—and with some reason—of really promoting "religion"? The following analysis makes no claim to provide a completely satisfactory set of keys to these puzzles. Still, it may help illumine some of the things that remain obscure and out of joint about the role of religion in a scientific society.

The Establishment of Science

We live in an *advanced* scientific and technological culture. That is the initial important element that must be understood. By "advanced," I mean that scientific inquiry and its technological consequences are thoroughly *established* in our common life. They are no longer on the periphery, as they once were, that is, confined to an educated and usually upper-class elite; nor are they kept out and kept under by an intellectual, cultural, and political "establishment" governed by other interests—for example, by the power and influence of religious institutions. Scientific and technological advance are now utterly necessary for the Pentagon, medicine, hospitals, industry, common services, and life in the home alike. As a result, since we are always willing to pay for what we feel to be necessary, federal, state, and foundational funds are almost without question expended to keep those advances going. Correspondingly, they quite dominate the curricula and the budgets of our universities and colleges. If there be a "queen" of the academic disciplines today, it is certainly natural science; if there is a "sacred knowledge" depended on and hence revered by everyone, it is scien-tific knowledge—for science represents to us *the* knowledge that promises well-being. The creationists are quite right: Science does represent an establishment in modern culture, much as religion once did—an establishment wielding vast financial, intellectual, and spiritual power.

Groups who enjoy a position of actual dominance generally do not like, for some reason, to admit it. They far prefer to see themselves still as "outsiders," dominated, even excluded and persecuted—certainly endangered—by other, oppressive groups. Thus, generations of Christians, as if they still huddled in catacombs in the pagan Roman Empire, have seen themselves as misunderstood by the world, as hardy martrys, whereas actually they controlled governments, lands, and gold. For example, the Southern Baptists especially enjoy this self-image of unworldliness and yet own or control most of the industries, banks, legislatures, and public universities of the South and Southwest. This is perhaps because the aura of virtue surrounds those who are oppressed and not those who dominate, and because aggressive action on one's own behalf seems justified if survival against entrenched hostile power seems to be at stake.

In any case, this is also true of the contemporary scientific community.[1] Even though its members may hold the key to national, military, industrial, and academic preeminence, and especially survival, and hence the key to the national treasury, they like to think of themselves as they once were in the sixteenth, seventeenth, eighteenth, and possibly even the nineteenth centuries: brave "free-thinkers," hounded by an implacably hostile establishment that would crush them if it could. In the establishment represented by "Christendom," the Church ended up owning one-third of the land in Europe. Science has not reached *that* level of financial dominance, but, compared to other intellectual disciplines in our day, it is running fairly close!

It is very important that established communities understand realistically this sociological fact about themselves. Only then can they comprehend and creatively respond to the bitter antipathy they frequently engender in those who are aware of their dominance and disapprove of its consequences. The Church would have been far more creative in European history if, much earlier, it had realized that it was made up largely of rulers and not of saints, and thus that it was more continuously tempted by self-concern to secure its own interests than it was impelled by virtue to sacrifice them.

Correspondingly, if the scientific community were more aware of its position of social and cultural dominance, it would be more cognizant of its intellectual and spiritual power and more careful of (and educated about!) its role vis-a-vis other aspects of our common life. In recent years, this community has frequently worried about what it likes to call its "public relations" —a euphemism (whether by church, industry, or science) for the situation of a large, powerful body which, in the face of obvious antagonism, wishes to maintain (at least to itself) its own innocence rather than to look carefully at its power and the often baleful uses of its power.

One of the causes of this controversy—not the only one, surely, but still a significant factor—has been the irresponsible use by the scientific community of that very cultural dominance. It is evident that creationism is a *reaction*, bitter and misguided to be sure, but a reaction nonetheless to the careless identification of the *scientific* knowledge of origins with an *exhaustive* knowledge or understanding of origins, and thus a reaction to the easy, and often superior, dismissal of religious views as primitive and therefore false. As we have noted, each time a child comes home and says to his or her parents, "My teacher told us today that science now knows that Genesis was wrong about our creation," two new creationists are produced. Science not only generates power over the natural world; it presently exercises power in the social world, especially the academic world. As one of the rulers over our cultural life, quite probably the dominant one, it must understand much better than it has its own procedures, their limits, and the relations of those limits to other elements of that cultural world over which it presides—if its rule is to be wise, fruitful, and secure.

Science Permeates All of Society

Another consequence of an advanced technological society is that science as well as technology now penetrates down to every level of that society, shaping and redirecting every aspect of society's life. This penetration throughout the social fabric has been evident for many decades with regard to technology; for example, the automobile, the telephone, the TV, and processed foods characterize the daily life of every class of society. It comes as some surprise, however, to realize that "science"—far from being confined as it once was to the upper intelligentsia—also appears at every level, at, so to speak, the "popular" as well as the elite level.

Even as late as the Scopes trial in 1925, this permeation of all society was not the case. Then, fundamentalism pictured itself as anti-science, as defending a sturdy, virtuous, believing, "down-home," rural America representing true religion against the decadent, sceptical, urban elite and academic world representing science.

Now all this has rather drastically changed. Doctorates in science, as in other disciplines (except theology and Biblical studies!), are no longer rare in fundamentalist groups; religious doctrines picture themselves as science; and perhaps most important, the myth that all truth is factual and concrete—"scientific fact"—prevails on the popular level in fundamentalist religious groups as well as throughout the wider technological society.

After all, these same groups have long since appropriated and mastered the techniques of commerce and
communication in modern society, and they have established a number of ultra-conservative Bible or "Christian" universities. It should be no surprise, therefore,
that they have now entered the laboratories and lecture
halls of science, and are seeking there—as in a number
of other cases in twentieth-century cultural life—to use
science in the service of their religious convictions and
aims.

As an established religion (for example, Catholicism
in, say, Spain, Italy, and Greece) appears among the
elitist and educated classes in very different form from
the way it appears on the popular, peasant level, so an
established science now appears in a number of different forms and at various different levels in our society:
in the elitist and upper academic forms of our major
universities and scientific associations, and also in the
form of "popular science." Fundamentalist science, or
creation science, represents, therefore, one of these
popular varieties. The intellectual, liberal, and generally elitist forms of religion seem to those who share in
them to be "true religion," "what Christianity really is."
Correspondingly, the science of the American Association for the Advancement of Science seems, to its participants, to represent true science, whereas the rest
represent a betrayal or even a mockery of science—and
on the whole, I agree with these judgments, as this
volume attests. An established spiritual force tends to
lose its clarity of definition and its purity—even its
moral excellence—and to appear on different levels and
in widely different forms, in popular and dubious as
well as in elite and noble forms.

Still, there is no doubt that as popular Christianity,
however unpalatable to aristocratic theologians and
bishops, is nevertheless a form of *Christianity*, so fundamentalist science, produced by persons trained in science, remains one variety of "science." Such forms of
popular science, strange as they are, could appear only

in an advanced scientific culture that has become "scientific" from top to bottom, and yet that remains at certain levels religiously literalistic and dogmatic.

In our century we should have been aware of this syncretism in relation to science as well as to religions, but for various interesting reasons we were not. It has been an important part of twentieth-century experience that different cultures, with different ideologies, have incorporated modern technology and science into their life and as a result have produced variant forms of both. If one can be sure of anything, it is that every modern culture is deeply intent on incorporating into itself technology, industry, and science. However, as the examples of China and Japan show, each one seeks to do so on its *own* terms, to reshape it by means of its own most significant cultural and spiritual structures. Thus the forms that technology, industry, and especially science take, shift interestingly as they become embodied in different social matrices, many being, in one way or another, strikingly deviant forms from the point of view of the science of our own elite Western culture. Nazi Germany was scientific, and with minimal resistance it incorporated all the universities and laboratories of modern Germany into its ideological life; Stalinist Russia did the same, as did Shinto Japan. And each one *reshaped* science into a "deviant" form, significantly different at some point from the normal and normative science we take as "science."

Believing in the universality and necessity of our own form of science, we took each of these as mere aberrations, and they were. Still, consider that Maoist China would have been another differently shaped example had it lasted, and possibly Khomeini's Iran will prove the most bizarre of all. Surely, we cannot be so naive as to think that the vast number of Sunni and Shi'ite students at our technological and engineering schools will return to their lands to reproduce there M.I.T. and the Charles River Basin rather than help create an *Islamic* form of modern culture and so of science in Iran or in Saudi Arabia! Each of these represents a different union, to us possibly bizarre and even menacing, of science and the religious. Our liberal understanding of science and of technology thus reveals itself not as the *one necessary* or guaranteed form of scientific culture, but as *one* option, one developed by and indebted to the liberal, democratic, humanistic, and capitalistic culture of the European Enlightenment. Quite naturally it remains for us "true science." But we may be sure that it is not the only form of science, of technology, or of industrialism that developments in the immediate future will produce.

The long association in the West of science with liberal social ideals, with religious tolerance, and with universal humanitarian aims is by no means merely accidental; science and its community have helped to nurture and shape these humanistic values. Nevertheless, that historical association, assumed to be essential and perpetual by the scientific community, may have been more dependent than is often realized on the cultural and religious traditions of the European West and on the university-educated, upper-class character of Western science in the eighteenth, nineteenth, and early twentieth centuries.

Thus that association of science with a liberal viewpoint is by no means necessarily characteristic of all subsequent forms of science wherever they may arise. After all, the major portion of the German scientific community accepted, prospered within, and worked for both the Nazi "religion" and the Nazi state, and present-day Soviet science has flourished amid Communist ideology. An advanced scientific society can take a number of different, and often bizarre, social and ideological ("religious") forms. Each one, because the culture is at base a scientific culture, produces its own unique, probably deviant, and (to us) utterly unacceptable form of appropriate "science." For powerful cultures *reshape* science as they do religion whenever they import either one. (We must remember that although noodles were invented in China, they became before long thoroughly "Italianized" as *spaghetti* after Marco Polo brought them back!) Each one represents a *union* or *synthesis* of science and the religious, not a separation of them, and certainly not a conflict or warfare between them.

If there be any "warfare" in such a situation, it will be a conflict—as in the case in Arkansas—with liberal religion and liberal science on the one side, and absolutist religion and its appropriate "science" on the other. In Germany, there were religious and academic/scientific groups on *both* sides, both supporting the Third Reich and resisting it. Significantly enough, however, there was more resistance to this Nazi union of science and the religious from church than from scientific and academic groups.

The problem in an advanced scientific culture is not that the forces of religion fight for dogma, ignorance, and dominance against the forces of scientific light— this is a nostalgic myth.[2] The problem in such a culture is that scientific knowledge and religious belief may unite—and in a scientific culture, they *will* unite—in very dangerous ways. Scientific knowledge and technical know-how seem only to add *force*, not restraint, to religious fanaticism; for the scientific and technological communities, like any others in a shaken society, are also vulnerable to participation in that fanaticism. Again, it is incumbent on the scientific—as well as the humanistic—community to be cognizant of this characteristic danger of its community in an advanced scientific culture.

Finally, to complete our general remarks about an advanced scientific culture, it is also true that—contrary to the modern myth—most "advanced" cultures in fact tend to become increasingly religious. We shall analyze this point in more detail later in this chapter. Suffice it here to remind ourselves that in fully developed and thus waning cultures, the religious reappears with surprising, often terrifying, vigor. The best example from history is the period of the late Roman Empire, when religious movements flooded that declining world. Sometimes this reappearance is in the form of cults or movements quite new to the culture (in the case of Rome, Indian and Near-Eastern cults, Christianity, and Judaism); sometimes it comes in a revivification of traditional religions that had for a period become weak. Ours is surely such a period: Asian religious groups, home-grown "sects," and reawakened forms of conservative Christianity, Judaism, and Islam abound around us. And no one aware of our present national scene can fail to note the new appearance at the very center of political power of fundamentalist and intolerant religion. We are more in danger of an evangelical theocracy than of a skeptical secularity. But it is also true that the two "breed" each other.

The question that is appropriate for us to ponder in the present connection is, therefore, What forms does the reappearance of the religious take in an advanced scientific culture? And here, of course, creation science is most illuminating, for it clearly unites in itself both of the elements that might be expected to appear in an advanced scentific culture: the element of religious conviction plus that of scientific demonstrability. On the one hand, it offers to its adherents the supreme value of religious certainty, so important in every such period of doubt, uncertainty, and relativism. And on the other, religious certainty is here united with the certainty and factuality provided by the dominant cultural forms of knowing, namely empirical science. Just as the early Christianity that appealed to sceptical Roman intellectuals portrayed Christian truth as "a revealed and therefore absolute form of philosophy," so in a scientific culture, Christian literalism appears as a form of "science" and is based on "scientific facts" and "scientific evidences."[3]

In a scientific culture, therefore, religious movements, even fundamentalist and literalistic groups, take on the lineaments of science. We have seen this repeatedly in the case of creation science: (1) the advanced scientific training of its major leaders; (2) the appeal to religious truth as "scientific"; and (3) the understanding of truth, even of religious truth, as factual and literal. To be sure, scientific rationality itself is actually theoretical and symbolic; creative scientific thinking is impressively imaginative, speculative, and anything but imprisoned in the literal. Nevertheless, the *culture* that builds itself around scientific thought tends to be factually oriented, to distrust symbolism and the sense of mystery that accompanies it, to appeal to the concrete, to the "data," and to regard science (just as fundamentalists regard revelation) as establishing undoubted and quite literal "facts." As a result of this dominant influence of a scientific culture, creation science embodies a common error of our cultural life, that all relevant truth is of the same sort: factual, empirical truth, truth referent to secondary causes—in a word, "scientific truth." It is for this reason that even the religious doctrine concerning God's creative act is transformed into (or reduced to) a "scientific truth," a set of literal propositions in which God's actions are regarded as parallel with the actions of the secondary causes which science studies. In a scientific culture, all truth is taken to be scientific truth. It is no surprise, therefore, that religious groups in that culture should conceive of their own religious concepts as scientifically established and scientifically valid. Only in such a wider cultural situation is "creation science" possible.[4]

Religion and the Religious

Before we continue our analysis of religion in an advanced scientific culture, it might prove clarifying if an important distinction, implicit in our whole discussion, was explicitly though briefly articulated. This is the distinction between *religion* on the one hand and *the religious* on the other.

When we refer in these pages to *religion*, we refer—as does our ordinary speech—to the beliefs, practices, and institutions of a specific community explicitly devoted to a particular religious point of view, as for example, Judaism, Christianity, or Islam. This usage may be legitimately criticized on a number of grounds,[5] but it is close enough to ordinary discourse, and it is helpful enough, if carefully used, to be justified. In this sense, the creation science movement is clearly a wing, a minor one to be sure, but a wing of the Christian religion. But *the religious* is something different. Here we may speak of the religious dimension, or the religious aspect or characteristics, of culture. And we may refer either to some *subordinate* or *special aspect* of cultural life —for example, its political life, its social structure, its ideology or reigning social theory—or we may speak of the religious dimension of a culture as *a whole*.

The point of this usage is, of course, to articulate that many "secular" elements of social existence can, and usually do, have religious aspects or dimensions. For example, the political ethos of a nation (or of a city-state or empire) can take on an aura of ultimacy and sacrality that requires absolute assent, obedience, and devotion; correspondingly, political leaders can in effect become absolute, directing and dominating all aspects of life, as in Nazi Germany or in Stalinist Russia. Such dominating political ideologies and rulers are clearly "religious" in their characteristics; nevertheless, the former are not helpfully called "religions," nor are the latter "priests."

On the other hand, if these religious aspects of the political are overlooked, the cultural reality under discussion is not thoroughly or helpfully understood. Our point is, then, that culture, even if it is secular in intention, participates in the religious dimension in much of its life, especially in those aspects of its life that are central and crucial to its security, its well-being, and its

-172-

hopes.[6] Obviously, this religious aspect of a culture can be benevolent and creative, or it can be destructive and lethal. In either case, it poses for society an essentially *religious* rather than a scientific, technological, or administrative problem. Now let us continue our analysis.

*　　*　　*

The Effects of Establishment on Science

Ours, we have said, is an advanced scientific culture. That is to say, science has for at least three centuries played a dominant, possibly *the* dominant, role in that culture. It has provided modern society with its most reliable and most useful mode of knowing, and thus through science the culture has been confident that it could both *understand* its most puzzling mysteries and *resolve* its primary and most threatening problems. Science provided the most important and most necessary knowledge, and it promised to provide the well-being that each society seeks. Any discipline or art that offers those two (as, for example, theology did in the medieval period) attains a special, almost priceless, status not only to those who participate in it but, more significant, to the whole community that admires and depends on it. A penumbra of the sacred begins to hover over every aspect of the scientific enterprise: It becomes, as Tillich would have put it, an ultimate concern, necessary for defense, for industrial progress, for health, for agriculture, for knowledge about the world, for the technological wonders of modern daily life. Almost every worthwhile and creative endeavor—except possibly art —then yearns to be associated with science and begins to regard its theoretical structure as scientific—as the claims of, say, both Marxist and Freudian theories to be science vividly show.

Moreover, the scientist possesses a special character not only as *the* knower, the knower of the most important or sacral secrets, but also, if he or she be a scientist involved in practice, as the "doer" of the most beneficial and saving deeds—as the roles of the doctor and the psychoanalyst in our cultural life, not to mention the magic of the white coat, also show. The priest once enjoyed this transcendent authority, respect, and esteem when what he knew and what he could do seemed utterly essential to life.

Each culture has a sacral form of knowledge and of expertise which it values inordinately and therefore rewards lavishly. Whatever is ultimately important to a society, to its security, its well-being, its fundamental styles of life, and its hopes, will participate in such a "religious" aura and will be an important aspect of that "religious center" around which each creative culture builds its life. In an advanced scientific culture, this is understandably true of science, with its knowledge and its authority. It is thus not surprising that as the effort to be scientific had characterized much of religion in our society, so in turn a religious dimension should appear in much of that society's dominant science.

In speaking of this religious aura, I do not refer only to those things interesting to the sociology of science— for example, to the prestige and wealth (relative to other intellectual professions) that the wider society provides for those persons and institutions engaged in science in its many forms. At this point, I am more interested in the "sacred status" in the intellectual or cultural sphere granted to scientific inquiry and scientific knowledge in an advanced scientific culture. For this religious aura connected with science is, I think, an exceedingly relevant factor in the development of the creationist controversy.[7]

Throughout the trial, it was evident that for both sides (more particularly for the creation scientists, but

-174-

also for many of their scientific opponents) an *expansion* or *enlargement* of science had taken place. As we have seen, scientific inquiry is limited by its very nature to posing only certain sorts of questions. It omits a wide range of important questions, especially philosophical and religious ones: questions, for example, about the nature of the real, the relation of the knowing subject to experience, the variety and interrelations of the forms of truth, and the meaning and destiny of human existence. It confines itself to what empirical inquiry can uncover about the necessary, universal, and observable causes or invariable factors that bring about material events. Much in experience is thereby ignored or overlooked—for example, again, the question of personal decision, of the personal origination of action, of knowing the truth, of enjoyment, of purpose, and of fulfillment—all obvious and important ingredients even (perhaps especially) of scientific inquiry itself.

Now to be sure, one *may* take as definitive a "scientific" explanation of these excluded factors or levels of experience and give to them (and to the knowing subjects of these thoughts) a *purely* physical explanation, and to their origin, a *purely* physical source. But such an interpretation of these aspects of experience is not a scientific conclusion, a tested hypothesis resulting from scientific inquiry. On the contrary, it is a *philosophical* conclusion, a speculative answer to the speculative question, What is the primary effective factor in experience, or what is the "really real"? Such questions may seem esoteric and irrelevant; but anyone who assumes that a scientific answer to these questions is definitive has already assumed a materialistic or naturalistic metaphysical position. It is also an answer with religious overtones, for it specifies and expresses a radically atheistic and humanistic life-stance.

To take scientific explanations as total explanations represents, therefore, a philosophical position, not a scientific one. It represents an expansion or an enlargement of the cognitive method or rule (the heuristic principle) essential to scientific inquiry, "I will regard only past, sensible, material, and universal causes or factors as relevant," into the metaphysical/theological stipulation, "Only observable, material, and universally determinative causes are real and effective"—a very different, undemonstrable, and in fact, in the end dubious (because self-contradictory) proposition. Naturalistic humanism has its own deep philosophical and theological difficulties; it is by no means a conclusion from scientific inquiry, however much it may seem historically and psychologically to be associated with science. It represents the most common philosophical assumption of large segments of the academic and intellectual communities in an advanced scientific culture; it is itself part of the "religious aura" of science, not a part of its theoretical structure.

Not surprisingly, therefore, this assumption that scientific explanations of any event represent *total* explanations of that event dominated both sides of the creationist controversy. On the one hand, as we have seen, the creationists assumed that any scientific explanation of origins represents a *total* explanation of origins. Thus, when what they called "evolutionary science" pictured the world as arising only from material causes universally at work in nature, and found no place for God in their explanations, evolutionary science represented to them a materialistic, atheistic, and humanistic philosophy or religion incompatible with Christianity. On the other hand, a multitude of scientists, or spokespersons for science, have made a parallel assumption about science: Because modern astronomy, geology, and biology have found no need or place for the hypothesis of God in their explanations, therefore they conclude that religious explanations represent "pre-scientific" ignorance. What science cannot and does not speak about cannot be real. As a consequence, in a scientific culture religious belief in God is apt to seem illusory and anachronistic, no longer either credible or relevant for a culture that "now knows how to know."

This expansion or enlargement of the principles of scientific inquiry from valid and useful conclusions about what is real and effective in the totality of experience into the *only* valid knowledge of what is real is strange. One might even call it weird when one considers it omits the creative and effective scientific *subject*, the scientist himself or herself! It can, however, be understood when we appreciate the power of science in a scientific culture. For this culture, science has (rightly) represented the predominant mode of knowing, and its conclusions and discoveries (a good deal more dubiously) represent the key to that culture's security and well-being. Thus, as we have noted, scientific knowledge and the principles of its uncovering appropriated to themselves a sacral aura: Science has become for many the supreme form of knowing and the key to effective action. From this position it is, of course, merely a step to believe that science therefore represents the *only* form of knowledge, the only reliable clue we possess to what is real or, as the analytic philosophers liked to say, "our only cognitive touch with what is the case."

Historically, whatever is said by a culture to be "known," that is, the referent of the word *knowledge,* is generally what that culture considers to be actual or real; knowing specifies a relation to what is taken in that culture to be real, and hence not illusory. In ancient religious cultures, for example, the divine was assumed to be *the* reality, and knowledge of the divine was regarded as *the* form of knowledge. Correspondingly, in ancient Greek culture, where the forms things embodied were regarded as representing reality, knowledge of forms was also regarded as *the* form of knowing. And, as is well known, in medieval culture the predominant form of knowledge—the "queen of the science"—was theology, the knowledge of God who was the ultimately real. In other words, whenever we say we *know* something, we take that something known to be *real*.

On the other hand, whenever we refuse to use the word *knowledge* in relation to a given subject matter (the material world, for example, in Indian or in Platonic thought), then generally we imply that that subject matter is at worst fictive or illusory (*maya* in India); or it is at best a product of our imaginative subjectivity, or only partly "real." Knowledge and reality are assumed to be correlative concepts.

Thus where a certain form of knowing becomes so predominant as to represent for many the exclusive mode of knowing, as has frequently been the case with empirical science in modern culture, then whatever that form of knowing "knows" will represent the sole relevant and actual aspect of reality. In this way, scientific truth becomes the normative and, in fact, the exclusive form of truth, and scientific explanations represent the total and solely relevant explanations of whatever is. As we have seen, it is out of this error, which can be called the error of "scientism" or positivism, an error characteristic of an advanced scientific culture and shared in different ways by both sides, that this controversy about evolution has been generated.

The Effects on the Humanities

Any important intellectual error on the part of a culture as a whole has multiple consequences for the total life of society, consequences far more serious even than the present controversy. Such is the case when a scientific culture holds that there is only one form of truth: that generated by scientific inquiry and characteristic of scientific discourse. Consequently, in that view, other levels of truth and other modes of discourse need hardly be taken seriously. Artistic expression, literary discourse, philosophical speculation, argument and discussion, religious awareness and affirmation—these are not considered to represent *complementary* levels of truth based on other sorts of relatedness to actuality and therefore other modes of cognition. On the contrary, they are regarded as purely "subjective," generated out of the inner turmoil of the natural psyche, expressive at best of its dreams and hopes, at worst of its nightmares and repressed hostilities.

To be sure, enough of the educated population has a fondness for art, literature, and critical discussion—in effect, for the humanities—to warrant their continuing presence in education and in cultural life generally. But since the humanities do not represent ways of encountering, understanding, and dealing with *reality*, but only subjective preferences of certain types of intellects, they are regarded as hardly essential to the culture's life or to science. Thus a scientific culture in general, and the scientific community in particular, has tended to ignore as irrelevant these non-scientific aspects of cultural life. In the end, of course, this indifference to other aspects of cultural life can prove fatal.

Another truth an advanced scientific culture reveals is that science and technology can be creative and not destructive in social existence *only* if these other complementary aspects of culture—its literature and art, its law, morals, and social theory, its philosophical and religious assumptions—are also strong and creative, and if the relation of scientific and technological developments to them is rationally assessed and humanely enacted. The confinement of knowledge and of rationality to the scientific and the technological enterprises alone is the dark harbinger of historical chaos, not of increased social enlightenment.

Among the casualties of a scientific culture is the misinterpretation of religion, and with that, the misinterpretation by that culture of itself and of its own life. As we have seen, in such a culture the humanities are interpreted generally not as responses to a rich and varied reality which we encounter in a number of diverse ways, but as subjectively generated, as manifesting only the inward life of the human psyche. This tends to make literature, art, and speculation trivial and esoteric. It makes religion—because religion is sustained only by the claim to denote what is objectively real—superstitious at best and pathological at worst.

To scientism, therefore, religion is caused by two unfortunate but diverse characteristics of human subjectivity; fortunately (so this view goes), both of them will easily be overcome in a scientific age. One is simply *ignorance,* ignorance of how the world really works, of the effective factors in nature and in history, and of the characteristics of what is real. Since to live amid what is unknown, and therefore uncontrollable, is nerve-wracking and thus unbearable, in a pre-scientific age men and women peopled the world with gods whom they might cajole, if not control.

For scientism, the other cause of religion is psychological and social-pathological, namely, *wish-fulfillment,* the picturing of the world in terms of what we wish to be the case in order to be able to bear what is a cruel and arbitrary reality. Out of ignorance, fear, and suffering, religion arose as a projection of mythical dreams upon the real world. Religion represents, then, pre-scientific efforts to know, and pre-technological efforts to reshape, the puzzling and difficult reality which surrounds us.

Thus, as scientific knowledge accumulates, the ignorance represented by religious myth will be dissipated; and as technology develops and spreads, the problems that in a pre-technological age seemed to call for religious resolution will be eradicated by realistic means.

In this view, the knowledge guided by science *replaces* the knowledge derived from religious commitments; and modern scientific technology in its broadest sense *replaces* the benefits brought by religious devotion and practice. As this understanding of religion and of itself—an understanding characteristic of much academic and intellectual culture—shows, a scientific society sees history as made up of "two ages," a pre-scientific and a scientific age, an age of religious superstition and bondage on the one hand and an age of rational enlightenment and technological capability on the other.[8] This is scarcely a helpful interpretation of religion and of the role of religion in human existence, including modern existence. And, as the characteristic dilemmas of an advanced scientific culture indicate, it could hardly be more in error about our own advanced scientific epoch.[9]

The errors of scientism, as well as the views of itself and the real world that are normative for a scientific culture, are by no means the fault of the scientific community alone. No community representative of a powerful or predominant cultural force is solely to blame for that culture's characteristic illusions. Priests did not generate the awe, respect, and power which accrued to religion in the medieval period—though they might well have *sought* their best to do so! Rather, it was the entire society, the *people* in that epoch—those who viewed the world religiously, who revered religious knowledge and who yearned for religious benefits— that gave to the community centered around religion, to the medieval church, the dominant power over mind, spirit, will, and purse alike (and over political rulers), which religion enjoyed.

So it has been with science. At first, only the upper levels of society, and then slowly almost all its levels, have revered scientific knowledge as supremely reliable and useful, and have welcomed the developments of technology as primary answers to their own central problems. It is such widespread and ultimately uncoerced social assent, approbation, and support—yes, adulation—that creates social power and dominance, that "establishes" a form of religion or a form of cognition, or both together, in a given society. By contrast, wherever a form of religion or of knowledge is the result of external coercion alone—as in the Moslem conquest of India, in many Reformation territories, or in present-day Warsaw—it breeds no such cultural or spiritual dominance. The dominating scientific community as such is as much a symptom or an effect of the power of science in modern culture as it is its cause. In effect, the scientific community has *received* its positions of dominance rather than *caused* it; it has received it from the quite understandable veneration with which science is regarded by modern populations. Nevertheless, there can be little question that the community of scientists, and not least, the community of educators in science, bear some responsibility for the "scientism" which, as we have seen, has been a major cause of this controversy about evolution.

The Effects on Scientific Education

In a culture increasingly centered on science, the idolization of science both as a form of knowledge and as the unambiguous key to human betterment was quite natural, especially for those engaged in its arduous labors. Specifically, this idolization took the form of a belief about science that tended to separate science from other aspects of culture and to raise it high above them. While these other aspects of culture were thought to be relative to culture, changing as culture changes, and so in the end unobjective and subjective, science was viewed as autonomously based only on itself, and its conclusions were seen as rationally and universally valid. It pictured itself, therefore, as dependent only on experiment, logic, insight, and objective validation, as firmly grounded in objective reason and free of prejudice, and above all, as quite independent of the myths and assumptions, the preferences, the moods, the unsupported beliefs and biases of the unscientific culture around it. While all other disciplines—the human sciences, the social sciences, the humanities, especially philosophy and religion—depended on scientific knowledge for whatever contributions to knowledge they might muster, natural science alone depended only on itself to advance further: on its immediate past tradition; on its laboratories; on its ancillary disciplines, mathematics and statistics; and on its genius. Thus the scientific community believed that in order to be scientific, it did not need to understand the rest of culture, for science is independent of it. Furthermore, since its knowledge is cumulative, it need not even understand its own past to understand itself. This picture of an autonomous, simply cumulative, and objective science is, of course, quite inaccurate;[10] the problem is that it can, like any myth, do a good deal of damage when it is enacted socially.

This mythical view of science as independent of the rest of culture for its development (except possibly for popular admiration and support and for the funds which result from them) and as simply cumulative in its knowledge has been objectively expressed in university graduate programs for the training of scientists. In all but a few there is little provision for the study, by prospective scientists, of the history of science or of the philosophy of science. The history of science sets (or could set) the development of science squarely in the midst of the cultural life of each epoch and thereby could reveal the dependence of creative science and of novel hypotheses on assumptions and concepts in other fields. It also could reveal how the use of scientific knowledge depends upon the political and legal structures, the aims and values, and the fundamental social, philosophical, and religious notions of any epoch. The philosophy of science examines (or could examine) not only the logic and assumptions of scientific method but also the relation of scientific knowledge to other modes of knowing: to art, morals, social and psychological theories, philosophy, and religion.

Knowing its own history and philosophy is invaluable to any community within society, such as the scientific community, that has achieved leadership, or even dominance, within the wider scope of modern culture. These two disciplines would prepare future scientists to recognize the prominence and hence the ambiguity of their own role in culture, and to deal with the questions of the relations of scientific knowledge and its technical capacities to law, morals, the arts, philosophy, and religion. To be unprepared in these areas is to deal with such problems—and they cannot be avoided—naively and crudely relying only on the "folk wisdom" learned in graduate school. Unfortunately, however, history of science courses are in the history department, and philosophy of science courses are in the philosophy department—and few future scientists find themselves pondering these matters as a part of their training. Yet as far as I know, the natural sciences represent the *only* set of disciplines that are taught without substantial reference to their own history and their own philosophy. And there is no discussion at all in the training of scientists of the relations of science to other permanent and significant aspects of cultural life.

The question of the relation of the scientific knowledge of origins to religious views of origins is just such an issue of the interrelation of different aspects of culture. It represents an intricate interface involving two different and yet variously interrelated modes of speech and of knowing, one scientific and one religious. To understand this question also involves some acquaintance with the way modern religious communities interpret their "doctrines" in a scientific age. And it requires some facility in interrelating these two in class discussions, specifically the theories representing scientific explanations of origins on the one hand and the diversity of relevant religious interpretations of origins on the other. How else is a biology teacher to broach these matters helpfully? And how can a science teacher avoid discussing the relation of science to Genesis? Merely to use a crude approach such as "The scientific views we are learning have replaced religion's pre-scientific myths" badly misleads students about both modern science and modern religions. But even more, as noted, it becomes one of the major "breeders" of the creationist reaction. Our culture is scientific through and through. That means that the scientific community must have the capacity creatively to reflect upon the interrelations of its methods, its knowledge, and the technical consequences of science with other aspects of culture. In turn, that means a definite *reorientation* of scientific training towards relating all aspects of science to the wider life of culture. Only thus can the massive effects of science and technology upon society's life be reasonably and humanely effected through the participation of the community of scientists itself.

The Responsibility of the Churches for the Controversy

This critique of the scientific community and its relation to the wider culture should be more than balanced by a similar critique of the communities representing religion: the churches. It is incumbent upon these religious groups, as well as upon the scientific communities of our society, to recognize that this is an advanced scientific culture and that it is also *their* responsibility to be cognizant of that fact and to deal effectively with it. A rapprochement or concordat between the natural science developing in modern culture and the Christian and Jewish traditions has been in effect among scholars, theologians, and educated pastors, rabbis, and laypersons for almost two hundred years. This rapprochement has gone through a number of quite diverse phases, some more liberal and some more successful, lasting, and "valid" than others. To argue which mode of rapprochement with modern science is more appropriate—that of liberals like Schleiermacher or Troeltsch or of neo-orthodox thinkers like Karl Barth or Thomas

Torrance—is not to the point here. What *is* at issue is that the theological rapprochement of science and faith in its various forms has been an actuality for well over a century; that by the early twentieth century, most of the major religious communions of the Christian and Jewish faiths recognized and applauded one mode or another of it; and that almost without exception, the study of that rapprochement has for decades formed a major element in the curricula of accredited theological and rabbinical seminaries.

In sum, at least since the beginning of the twentieth century, the *leadership* of the mainline churches and synagogues (though this is mainly a church problem) has been well aware that scientific theories of origins do not conflict with the religious belief in creation, and all have recognized that a person can be a believing Christian or Jew and at the same time a student of the latest geological and evolutionary theories. There is hardly a ministerial conference where this rapprochement is not as thoroughly assumed as has been, say, that between Christian faith and democracy, or between Christian faith and psychoanalytic theory and practice. At the leadership level of the Church's life, therefore, there simply is no intellectual or theoretical problem concerning the relation of religion and science, or if there is, it concerns only the question of how most appropriately one is to understand the differences and the relationships between these two modes of truth. Just as among scientists arguments continue to take place about *how* evolution is to be understood, not about *whether* it happened, so among the intellectual leadership of the churches there may be debates about the most felicitous philosophical or theological interpretation of the relation of science and religion, but not about whether they do conflict.

Nevertheless, despite this almost universal agreement among religious leaders, *the wider public*, both those who attend church and those who do not, remains apparently quite unaware that there is no longer any such conflict between science and religion, between evolution and Genesis. The century-old rapprochement between science and theology is the best-kept secret in our cultural life. Much of the lay public assumes that Christian belief, and certainly Christian theology, are as anti-scientific as the Roman Church was with Galileo, as some (though not all) religious leaders were with Darwin and Huxley, and as present-day fundmentalist preachers are—an error almost as bizarre as if most of the public thought that the majority of contemporary doctors *bled* their patients regularly as they were wont to do with deadly effect less than two centuries ago!

The extent of this ignorance of developments in theology—that is, ignorance about how the beliefs of the major churches are interpreted in the contemporary world—can perhaps be indicated by two experiences in the author's recent life. Four years ago, when my son was attending the sixth-grade science and social science classes at The University of Chicago Laboratory School (the "Dewey School"), I received a long letter from the two teachers of those classes. They were, they said, aware that I taught theology at the University Divinity School; and, seeking to be quite fair to me and my beliefs, they wanted to give me ample notice that Amos would soon be learning about biological evolution and the early development of hominids. So, in order to give "equal time" to each view, they wished as well to invite me to explain to the class how we in the Divinity School "did Biblical dating"!

After I had recovered from the mingled shock and amusement at receiving such a letter in my office at the Divinity School—famous, or perhaps infamous, as the seat of modernist religion—I realized that I neither knew how to do Biblical dating nor was I acquainted with anyone who did. Not sure how to deal with this problem, I sat down and began a letter that, in the end, comprised a dozen or more pages. In explaining my inability to accept their invitation, I outlined some of the history of liberal theology beginning in the eighteenth century, the rise and growth of the critical and historical approach to Scriptures during the same period, the development of the symbolic interpretation of creation in nineteenth-and twentieth-century theology, and I ended with five pages on the founding of the University of Chicago Divinity School in the 1890s on liberal, cultural, and historical principles, and its subsequent career as "the mother of liberals."

After they read this letter, these two otherwise well-educated and certainly intelligent young men proceeded to congratulate me on it, expressed amazement at its contents, and said enthusiastically that since it contained so much "wonderful stuff," I should publish it as an article at once! Ruefully, I pointed out that, as novel as all this might seem to them, it was not at all new; in fact, every library was full of literally shelves of materials on the history I had so briefly outlined. To them, religion and theology *meant* fundamentalist religion and dogmatic theology; that this was not the case was a very well-hidden truth.[11]

A second example took place at the trial at Little Rock. After I had stepped off the stand, an intelligent-looking, well-dressed young man approached me and identified himself as the reporter at the trial for *Time*. He said, "I have a strange question to ask you."

"Go ahead."

"You say you are a theologian. Is that right?"

"Yes, sure," I said, somewhat on guard at this phrasing.

"And I suppose you believe in God?"

"Yes, of course I do," I replied, even more wary.

"Then, how on earth can you be here as a witness for the plaintiffs and accept Darwin?"

I looked at him in amazement: Had he been the reporter for a local paper in Arkansas, say the *Pea Ridge Country Times*, his question might have been understandable—but *Time*! Since I felt that he certainly should know better, I decided to muddy the waters even further. So I replied.

"On a number of counts I don't accept Darwin at all. In fact, most of the biologists I am acquainted with maintain that there are good scientific reasons for questioning important elements of Darwin's theory. His theory is, I gather, now quite out-of-date."

At that, the *Time* reporter said, "Now I'm really confused." Before he wandered away, I said I agreed with him, he *was* confused, and I suggested that he refrain from writing an article about the trial.

Surely this was a commentary on the level of reportage that *Time* sent to the trial. But it was also a clear indication of our present point: The existence of liberal religion, of forms of religion that have no problem in seeing the congruence between themselves and modern science, was as hidden to this young man as it had been to the two teachers at the Laboratory School. One can only presume that the leadership of the churches has been strangely, and yet effectively, silent about the Church's accommodation to the science with which its parishioners daily live.

Why has there been this silence in the pulpits, the classes, the discussion groups of our churches—a silence so complete that no one seems to know anything about the central beliefs, or the interpretation of those beliefs, of the main churches of our land? Certainly there must have been a dearth of theological preaching —that is, the attempt to spell out clearly what those beliefs might mean in our day, whether that meaning be intellectual (vis-à-vis science, and so on), personal (existential), or ethical (vis-à-vis individual and social moral issues). But, more specifically, the way the churches interpret Scripture, especially Genesis, and the consequent new relations of Christian faith to science, especially geology and biology, must also have been scrupulously, and deliberately, avoided in pulpit after pulpit, in class after class.

The reasons for this are probably diverse, but two are obvious. The first is probably a feeling of intellectual inadequacy on the part of the pastor in dealing with issues of science, philosophy of science, Biblical interpretation, and theology—though all this is precisely what he or she, as an educated pastor and teacher of the faith, is supposed to know. The second is a detestation for, a shrinking from, controversy in the Church. Most of us can rouse ourselves to do battle for the faith only when absolutely necessary (if then!)—and it is easy to put off until later a sermon or a class explicitly challenging and revising the strict literal interpretation of the Scripture. After all, there are many other important topics too. Especially we put it off when we fear that offended lay members may leave and join one of the conservative churches down the street. Thus, while "God's creation" may frequently be ringingly affirmed, a careful and explicit interpretation of creation as in accord with modern science rarely appears—and the secret is kept well under cover.

In short, then, if the scientific community is partly to blame in this controversy for heedlessly assuming before the public that scientific theories simply replace "religious myths," so the leadership of the churches is as much to blame for querulously avoiding an important issue and thereby keeping the actual fact of a theological *aggiornamento* (updating) quite hidden from view.

*   *   *

The Persistence of Religion in Advanced Cultures

One of the major surprises of an advanced scientific culture is the persistence of the religious in its life. This theme has been present throughout our present analysis: in the reappearance in power of fundamentalist groups not so much against the science and technology of the culture of modernity as in a strange alliance with them, and in the presence of a "religious aura," as we have called it, enveloping the established enterprise of scientific inquiry itself. The persistence, even the growth, of the religious in a scientific culture comes as a surprise because, as we have noted, the self-interpretation of that culture, its image of itself, was of an increasingly rational and "humanized" society, one in which scientific knowledge and technological capability would gradually replace the religious superstitions of previous epochs. That this advanced scientific culture would at almost every turn find itself involved in disputes about the religious, in conflicts and dilemmas a significant part of which can only be characterized as religious, was therefore hardly to be expected.

Nevertheless, as we have seen, one significant aspect of this controversy between "creation science" and "establishment science" has been precisely such a clash of religious perspectives, that of a new "fundamentalist science" on the one hand and that of a relatively new "naturalistic or atheistic scientism" on the other. Significantly, neither one in this form is a mere carry-over from the traditional religions of Western culture. In fact, the traditional (mainline) churches and synagogues find themselves in uneasy conflict with *both* the literalistic creationists and the naturalistic scientists. Both fundamentalist science and naturalistic scientism have arisen out of, in conjunction with, and because of modern scientific technological culture. It is therefore this persistence, or reappearance, of the religious that we must now seek to understand if we are to comprehend the full scope of the roles of religion and of science in current society.

If one asks, "Why is religion so persistently *there* as to seem to be a permanent and irrepressible aspect of human existence?" one poses a strange, almost paradoxical, question. For any answer to this question itself presupposes a perspective about religion, and any such perspective about religion itself reflects a "religious" perspective. There is no objective answer to this question, but only answers implying an involvement on the part of the answerer in the subject matter of the question. Thus, as we have noted, the explanation of religion as a subjective projection because of ignorance, fear, and hostility on the one hand, and because of frustrated wishes and dreams on the other, reflects a viewpoint of naturalistic humanism which regards religion as pathology or alienation—that is, as illusion, its imputed objects or referents as unreal, and its consequences as baleful. Generally, of course, those who have regarded religion as an illusory projection, as an alienation from true humanity, a neurosis (for example, Feuerbach, Marx, Freud, Frazier, Julian Huxley), have looked forward to its progressive demise as scientific rationality and the "reality principle" enlarge their scope. Few of them (except Freud, in some moods, and Durkheim) could bear to recognize religion as persistent and permanent—a *permanent* neurosis presents a debilitating prospect indeed! Thus the reappearance of the religious in our present cultural situation raises difficulties, to be sure by no means insurmountable, but nevertheless real, for the projection theory: If human existence is permanently alienated, then the optimism of rational humanism about the human condition, an optimism essential to its message, seems dubious indeed —and the entire position is set awry.

On the other hand, if one asks a religious thinker, a theologian, this same question, the answer will almost certainly be: "Religion arises as a *response* to the sacred character of reality; and it is persistent and permanent because our lives are consistently lived in the presence of that sacred reality." The various religions encounter, respond to, and formulate or name this "sacred reality" differently. The Christian religion names it God, and describes God so identified in terms of its own traditional symbols and of its own experiences of that encounter. To me, only some such *religious* interpretation of religion and of the religious in terms of response makes sense not only of the data of religion but of the obvious religious dimensions of culture, history, and personal life.[12] And it makes sense not least because the religious reappears in numerous unexpected forms even in those cultures (e.g., Marxist Russia) that have deliberately sought to diminish, even to banish, it.

But such a theological explication of religion and the religious, valid as it may well be, entails so many prior assumptions about the reality and nature of God, as well as about human beings, that it is hardly helpful in an analysis such as the present one. So let us simplify this account and seek to understand the persistence of the religious in terms of the needs as well as the capabilities of human beings, particularly *social* human beings. These are needs and capabilities evident in every past social context and also elegantly manifested in our own modern society; and they are needs and capacities which in turn become intelligible only if one assumes this encounter with, and dependence on, the divine.

The Social Role of the Religious

There is, first of all, the need of any community for a credible system of symbols giving structure, meaning, and direction to all of experience: to nature, history, society, and the self. The symbols thus unifying all of experience tend inexorably to take on a religious character, even if they are not directly drawn from and expressive of the community's traditional religion. Since they encompass all of experience, shaping it into a coherent whole, these symbols tend towards ultimacy and sacrality. And since they give meaning and direction to the human lives lived under their aegis, they become immensely important, even absolutely central, to the lives of the community they shape and direct. In short, they represent matters of "ultimate concern."

In traditional societies, the established religion of the community performs this function. An important aspect of any religion is its system of symbols, the "grammar" with which it interprets all of experience. Correspondingly, the political life, the military defense, the economic and social arrangements, the structures of education, and the patterns of personal and civil behavior in such a traditional society receive their foundation and shape, their norms, and their aims from this centering religious symbolism—as the traditional cultures of China, Japan, Egypt, India, Persia, and Greece show, and as medieval Christendom also illustrated.

To our surprise, even after the separation in the West of the Church from public rule in the eighteenth century and the consequent attempt to construct a "secular" society without Christian foundation, the religious as an aspect of social unity and social structuring has persisted. Ideologies have replaced traditional religion in providing such a unifying, directing, and empowering system of symbols for political structures and policies, educational aims, fundamental social institutions, and personal behavior. Not surprisingly, these ideologies (for example, Marxism as embodied at the center of a society) take on the characteristics, often in history unlovely indeed, of traditional religion: The distinction between orthodoxy and heresy reappears, dogmatic truths abound, theoretical authorities ("theologians") are called in,[13] and each society governed by an ideology seeks to "missionize" other communities through its instruments of propaganda. Whenever these elements appear, something very like a "religion" has appeared; this is one reason we term this the "religious dimension" of an ideology.

Once it had gradually broken free of the traditional Christian foundation for society in the sixteenth and seventeenth centuries, the modern West did not, as it had hoped, escape this need for a "mythos," a guiding symbolic interpretation of its existence, on which it could live. Rather, it found that myth in a new conception of history centered around (1) the science developing in its midst, (2) the social implications of its new commercial life for individuals, and (3) a new political vision of society. Thus appeared the vision or myth of the Progress of Civilization: progress through science, technology, industrialism, and democracy. Like all such symbolic visions, this one took in all of human experience—in this case, historical experience.

According to its view, human society, beginning with the ancient world, has steadily progressed up to its present unequalled heights, represented by European, and later, American, civilization. Because of the now-sophisticated scientific method, deliberate technological advancement, industrial individualism, and social democracy, this progress is now explicit and assured: History is in the process of achieving its fulfillment under the present North European and American leadership. Moreover, soon this fulfillment will encompass the entire globe—if the return to barbarism represented first by Fascism and now by Communism is diverted!

This myth has every potentiality of accruing to itself the same religious characteristics that we noted in connection with its contemporary sibling, the Marxist mythos. Though it has some important intrinsic anti-ideological safeguards built into it, nevertheless, as our own growing American Right Wing illustrates, it is evident that under certain circumstances it too can become a dangerous ideology and thus take to itself all the baneful characteristics of a new modern religious mythology. Although this wider myth can have theistic and Christian variants, nevertheless it is clear that the scientism and the "two ages of history" described earlier depend upon this vision of history and thus represent central elements in the wider religious myth of Progress.

Our present subject is not contemporary visions of history, however relevant they may be to much of this controversy. The point is the persistence of the religious in the public life of any society, even an advanced scientific and technological one. Not surprisingly, the myth around which such a society centers its life is, in turn, centered around science and its developments, as in an agricultural society religious myths concern the difficulties and the prospects of the arts of agriculture. The image of the warfare of science and religion is one *part* of this scientistic and positivistic myth, the part explicating (as so many traditional myths in religious history do) the way the new and finally valid "pantheon" (in this case, scientific and rational social theory) is scattering, demolishing, and ultimately will eradicate, albeit with great danger and difficulty, the preceding set of reigning deities (in this case, the entrenched forces of bigoted religion).

The Role of Religion in a "Time of Troubles"

The role of the religious, however, is not confined to the creative, developing, waxing period in a culture's life, when a new cultural complex is born and grows on the basis of some new vision of nature, history, society, and the self—as in the case of both liberal Progress and Marxist Communism (both, as noted, founded on the determinative role of science). For cultures have their ups and downs, and apparently in the end all decline and disintegrate, however hard this is for a powerful society to contemplate or admit. With that decline, on the one hand, the founding religious vision or mythos, the ideology supporting, shaping, and empowering that culture, itself begins to become vulnerable, to encounter doubt, radical scepticism, protest, and bitter antagonism—as the theology of medieval and early modern Christendom did when the latter began to come apart. And that theology received this barrage of negativity from precisely those intellectuals and critics in the seventeenth and eighteenth centuries who helped to formulate the modern myth that replaced it. On the other hand, in a period of decline *other* forms of the religious appear in renewed power, providing another mode of security, meaning, and hope, once founded upon the now-weakened established religion—as occurred in the proliferation of cults in the declining Roman Empire, and in the varieties of "outsider" religious movements at the end of the medieval period.

Our own age has produced both of these critical and cultic forms of the religious: the radical criticism of and protest against the reigning social ideologies of our time, expressed in revolutionary and liberationist movements East and West; and the proliferation of non-establishment esoteric, mystical, and occult groups, some older ones from outside Western culture, some new ones home-grown. Everywhere that one now turns, whether at home or abroad, one encounters the religious, sometimes healing and creative, sometimes terrifying and cruel (sometimes both), always there with renewed power and authority. It should be no surprise that in such a religious age, fundamentalist religion should be on the rise as representing newly-revived, dogmatic, and extremist forms of a traditional religious faith—much as the fundamentalism that has swept Iran represents an extremist form of traditional Shi'ite Islam.

If one asks why the religious appears in new strength in periods of social and cultural breakdown—in "Times of Trouble," as Arnold Toynbee called them[14]—the answer is multiple. The rapid transformation, the shaking, and even more, the possibility of collapse of the essential structures of society—economic, political, and social—obviously represent a cumulative threat to the security and the meaning of the lives of individuals in that society. Suddenly, that very ground on which they stood begins to shake and disintegrate—and they seek desperately for other bases for the security and meaning of their existence.

Along with this experience, they find that the mythical certainties, those symbolic structures associated with the established institutions, become uncertain—as the truths of Marxism seem radically uncertain in much of Eastern Europe at the present, and those of democracy/capitalism in most of Western Europe. The need for a new and more certain symbolic structure of experience arises with surprising urgency. Because of this need, religious symbols that would have seemed incredible a short time before become desperately-held convictions now, and any intellectual sacrifice will willingly be made for them.

As we have said, a scientific culture thought it was essentially immune to this sort of anxious uncertainty and to these excesses of religion. Its method of doubt and of empirical testing, its practical orientation to "real" problems, its openness to ever-new hypotheses, seemed guaranteed to eradicate permanently the need for absolute answers, unquestioned certainties, and transnatural means of grace, the questionable and dangerous paraphernalia of religion. The problem has been that as the scentific culture has developed, it has been precisely *its* science and *its* technology that have been in large part the causes of, not the antidotes for, new levels of uncertainty. It has been science and technology, not religion, that have bred the dilemmas, the anxieties, and the dread of mortality characteristic of modern culture.

Many other factors have also been at work here: social factors, such as racial and class antagonisms; insoluble economic dilemmas and radical economic inequalities; changes in political balance; and, above all, the relative decline of the power, influence, and security of the West. All of these have helped to create our "Time of Troubles." But essential to the relation of science to the rise of the religious in our age has been the fact that the vast developments of science and technology in the twentieth century have, more than any other factors, led to a great increase of anxiety about the future—the future not only of our civilization, but even more, of the world itself.

There is no need here to rehearse these present dilemmas and mortal threats: The key point is their direct relation to developments in science and in technology. They include the endangering of the quality of life, private and public, by the spread of a technological, industrial civilization; the apparently uncontrollable population explosion generated by scientific medicine, agricultural improvement, and industrial expansion; the seemingly unavoidable crisis of the environment, the depletion and exhaustion of its resources, brought about by expanding technology and industrialism; and the ultimate terrors of a nuclear conflict bringing with it an apparent end, or the possibility of an end, to both nature and history, and to *us* through that double death.

These threats to our common future, especially the last two, are unparalleled in their intensity and their ultimacy. They have caused an almost complete reversal in our assessment of that future: from one of bright promise to one of darkest menace. As the promise of a coming scientific and technological utopia seemed to make religion irrelevant to many, so it is intelligible that the present dark menace of our impinging future makes religious certainty, religious promises, religious grace, seem to many to be utterly necessary. In short, it is the dilemmas and threats created by a *scientific* culture that have in large part called forth the reappearance of the religious. As an advanced scientific culture experiences difficulties, it enters a religious phase, just as did previous advanced cultures; but its dilemmas are generated precisely out of its scientific and technological advances—which itself raises puzzling though fascinating questions about our common human destiny.

The Religious Dilemmas
of an Advanced Scientific Culture

These questions are by no means irrelevant to the reappearance of the religious. For they are, in fact, religious questions, just as the dilemmas represented by the threat of natural and historical extinction are, in the end, religious dilemmas. If it is a fact, as it seems to be, that developments in science and in technology, which theoretically we should welcome, are in actuality the ground of the menace of our future, then a strange paradox, even a contradiction, faces us. These are the developments in scientific knowledge, technical know-how, and industrial organization of which we were once (and with good reason) supremely proud as a culture, and on which the bright promise of our future has been securely based. They were the grounds of the future Progress we believed in. Now they appear in a quite opposite guise, as the bases of the future's menace. What does this reversal mean? That applied intelligence, that verified theory, that technical ingenuity, are *evils*? Or that in the end they are self-destructive, possibly our race's "fatal flaw," leading to our extinction (instead of our permanent ability to adapt)?

Some in our culture have concluded precisely this, and have turned to esoteric religions. At the least, this cultural "Time of Troubles" in an advanced scientific culture shows that science as knowledge and as technical capacity is *ambiguous*—that is, capable of creative but also of destructive use. It all depends upon the *use*; and, in turn, the use depends upon the political and legal health of the society, and thus ultimately upon the moral strength, the wisdom, and finally, the spiritual depth of the culture itself—in short, on the inward life and power of the *persons* in the culture.

With that realization, the dream of an independent, self-sufficient science as the center of a steadily progressive secular culture vanishes. For the creativity of science is now seen to be *dependent* on something outside itself: on the character and aims of the users on the one hand, and on the spiritual health of the cultural matrix on the other. The creative use of scientific intelligence (as opposed to its demonic, destructive use) is now a function of the human will that uses it and of the culture, and thus of the historical situation, in which it is used. This changes the whole relation of natural science to the humanities and social studies, and not the least, of science to religion; and it changes these relations to ones of mutuality and interdependence.

The ambiguity of intelligence and of ingenuity poses a religious dilemma on several counts; but one is surely primary. If the creative use of scientific intelligence is not merely to be taken for granted as a function of any advanced scientific culture, but depends on the character and aims of the persons who use it, and on the character and aims of the wider society, then immediately the whole locus of the human problem and of its possible resolution shifts. It shifts from the external accumulation of knowledge (the banishing of ignorance) and the cumulative developments of techniques (the banishing of powerlessness) to the internal development of self-control, of wisdom, and of the capacity for self-sacrifice.[15] This shift raises urgent questions about whether our modern confidence in ourselves and in our natural powers of intelligence and will has been well placed, and it raises even deeper questions about our confidence in future history.

These are religious questions and issues. They reflect a sobering, even frightening, experiencing of our *limits* —of our ultimate dependence, powerlessness, and alienation from ourselves. Yet it is these sorts of experiences that have in every age set the conditions for religious commitment, religious faith, and the experience of religious renewal. For when assumed values and certainties are radically questioned, when social structures are shaken, when customary styles of life seem more treacherous and destructive than beneficial and creative—*then* the need for some other base for existence is urgent indeed. And eyes and ears are opened for a religious message, a religious technique or program, and a religious promise unneeded, unwanted, and thus previously unheeded.

In short, it is directly out of the dilemmas and anxieties of an advanced scientific culture that the *need* for religion has arisen; and so it is by the nature of its own career that that scientific culture has called for the reappearance of the religious—a reappearance that has characterized our age.

One final point. The religious as it reappears is by no means always healing and creative. It may well be itself destructive—in fact, to use a religious category for it, "demonic." Religion always involves a relation to the ultimate and to the sacred: to what is taken to be ultimately real, ultimately true, and of ultimate value. This relation is characteristic of all human existence; it is at some times more obvious than at other times, but it is always there, as we have argued. This relation to ultimacy is surely the basis of what is creative in life: It is present in the establishment of creative cultures and in the immense intellectual, artistic, and moral energy and creativity of individual persons—as we have in part noted.

But ultimacy pervades all aspects of human existence, and it characterizes human evil as well as human good. For when any human force, movement, or community *claims* ultimacy and sacrality to *itself*, it becomes a terror and a mortal threat to all else in its world. Then appear the fanaticism, the dogmatism, the exclusivism, the intolerance, the oppressive and aggressive spirit, the infinite cruelty, that characterize the great evils of history, that establish oppressive and tyrannical rule, that engender wars. It is precisely the *religious* dimension of social forces that makes them particularly dangerous, whether in the form of tribalism, nationalism, class ideology, or racism.

The demonic character of the religious reaches its apex within religious communities themselves, communities peculiarly tempted to claim ultimacy and sacrality for themselves—as the history of religious persecution, religious wars, and religious intolerance reveals. The great ambiguity of religion, as creative and yet as demonically destructive, is clearly manifest in our own day, not only in, say, the rise of fundamentalist Iran, but also in some of the more destructive cults now so widespread in Western culture. Some of the new religious movements have great healing and redeeming effect, yet others seem to be the quintessence of the destructive. With the removal, however, of explicit religious communities—for example, the churches—from central political power, the problem of the demonic in the religious has not receded as was once hoped. For secular ideologies can also partake of the demonic claim to ultimacy and sacrality and can require total devotion for themselves and absolute scorn for the other. The religious, in both its creative and its demonic form, is as characteristic of our so-called "secular" age, and of a scientific and a technological culture, as it had been of human history. And this sets the peculiar problems for the present, as that scientific culture moves into its "Time of Troubles."

The danger is, of course, that a scientific and technological culture can well be taken over by a demonic religious mythology that leaves the culture's scientific knowledge and its vast technical powers virtually intact. We have already seen how such a culture is vulnerable to the mild, only relatively ambiguous self-adulation of scientism and of Progress. That these, benevolent as they seem to us, can have the force of an ideological imperialism is evident from the way an aggressive Western culture has dominated other cultures in the name of this progress, in the name of an industrial, even a "free," scientific civilization. But contemporary radical Right Wing interpretations of our technological, industrial, and capitalistic society, newly combined with Christian fundamentalism in the Moral Majority—and, let us not forget, creationism is an ally, even a part, of this religious-political force—shows the possibility in our own midst for a takeover of our scientific, technological, and industrial society by a demonic ideology, demonic precisely because of its religious aspects.

And if we look beyond our own borders, we can see such a takeover in a number of other advanced industrial and scientific societies. In Italy, in Germany, and in military Japan, a religious ideology (quite different in form in each place) once dominated, empowered, and directed a destructive industrial, political, and military force, in each case made all the more destructive because of the excellence of the science and of the technology that had been captured and employed. Obviously, the same dominance and direction of an advanced scientific and technological culture characterizes Russian society as well.

One of the lessons our age has taught us is that scientific knowledge and the technology it makes possible are not, as was once believed, purely benevolent. Rather they can both be terribly ambiguous, creating evil as well as good, instruments of self-destruction as well as of survival. Thus they and their use are *dependent* on other aspects of culture: on its political and legal structures and processes, its moral integrity and courage, the forms of its religious faith. Correspondingly, as I have here argued and as this case shows, our century has also shown the persistence, the permanance, the ever-renewed power, as well as the deep ambiguity, of religion. Modern secular culture has been thoroughly aware of that ambiguity; it has long looked at religion with suspicion—and rightly; and it has looked forward to its demise. What, therefore, it has not accepted, and probably still does not accept, is that persistence.

Religion in one form or another, however—and its forms are almost infinitely various—is and will be there, like science, and it will be there in demonic or in creative form. Thus the relations between these two essential and permanent elements of culture represent a recurrent and foundational problem. Those relations, therefore, are an issue on which each of our communities, both the religious and the scientific, should be informed, about which each should reflect, and to which the training of each should in part be directed. Critical and reflective interpretation of *both* science and of profound religion should be a part of the self-understanding of *both* communities, as much of the scientific as of the religious.

If such self-reflective and critical interrelation is not the case, if significant religious groups fail to understand science, and if large segments of the scientific community ignore or misinterpret religion—as this trial illustrated they do—then the culture as a whole will suffer gravely. Science is surely going to remain the dominant intellectual force in modern life; this is widely recognized and prepared for in our educational curricula. Any large group quite ignorant of the character and implications of science will mislead us rather than lead us.

What twentieth-century experience shows in this case, however—and it is a surprise—is that religion too is not about to wither and die. If then the professional and especially the scientific and engineering classes— the intellectual leaders—are quite ignorant of the religious, and particularly if they think it merely anachronistic and harmless, then the situation is ripe for the sort of tragic consequences our century has frequently witnessed. We can only expect that, in that case, a scientific and technological culture whose intellectual leaders refuse to reflect on the religious, will find itself in the end ruled and directed by an irrational, not to say demonic, *form* of the religious—as in the case of Nazi Germany, Stalinist Russia, or our own new Religious Right.

In a "Time of Troubles" such as we are entering, the religious dimension tends to expand and, unfortunately, to grow in fanaticism, intolerance, and violence; science and technology tend accordingly to concentrate more and more on developing greater and greater means of destructive and repressive power. This combination represents, as we can all agree, a most dependable recipe for self-destruction.

Let each of our communities, then, the scientific and the religious—and ideally of course, the whole academic community—rethink its own role in this light, and especially rethink its relations to the other communities in our total social life. Only then can we prevent the proliferation of laws such as this Arkansas law—laws which unite science and religion in ways destructive of the genius of each. Science and religion will unite in some form or another in any case: in theocratic or fundamentalist form, in political, ideological form—or in the more desirable form of a relation respectful of the autonomy and yet the creative power of each. Such a desideratum, however, requires critical reflection *both* ways, true dialogue between both religion and science, joint deliberation—above all, mutual respect, interest, and forbearance. It is not too late for these two important communities to embark on such mutually vital communication.

Forms of Unity of Science and Religion

As the argument just completed indicates, an apprehension of the wider *unity* of science and religion, of scientific and religious discourse, is in the end as important for a creative culture as is an awareness of their *distinction* from each other. Clearly if scientific and religious thinking are kept strictly apart rather than coherently related, the destructive consequences outlined above will be realized—probably by a relatively primitive form of the religious, as in Nazism, taking over the scientific elements of culture. It is, therefore, not

-206-

enough merely to distinguish these realms of discourse from each other, as the immediate necessities of this trial called upon us to do. As we have shown, if these two levels of thought are not distinguished, if truth is regarded as represented by only *one* sort of truth, then either the humanities and religion suffer slow but sure extinction in a dominating scientific culture, or valid and creative science is extinguished by a victorious fundamentalist culture. Nevertheless, the continual effort must be made to bring these two *distinct* levels of inquiry, of thinking, and of truth into *unity*. For after all, each of us participates in both sorts of thinking and doing, and the culture as a whole embodies and depends upon both. And in each case, a divided self and a divided culture are both in danger of self-destruction.

The effort to think through the relation of scientific discourse to religious conviction, thought, and speech is, of course, primarily a philosophical effort, just as the interrelating of all the diverse aspects of cultural life is a philosophical enterprise. In the case of science and religion, it concerns primarily the philosophy of science and the philosophy of religion, with the philosophy of language, epistemology, metaphysics, and the philosophy of human nature acting, so to speak, as mediators. If in our age this effort is to include the religious, and to include it as an actively contributing factor to truth and understanding, then probably the word *philosophical* has to be supplemented by the phrase *philosophical/theological* or, as it is usually termed, *philosophical theology*. For that unifying work must presuppose reflection from within a religious as well as a given cultural perspective—if, that is, the two are to be actively united.

Perhaps, then, the major philosophical and theological task of our time is represented by this question, as old as the tradition of reflection itself: How are the many diverse ways of thinking in a culture—its technical and scientific thought, its social and political thinking, its artistic and moral experience and reflection, and its deepest or religious convictions—to find *unity*, that is, together to achieve coherence, mutual credibility, and effectiveness? That such a crucial enterprise of thought as this should seem strange, esoteric, and useless to much of our current cultural life, especially to much of its official philosophy, not to speak of its scientific faculties, is itself possibly the strangest truth of our present cultural existence!

8

The Shape of a Religious Symbol
and the Meaning of Creation

Our analysis of religion and science in an advanced scientific culture as manifested in the creationist controversy is virtually complete. But our discussion has raised certain questions whose answers have been more assumed or glossed over than explicated. Since these questions are in a way more theoretical than descriptive, or, to put it another way, since they represent, in fact, presuppositions of our descriptive analysis of an advanced scientific culture rather than aspects of that description, it seems sensible to close this book with a brief discussion of two of them. This discussion may, therefore, also serve as an introduction to the position or viewpoint from which this volume has been written —an entrance, let us say, into the philosophical theology, or a part of it, lying back of this interpretation of the event of the trial and of the culture in which it occurred.

The Meaning and Use
of a Religious Symbol

The first question broached in our discussion has been that of the character and role of the *religious symbol*. The category "religious symbol" has come up in a number of varied contexts: (a) in relation to the creationist model itself; (b) in relation to the concept of *creation out of nothing* in the entire Christian theological tradition; (c) in relation to the naturalistic, materialistic, and atheistic philosophy—that "scientism" which, we said, characterized the ultimate viewpoint of much of the intelligentsia in modern scientific culture; and finally (d) in relation to culture generally, namely, those most fundamental "religious" symbols or concepts which unify into a coherent vision a culture's view of things and represent, for good or for ill, the spiritual center of that culture's life.

As these four different referents for the notion of religious symbol indicate, these sorts of symbols characterize the speech *both* of what we have called "religions," namely, communities centered explicitly around a religious center, and of the "religious aspects of culture," that is, political, social, and intellectual systems that function as the unifying center for a culture's life—in short, ideologies.

One of the grounds for using the same category of the "religious" in connection with both of these is that religious symbolism, and with that, certain traits of religious speech, characterize both explicit religions and the religious aspects of culture. The rhetoric of cultures whenever they speak of their "way of life" is very close in linguistic form and in its vast seriousness to the rhetoric of religious communities concerning *their* object or objects of devotion. A *theological* analysis of cultural life —such as the preceding chapter has illustrated—is possible and relevant because religious symbols are an intrinsic and fundamental ingredient of the political, social, intellectual, and moral speech of culture. This is why an analysis of the religious dimension of the scientific enterprise, as well as of the scientific dimension of current fundamentalist religion, has been so central to a full interpretation of the creationist controversy.

Every culture has a spiritual center, a commonly-held vision of what is real, what is true and beautiful, and what is good. These visions differ markedly from culture to culture; and it is *this*, not its geography, size, technology, amount of knowledge, or even duration, that makes a given culture unique, that importantly differentiates Chinese from Indian from Greek—and all of these from modern culture.

This vision of reality, truth, and value is expressed in fundamental symbolic forms: mythical, theological-philosophical, social, and artistic. These symbols expressive of this vision articulate it, organize it, communicate it, and provide the possibility of discourse about this vision. And discourse about a vision in turn makes possible a conscious appropriation of it, explicit loyalty to it, and criticism and reformulation of it. Examples of such a symbolic structure are (1) the fundamental symbolic or conceptual elements of the Marxist vision of history, society, economic and political life, and human obligations and (2) those symbols or concepts that make up the Western vision of liberal, scientific, and democratic Progress so central to our own society. Because to both of these ideologies science represents the most fundamental of cultural enterprises, in both of their societies science has itself, as we have noted, taken on elements of "religious expansion"; and important speech about it, about its uniqueness and necessity for our life, participates in this common cultural symbolism.

In most traditional cultures this spiritual center for a community, or even for a culture, was identical with its religion in the explicit sense—though in both Greece and Rome a separation was beginning to take place. Gradually, however, as Western cultural life has developed and matured, the traditional religious communities and the "secular" elements of culture have separated and frequently have come into conflict. But the religious character of the fundamental symbolism remains as the spiritual center of the society, as it has in Marxism or in Liberal Democratic Capitalism, while the explicit symbolism of the religions characterizes the speech of only the special religious communities within that wider society.

It is no surprise, therefore, that tension frequently occurs between these two sets of fundamental communities of a culture and some of the traditional religious groups within the culture (as in the creationist case); or between the dominant political ideology of the society, as in Nazi Germany or Maoist China, and its special religious communities, its "religions" (in these cases, Jewish, Christian, or Buddhist); or between a reawakened theocracy and the secular culture (as in Shinto Japan and present-day Iran). In each of these cases, as we have argued, the picture of "science" as at war with "religion" is quite inaccurate; in actuality, it is two sets of religious symbolisms, both united to science, that are in conflict. Let us note further that, even from this brief list, what we have called "the demonic"—an intolerant, exclusivist, dogmatic, cruel, and so infinitely destructive faith—can arise *either* from those communities that represent traditional religions *or* from the religious aspects of secular culture itself. But in either case, it is always the *religious* component, the claim to ultimacy and sacrality, that causes the lethal character of the conflict and that increases the scope of the destruction.

Religious symbols, as used both within the explicit "religions" and within the religious aspects of cultural life, have certain quite definite characteristics and functions as forms of speech. Religious symbols function in certain definite ways and say certain definite sorts of things.

First of all, they seek to encompass the *totality* of experience and of known reality; they tell us the ultimate character and the pattern of the whole of reality, so far as we know that whole. Thus even the earliest creation and foundation myths tell us how it *all* got started, what its founding powers or principles were, and what the normative pattern for the whole and all of its parts may be. And Marxist ideology gives us a clear picture of *all* of history from beginning to end, of its major ruling forces or factors, and also of its coming culmination.

Secondly, religious symbols set that vision of the totality of the real into a *meaningful* pattern, a pattern that enlightens us with regard to both the creative and the destructive forces of reality, of the career of good and evil in time. Thus they include norms, clear indicators about what we should support, what we should be and do, and how our individual lives and our social community should be structured. Religious symbols give *meaning* by centering on our most fundamental problems and showing us a "way out," a mode or hope of resolution of those problems in terms of our relations with the most fundamental structures of what is real.

Thirdly, as a consequence, religious symbols provide *hope* and *confidence* by showing how the creative forces of existence—either divine (e.g., God), natural (e.g., evolution), historical (e.g., the Material Dialectic), or human—can and will shape events to a resolution of our deepest problems. In modern existence, this resolution has been held to be *historical*, that is, at the end of history, as in some modern forms of Judaism and Christianity, and as in both Marxism and liberal Progress. In many other religious symbolisms, since history is seen to be endlessly cyclical, salvation cannot lie within history but is *trans*-historical, as in some forms of Christianity and in Hinduism and Buddhism. In either case, religion points to the ultimate meaning of existence, and it locates that meaning in conjunction with what is affirmed to be ultimately real.

Religious symbolism deals, therefore, with what is ultimately real and what is ultimately sacred or worthful. It is that envisionment of reality, truth, and value that shapes a culture's basic outlook and on which, therefore, the rest of culture is dependent. As a consequence, this vision is not directly concerned with what is proximate, relative, contingent, or, so to speak, in the foreground of cultural life. This latter is the "profane," the secular—that which may be related to the ultimate and the sacred but is not directly a part of it. While science, art, politics, and law, therefore, participate in and in part express this fundamental vision, nevertheless, the religious as an aspect of culture should not dominate or control these secular activities, else an oppressive theocracy, as in Shinto Tokyo, Nazi Berlin, Stalinist Moscow, or Shi'ite Teheran, appears. Obviously, keeping these two *distinct* (so that religious ultimacy does not tyrannize the rest of life) and yet *related* (so that the sacred is not irrelevant nor the profane empty and meaningless, but gains power and meaning through participation in the sacred) is perhaps the most difficult task, not only of philosophical theology, but also of individual and social religious existence.

One of the most common, because very helpful, ways to describe religious discourse is to say that it appears at the *limits* of experience.[1] Thus the religious refers to what grounds or establishes our existence, what challenges or threatens our existence, and what might rescue, release, unify, or heal it. The object of religious speech is, therefore, what shakes and judges us, what redeems us—as the pervasive patterns of the religions show, and as even a secular ideology such as Marxism will also illustrate. That which lies beyond our grasp, our power, our clear understanding, and the limits of our precise discourse is not thereby nothing, a blank; experience is continually and importantly related to this "depth" level in a number of positive and negative ways. We become aware of it whenever we experience on the one hand our dependence and our contingency, our helplessness, our waywardness, our deepest weakness and anxiety, or alternatively, whenever we have the deep experiences of creative power, of being alive, of health, of renewal—of acceptance, ecstasy, and hope. In these situations, we touch the *limits* of our powers and relate to something beyond them. Religious speech refers to this level: whether it be the principle of Brahman in Hinduism, of Nothingness in Buddhism, whether it refers to Allah, Jahweh, or God, or to Nature or Substance in modern naturalistic philosophy, or to the Material Dialectic in Marxism.

Since religious speech refers to a level of actuality beyond the ordinary because beyond our limits; it points to some form of transcendence: to the divine powers or gods, to one transcendent divine source or being, to Nature (with a capital N), or to the Dialectic of History. Here ultimacy and sacrality are located and joined, and thus our speech about it is not ordinary but symbolic speech. Negative in part, often picture language or imagist language, metaphorical, analogical, even paradoxical language, it expresses confident feelings as much as logical demonstration or clear conceptuality.

This symbolic or metaphorical character of religious speech is as characteristic of cultural religious speech (Progress, Dialectic of History, Democracy, and so on) as it is of orthodox or traditional language about God or the One. To require that all speech be *ordinary* speech, non-symbolic, univocal, and precise, is to seek to excise religious speech entirely. It is to assume that this dimension is irrelevant or nonexistent—and it is, therefore, to open the way for its return in demonic form. It is, in fact, precisely this error that dominated both sides of the creationist controversy: the error that religious speech and scientific speech are of the same sort, so that one of them excludes or replaces the other.

The direct purpose of religious speech is to express what creates, founds, or establishes life (its ground and ultimate horizon), what is experienced as most deeply disturbing or threatening to life (its most fundamental principles of evil or alienation), and what is experienced then as rescuing or restoring it (its redemptive or saving powers). In explicitly religious communities, therefore, religious symbols refer to the object or objects of religious dependence, worship, meditation, obedience, and faith; and religious speech appears wherever our relation to that object or those objects (Brahman, the Divine Energy, God) is spoken of or expressed. And religious symbolism appears *only* when that relation is talked about. It does not and cannot characterize "ordinary speech," when we are talking about the world around us, nature, society, ourselves, or others, as all of these appear and function in ordinary experience.

To take a Christian example, namely, talk about the Church, religious speech appears when we speak of *God's* presence in the Church's worship, in sacraments, in prayer, in belief, and in theological thought—not when we speak of the church's roof, electrical system, budget, or even its history or its officers and leaders. Then we use ordinary builders', electricians', firemen's historical and institutional speech—except when, perchance, we are concerned with each of these (especially the history and the leaders) in their relation to God. Then religious and theological speech immediately appears.

It is important to point out at this juncture that religious speech so described does not necessarily possess a different *referent* from ordinary speech. Rather, it can be said to refer or speak about a different, deeper *dimension* of that which common sense, sociology, history, or even natural science seeks to describe. To take our own recent example, when we speak politically or through sociological analysis about the churches, we refer according to the methods of political analysis or of sociology to those institutions and the participants within them that claim and seek to be representatives of the Christian tradition.

When, however, we speak *theologically* or "religiously" of those institutions and their participants, we refer to the *same* communities and persons, but in their relation to God. Correspondingly, certain historical events that are crucial to the life of these communities— for example, the exodus and exile, or the incarnation and crucifixion—can be referred to and described *historically*, by the appropriate modes of inquiry and discourse of the historical inquirer; and they can be spoken of *theologically*, in their relation to the manifestation, the presence, and the purposes of God within these events. In the case of the latter two, one is developing the symbols of Christology and Atonement.

Finally, nature (or the natural universe) itself can be spoken of *scientifically* with respect to its "origins" when we ask how certain forms that characterize present experience arose out of other natural forms assumed to have preceded them. Nature can also be spoken of *theologically* when we describe in religious and theological discourse how the divine power is believed to be related to nature's processes (as modern inquiry understands them) through the symbols or concepts of creation and providence.[2]

Although, as we have frequently argued here, these different forms of inquiry and of science are distinct, each with its own logic, methods, and modes of validation, nonetheless one notes that in these cases the "creaturely" referents are the same: nature, events, institutions, and persons all in their relationship to God.

The theological reason for this is that in the Jewish and Christian traditions it is generally accepted that God, whatever the divine nature may be in itself, is known and spoken about by us as God reveals his nature and purposes through creation, and especially through history and persons. We have difficulty, in these traditions, experiencing and speaking of God in himself. Thus we speak of God in *conjunction with* that aspect of the creaturely world—be it nature, history as a whole, or special events and persons or communities—in which God is present and through which God is manifesting himself. Religious speech, therefore, has two interrelated referents: the finite entity or entities through which the divine manifests itself on the one hand (exodus or the person of Jesus, for example), and the divine power and meaning present within that historical reality on the other, which we referred to earlier as the "deeper dimension" of that reality.

Thus religious and theological speech, at least in our tradition, is not directed exclusively at another realm separate from nature, history, and personal existence, at the divine *in* itself as experienced and known *by* itself. Rather, theological speech is directed at the points of intersection between God and the world, those places where a relation of nature, history, and personal existence to God occurs or is experienced. Religious thought witnesses to, reflects upon, and describes the ways in which, within each of these realms in, so to speak, the "foreground" of experience, the divine manifests its presence, its power, and its purposes. A "doctrine of God," therefore, is not devised by means of a cognitive tour outside of and beyond the created world of nature, history, and personal experience. On the contrary, a doctrine arises when the experienced and acknowledged manifestation of God within that world of nature, history, and personal existence is reflected upon and expressed in coherent and systematic form.

The Role of Religious Symbols in Culture

Religious symbols, however, function, as we have noted, in cultural life as well as in communities explicitly centered on the religious (what we have called "religions"). In cultural life also the role of religious symbols is to point to and express what is taken to be ultimate and sacred, to the creative sources or grounds of that culture's life, to the essential structure and obligations of human existence in that culture, and to the grounds or bases of the culture's confidence or hope. In traditional societies, this function of relating the society to its sacred ground was performed for the culture by its established religion. In modern societies, ideologies (secular "myths") have replaced religious myths and theology—but the characteristics of their speech remain nearly the same. The religious dimension of cultural speech then expresses the basic vision of the culture: its apprehension of what is ultimately real, what is ultimately true, and what is ultimately of worth and good. All of this is articulated in the mythical speech with which each culture expresses its way of life.

Frequently in these pages we have referred to the fact that there are certain presuppositions in a modern culture's life—about the real in experience, about knowing and its relation to experience, about what is important in life, about the history and development of civilization—that have made its science and its technology possible and intelligible enterprises. These presuppositions form a large part of the spiritual center (the "religious substance") of modern cultural life, and their expression in symbols—whether in the liberal forms of Western culture or in Marxist form—are examples of religious symbolism in its cultural form. These presuppositions are neither a part of science nor conclusions from its inquiries. As the intellectual *bases* of the method of science, they cannot be established or disproved by that method. Rather, they are its presuppositions, shaping and expressing the horizon within which scientific and technological development become possible and can be continued. The forms of education of our society depend especially upon this symbolic structure, for educational programs are directed at what is felt to be of most importance in the cultural inheritance, at that view of reality, truth, and value which continues the life of the culture.

Thus do Marxists and liberal educational systems differ widely—except that both emphasize science and technology as the bases of their respective societies. When, therefore, one seeks to express for each modern society the metaphysical or epistemological presuppositions of its science and of its technology, of its philosophy of education, and of the fundamental political and social norms effective there, or the vision of history animating the culture's life—one is delineating that structure of religious symbolism upon which the entire society depends.

The function of religious symbolism is not, as the preceding might seem to indicate, purely a conservative one, establishing, preserving, and continuing a cultural structure—though this is what most revolutionaries and reformers have thought in their consciousness of the sacral power of the culture they sought to dismantle. For each revolutionary challenge, critique, and transformation of a cultural structure itself presupposes and expresses a powerful vision of its own, a new vision of history, of society within history, and of human beings within society. Thus it too articulates and depends upon a "religious vision," and it uses religious symbolism for that articulation. The Enlightenment challenge to Christendom was in the name of Reason and Nature, and of autonomy, freedom, justice, equality, and community in this world—all of them "religious" symbols in the sense we have here described. And the Marxist challenge to that liberal, bourgeois culture was in the name of another ultimate vision of human society, history, and the future.

The *criticism* of society, then, as well as its *establishment*, expresses a religious vision. In this sense, all important political and moral speech, whether conservative or radical, has a religious basis. The religious, or the religious dimension, in this wider cultural sense, permeates modern cultural life and informs its center just as traditional religions permeated and informed the spiritual center of each traditional or "archaic" society.

When one asks, What is the ideal relation of religion as an explicit community to this religious center of a modern, secular culture, one asks an important but complex question. Two alternatives are immediately suspect.

The first, the theocratic, is otiose for a number of reasons. There the explicit religious center, controlled by a religious institution and by a religious hierarchy with political power (or a political hierarchy with ideological power), in turn controls or rules all aspects of cultural life: art, education, science, the intellectual realms, and daily customs. One sees this with dismay in Iran; one viewed it with horror in Nazi Germany; one sees it in prospect in the Protestant religious Right and its offshoot, creation science.

The other alternative is a "secular" society with no ultimate vision, no unifying symbols of reality, truth, and value at all. Here is represented a purely relativistic, pragmatic, profane culture where no sense of ultimacy or sacrality is present, envisioned, or expressed. Such is certainly the explicit aim of much of modern cultural life, past and present. As modern experience and these pages show, however, such a totally secular culture is not a human or a historical possibility. The religious reappears in every aspect of cultural life: in its science and philosophy, perhaps especially in its political and economic views, and in its social loyalties of nation, class, and race. Wherever ultimacy and sacrality appear, and they will, there the religious reappears. And if the historical stage is set in certain ways, it will reappear in demonic form, that is, without any internal principle of self-criticism or self-reformation.

Some form of "mixed economy," to borrow a notion from another realm, is therefore most creative. Here the explicitly religious communities of a culture both support and criticize the "civil religion" of the wider cultural life. They do not seek to dominate the various facets of culture by their own laws; they witness on the one hand to the genuine values in that culture's tradition (e.g., equality and justice) and on the other to cultural and social error and evil (in political, economic, and social matters) wherever they find the civil society clearly in the wrong. In such encounters, whether *supportive* of the efforts of the civil world to achieve justice, equality, and beauty, or *critical* of the aggressive, racist, intolerant, or vulgar modes of behavior of the civil order, there is, let us note, an encounter of *religious symbolisms* as well as of class, racial, and social interests —as there was when Christian protesters challenged the Nazi ideology of the Third Reich.

Religious communities do have a social role in support of creative cultural enterprises (such as science and art) and a critical role against uncreative cultural or social movements (such as the technological exploitation of nature). Their task is not to rule society and force it into their own restricted path—as one suspects many creationists would like in the end to do. Needless to say, it is also necessary for the health of these religious communities that the secular society in its legal, governmental, academic, and social institutions also both criticize and support—in much the same way—the churches, synagogues, and "sects." Church history shows that the Church has gained from responsible secular criticism of its errors and faults—and still does; and present experience of religious cults reiterates the importance of careful legal and even legislative oversight.

As indicated in the preceding chapter, this dual task of each religious community in its surrounding social world, a task of both support and critique, requires that each such community achieve some reflective and practical *unity* between the religious existence with God at the center of its life and its life within the world. The necessity of *distinguishing* religious speech about God (or, more accurately, speech about nature, history, and persons in relation to God) from scientific and historical speech about nature, history, and persons has been the central theme of these chapters. That distinction cannot, however, be the last word. In the preceding chapter, the necessity for a society's health of the unity of the religious dimension of culture with the other "secular" aspects of culture was made as clear as possible. At this point the necessity of their unity from the point of view of communities of religious faith is our emphasis.

There are three reasons (from the point of view of religious faith and theology) for the necessity of this unity of religious discourse (a) with scientific discourse about nature, (b) with social, scientific, and historical discourse about communities and history, and (c) with psychological and personal discourse about human beings or persons. These three reasons are:

1. The understanding of God in Christian faith appears out of the manifestation of God in special events, in particular human persons (e.g., Jesus), in history generally, and in nature. Thus since God comes to us *within* those "creaturely" realms, reflectively (that is, in our thinking), those diverse realms of cultural discourse must be united with and incorporated into any philosophical theology which interprets that religious faith. What is said of *God* must be said in conjunction with what is understood about persons, historical events, and nature since the divine appears within and through those realms.

2. Communal life and individual life are both lived within the divine presence, and they are supported, judged, and healed by that presence. Thus both social and individual existence are saturated, so to speak, with the ultimate and the sacred, with unconditionally serious questions of right and wrong, with experiences of judgment, inadequacy, and guilt, and with the longing for reunion, renewal, and fulfillment of life. To allow "secular" forms of discourse completely to preempt the realms of nature, history, and individual existence is thus to truncate and distort the actual character, integrity, and richness of those realms and to misconstrue their deepest problems. Such a sundering of religious speech from secular experience makes life within them intolerably profane and ultimately meaningless, and likewise renders the discourse of religion empty, irrelevant, and meaningless. It is therefore imperative that language concerned with God and our relations with God, with that in us which ties us to an ultimacy of being, meaning, and holiness, be intimately related in turn to our language and thoughts about our ordinary, daily environment and our ordinary selves within that environment. For the sake alike of ourselves and the world, we must bring into unity our relations to God

and our relations to ourselves and to all that surrounds us.[3]

3. Finally, the life lived actively and creatively on the basis of religious faith, a life expressive of it, must be lived within the world of persons, of historical communities and traditions, and of nature. Thus, the reflective (theological) language of the faith must be united with contemporary discourse about nature, society, and individual persons if our active existence in the world is to be morally creative, consistent with itself, and genuinely expressive of its religious center. On all these counts a *unity* between religious symbols and the natural, the social, the psychological, and the historical sciences must be achieved. The achievement and the articulation of this unity, both a reflective and a practical unity, is the major task of philosophical and systematic theology and ethics.

*   *   *

The Meaning of the Symbol of Creation

The religious symbol that has been central to this controversy is unquestionably the symbol of creation. It is this which creation science wishes to defend as "scientific truth" and to teach as a scientific model; and it is this which the naturalistic humanists in modern culture, both scientific and nonscientific, wish to deny in the name of another religious symbol: that of a fecund, blind, purposeless, and everlasting material Nature. It is therefore appropriate that we conclude with a brief discussion of the symbol of creation as much of the present theological community and most of the churches view it. What has this symbol traditionally said? What does it *mean* religiously? Or, if it is not asserting an alternative scientific theory, what *is* it asserting? And how can it be conceived in a positive rather than a negative relation to the conclusions of modern science?

Like most other religious ideas that began their careers many thousands of years ago—and this one can be dated somewhere, very approximately, from the tenth to the seventh centuries B.C.—the symbol of creation has borne a multitude of associated meanings or referents. Two sorts of distinct and yet interrelated meanings are immediately apparent in the traditional forms of this notion or doctrine. These two meanings became apparent as soon as speculative thought began to ponder, defend, and formulate this symbol, that is, when Hebrew religion (and its offshoot, Christianity) united with Greco-Roman culture.

First there is what we might call the "factual" meaning. Among other things, the belief in creation here *meant* to the ancient church tradition that was affirming it the conviction (or "knowledge") that the whole world had begun to be on a certain date; that that originating or primal event had taken place over six days of concentrated divine activity; and that this event was followed almost at once by the cataclysmic Fall and the coming of evils of all sorts into natural, animal, and human existence. Implicit here, obviously, were what might be called "Biblical" astronomy, geology, biology, paleontology, anthropology, and geography, as well as an account of ancient history, all capable of being developed out of a careful, and mostly literalistic, interpretation of the first chapters of Genesis. Both Origen (ca. 220 A.D.) and Augustine (ca. 400 A.D.), philosophical theologians of a very high order, questioned whether this sort of literal interpretation of Genesis was either important or helpful in understanding the symbol. Origen regarded it as merely a material parable of a much more significant "spiritual" creation; and Augustine said it was impossible to interpret it in a completely literal way, since the creation of all things included the creation of time, and so could not itself have taken place over six days of time.

Still, most of the tradition assumed this factual meaning as providing *the* valid information about how everything began, about "origins." And there were cultural as well as religious reasons for this assumption. Until very recently (say, roughly 1700), not much else was known or knowable about pre-history, the history either of nature or of the earliest societies; and the world's other religious or speculative accounts of beginnings, had Europe even been acquainted with them, would have been regarded by medieval and early modern Western people as clearly blasphemous and erroneous. In fact, the main outlines of the Biblical account were taken for granted as "true" by both clerics and lay intellectuals right up to the eighteenth century. Sir Thomas Browne, no prejudiced theologian, wrote in his *Religio Medici* in 1635: "Time we may comprehend 'tis but five days older than ourselves, and hath the same Horoscope with the world."[4] And in 1688 John Ray, one of the important founders of biological science, held that ". . . the number of true species in nature is fixed and limited and, as we may reasonably believe, constant and unchangeable from the first creation to the present day."[5] Both illustrate the fact that the entire culture assumed that the "Biblical history," beginning at a recent date with the creation of the world and its fixed species, and going forward from those initial events into recorded history, represented our only valid knowledge of origins. Western people were, at that point, quite ignorant of the vast extent of the history of nature and of the pre-history of the human race, as we now know of them. As a consequence, the Genesis account remained the accepted authority on such matters as these—that is, matters beyond our present experience and knowledge. The content of creation science is not at all new; what is new is just the twentieth-century claim that this content is "scientific."

Mingled with the factual, proto-scientific set of meanings of the idea of creation were what could be called its *religious* meanings.[6] These meanings appeared in and with—by means of, so to speak—the factual assertions; but it is clearly these assertions, not their factual "clothing," that have been and are important to religious worship, religious feelings and experiences, and theological reflection—as a careful scrutiny of Genesis 1-3, of the Psalms, of Amos, of II Isaiah, of the relevant New Testament passages, and of devotional and theological writings on this subject will show.

We shall expand briefly on these religious meanings in a moment. Suffice it here to say that they include the following notions crucial to both Jewish and Christian faiths: (1) that God alone is the source or ground of all existence, and thus is the sovereign Lord on whom all rightly depend; (2) that God created out of love, because "he saw that it was good"; and thus not only does God love all of creation, but also all of creation is replete with value, meaning, and possibility; (3) that nature, history, and human beings are not illusions or intrinsically evil but are real and good—and thus in some sense themselves free, creative, and originating causes; (4) that despite their clear weaknesses and even their manifest faults, history, society, and individual persons—and with them, nature itself—are all "going somewhere," under or with the aid of the divine sovereignty; they are not imprisoned either in a senseless prisonhouse or set on an endlessly-rotating wheel—as much of the ancient (and the modern) world has held. The concept of creation meant religiously, therefore, many important things: the sovereignty of God over all (it is clearly associated with monotheism); the potential goodness and creative power of all creaturely existence; the dependence of all on God; and the universal hope for all who live out their dependence on God. Again, let us note, these religious meanings represent the *primary* meanings of Genesis, and have done so since the beginning. Genesis and the concept of creation within it are not merely "pre-science."

What is interesting about the history of this concept —and this is true as well of other religious ideas and other religious symbols—is that these several religious meanings or assertions run consistently and without much alteration through the entire tradition, from its Biblical beginnings to its more recent theological articulations. On the other hand, the *way* these meanings were thought about philosophically and understood "scientifically" or factually tended to vary a good deal with the culture and the epoch in which the theological reflection occurred. Each age apparently thought about creation in terms of what it then knew about its world. That knowledge, based on the beginnings of science and on philosophical speculation, changed from age to age: a Platonic, unnaturalistic interpretation in the first centuries; an Aristotelian one in the High Middle Ages; a significantly different way of thinking about it in the Protestant Reformation, Protestant orthodoxy, and Protestant liberalism.

But in all, the same fundamental religious motifs listed here appear as *what* is believed, as the important religious content of the idea. Apparently, religious symbols can, in being reflected upon and articulated, take on the garb, so to speak, of the philosophy and the science of their time. Yet despite these material and factual differences, they can express the same fundamental religious convictions or ideas.[7] On this ground there seems excellent historical and traditional precedent for interpreting the idea of creation in the terms of what we now know scientifically and historically about the history of nature and the history of pre-historical men and women. And, what is more important, there is ample precedent for being confident that, despite the different factual content, the religious symbol expresses the same fundamental religious convictions or affirmations.

There was always a discernible difference between the factual content and the religious/theological meaning of the symbol—as there is between the *fact* of an event called the Fall of Adam and Eve in a given garden and the *symbol* of the universal alienation of men and women from their Creator. With the advent of modern science, and especially with the beginnings, in the late eighteenth and early nineteenth centuries, of sciences dealing with the *history* of nature (geology and astronomy), this difference became a clear distinction, and the two different meanings separated.

As geology, biology, and astronomy brought new knowledge of the age of the universe, of the earth and of its forms of life, and of the radical changes and developments each has undergone in the process of time, the *factual account* of creation associated with pre-scientific speculation (i.e., everything in its present form appeared all at once at a recent beginning) grew more and more incredible to those who created the new science as a dependable mode of knowing the history of Nature. It became evident that this factual account represented the "science" of the eighth- to sixth-century Hebrew world (B.C.E.), what they "knew" or thought they knew about their world and its beginnings. As a consequence, all this receded from theological reflection and was, by and large, no longer asserted as part either of Christian belief or of its theological expression. What was retained, however, and asserted in a variety of forms, perhaps more strongly in the twentieth than in the nineteenth century, was the *religious* meanings of creation (and of Fall) as fundamental to a Christian interpretation of nature, of history, and of human life, and as the basis for our religious self-understanding, obligations, and hopes.[8]

The idea of creation, now separated from the factual implications stemming from ancient views of origins, has been re-presented, therefore, in modern theology, now in terms of modern knowledge of the world about us and the history behind us—in other words, in terms of modern astronomy, geology, biology, paleontology, physical anthropology, and historical inquiry. Just as formerly, in earlier theology, the factual understanding of the world characteristic of ancient societies provided the expression of the *ways* God was thought to have created the entire system of things in a sudden series of acts, so a modern scientific understanding of the universe characteristic of a scientific society provides us with the *way* God is now seen by present theology to have brought the present system of things into being over eons of time. In this manner, the religious meanings of the concept or faith in creation are preserved and quite possibly strengthened and purified. Despite its adherence to the conclusions of science, therefore, modern theology stands firmly within the tradition of Biblical witness and of the historic affirmations of the churches: that all things come from God, are dependent on God, and are therefore good, potential of creative meaning and hope.

The religious meanings of the symbol of creation are crucial to the Christian interpretation of life. Because these implications of creation are multiple and pervasive, they cannot be discussed in any detail here. Clearly, though, they center around the relation of the creaturely world, and especially of men and women within it, to God. For creation establishes, so to speak, the permanent and crucial *form* of that relation as it appears in every other fundamental Christian idea or symbol. Since the existence, power, and meaning of each creature find their source in God, each part of creation is dependent on God for its life, its continuity, and its fulfillment. Thus are devotion and commitment to God, obedience to his ways, and trust in him central characteristics of Christian and of human existence. As God has created out of love, so each creature in turn responds to God, and to all else in creation, in love. The integrity, freedom, and value of each part of creation was assured in this symbol, for each is the work of the love as well as of the power of God.

Whether, therefore, we look at nature, at other communities, at other persons, or ourselves, we see beings of value (yet not of *divine* value, lest we tend to worship them!)—beings worthy of our care, our respect, and our love. This attitude toward nature, other communities, other persons, and oneself is far different from the one encouraged by the view common in our technological culture: that nature is clearly only "material object," and other persons are the chance result of blind forces. The understanding of the world as the divine creation is absolutely central to sane and human attitudes, and yet it is quite in accord with all the conclusions of modern natural science.

The Meaning of Creation for Modern Culture

In the long centuries in which Western culture was "Christendom," these religious meanings of the symbol of creation naturally penetrated every facet of that developing culture and left a permanent imprint there. In fact, it is apparent to scholarship[9] that the attitudes toward nature and toward history implicit in the idea of creation created just those fundamental assumptions most characteristic of, and creative within, modern Western culture and most important for the development of modern science and of modern views of history.

A nature created by God was, first of all, a nature stripped of gods, goddesses, and demonic forces and was thus a "secular" nature, capable of careful, empirical study leading to scientific theory and, on the basis of that theoretical understanding, capable of creative use. Nature was, moreover, *real*, not illusory; thus its physical relations, as known through the senses, were the locus, or "place," of its order. Nature manifested a *material* or *physical* order; matter and order were no longer antithetical terms. This order was known to be there, even if we had to look hard for it, because the God who created the material world was a God of order as well as of love.

As is evident, this view of nature as a *created material order* laid the foundations for modern empirical science: It made the empirical study of the habits or laws of nature a sensible and a worthwhile enterprise—which the idealistic philosophies of Greece and the a-cosmic pantheism of India never would have done. Modern science was conscious, and rightly, of arising as an alternative to the "Christian" world of medieval Europe; in fact, however, the rise of that science presupposed the view of nature as a created yet contingent order which the Christian idea of creation had established. Thus in this historical case, the symbols of a traditional religion helped to shape and establish the cultural presuppositions that later, in other forms, were to represent the (secular) religious base of modern scientific culture.

Correspondingly, the symbol of creation, deeply assumed for centuries, laid the foundation for the view of history characteristic of the modern West. In fact, the myths of Progress and of the Material Dialectic, characteristic of the two so-called secular societies of the present, are offspring or derivatives of this Christian (and Jewish) religious symbol. If God created time, then time has a purpose, and its unfolding leads to a culmination, a period of fulfillment for which we can realistically hope—a message clearly articulated in both the Hebrew and the Christian scriptures. Because of the symbol of creation—and the other Jewish and Christian religious symbols concerned with history—time becomes linear rather than cyclical; and correspondingly, history becomes a development toward a purposed goal rather than an endless round of frustrations and miseries.

The modern sense, then, that history is building meaning, that it is a progress toward a longed-for end, central to both liberal progress and Marxism, has its roots in the symbol of creation. That symbol—whatever its strange relations to present developments in modern science and modern historical and social thought—thus in fact provided the historical basis for those presuppositions about nature, time, history, and society most essential for modern science, for modern social theory, and for the modern sense of history.[10] Far from being antagonistic to modern scientific cultures—as *both* creationists and many in the scientific community believe— the conception of divine creation has been one important historical ground of that culture; and quite possibly, it remains its firmest and most creative basis.

As modernity developed, however, the attitudes toward nature and toward history which had been received from the Christian inheritance, and especially from the notion of creation, soon abandoned this received basis. For a number of understandable reasons, they took off, so to speak, on their own. This new "modern" nature was not seen as God's creation, and so was not viewed as of inherent value with an integrity balancing that of the human. Rather, it was perceived as a nature that was in itself purposeless, an objective, material realm void of value in itself, and hence was a realm of concern (i.e., of value) to humans solely in terms of its *uses* for them.[11] And with this new sense of the dominance of human intellect and power over nature, unlimited technological exploitation founds its intellectual charter and spiritual legitimation.

In history, men and women again found themselves "alone," free now from divine sovereignty and therefore free apparently to create whatever world they pleased, to build utopia by their own scientific intelligence and moral will. They have, however, found themselves able to build nothing resembling utopias. The continuation of oppression and tyranny, of injustice and conflict, the exploitation of nature, the invention of terrible weapons, and the reappearance of the demonries of nation, class, race, and social ideology have faced us with a future apparently replete with menace and void of promise.

The symbol of the divine creation of nature, of history, and of each of us, and its implication—the affirmation of the divine center for all of life—remain peripheral to our scientific and technological culture, crucial as each once was to the establishment of that culture. Possibly in the "Time of Troubles" now facing that culture, the relevance, power, and beauty of that symbol will reappear, and the centrality of the divine to which it points will return. Such a reappearance might reshape many of the attitudes now destructive in an advanced scientific culture, as once creation functioned to establish that cultural way of life. In both cases, however, as both the principle of the establishment of our being and the principle of its renewal and fulfillment, the religious symbol appears as the deepest ground of creative science and of a healthy technology, and not as an antagonist to either one.

Notes

Chapter 1—The Initiation of a Witness

1. For understandable reasons, it is usually assumed that only natural science classes, and particularly biology classes, are vulnerable to the "equal time" or "balanced treatment" insistence of the creationists. This is not so, although so far only the issue of the conflict of the "Biblical view" with that of evolution has been publicly raised. Not only are astronomy, geology, and botany classes also implicated; so is almost every conceivable high-school subject, as the following quotation from the paper of Gerald Skoog, Professor of Secondary Education, Texas Tech University, Lubbock, Texas, makes clear:

   State and religion could become entangled in other curricula areas if creationists achieve their goal. The ICR goals for 1981 included the development of "two-modeled" books in every subject and at every level (Morris, 1981) [Henry Morris, Scientific Creationism]. During the 1981 Texas Textbook Adoption Proceedings, there were several demands that specific areas in textbooks be neutralized by biblical ideas. For example, social studies textbooks that discussed the human transition from nomadic hunters and gatherers to farmers were criticized for not including Cain's "theories." According to this so-called theory, farming could not have been preceded by hunting and gathering because Cain, the son of Adam, was a farmer. Psychology textbooks were criticized for not including Judeo-Christian viewpoints. Textbooks were criticized for contradicting or not including biblical ideas on the role of women, marriage, sex and child-raising. One petitioner argued against the inclusion of the metric system in an earth science textbook because "if the Lord had meant for the decimal system to be used, he would have had ten apostles" (Texas Education Agency, 1980, p. 78). This paper was presented at the annual convention of the National Association of Biology Teachers, Las Vegas, Nevada, October 24, 1981.

2. For a more complete discussion of the relation of creation science to "scientists" and to science itself, see Chapter 2, pp. 0-0, and especially note 3, and then further in Chapter 7.

3. For examples of this "friendly yet critical" treatment, see the author's *Religion and the Scientific Future* (New York: Harper & Row, 1970), especially Chapter 3—now published by Mercer University Press; and *Society and the Sacred* (New York: Crossroad Press, 1981), especially Chapters 6, 7, and 8.

Chapter 2—Preparation for the Case

1. This brief history is owed to a document on creationism written and circulated by Professor Franklin Parker, Department of Education, West Virginia University.

2. A goodly number of representatives of the scientific community have objected to this identification of some of the supporters of creationism as "scientists," despite the latters' impressive doctorates in hard science and their tenured positions. As one insisted, "Scientists are those who *do* science, and these persons do not." Well and good.

It should be noted, however, that this is a *normative* definition of scientists, i.e., what scientists *ought* to be doing to deserve that title and honor. It is not a *descriptive* definition of scientists. A descriptive definition represents a quite different sort of definition. It tells us, not what a scientist ought to be like, but what those who function as scientists in society are actually like—that is, what their objective professional credentials are, how they perform professionally in society with regard to their professional role (as laboratory researcher, professor, e.g.), what sorts of groups in society they participate in, and so on. Such a definition, therefore, describes people in society who are *called* scientists and who call themselves scientists, not what those names or titles ideally might denote.

The vast difference between these two sorts of definition can be seen by a couple of parallel cases. One can speak of "real" doctors and thus, of course, omit entirely those "so-called" physicians concerned only for income and prestige, those who seem quite indifferent to real healing, those who ignore their patients, those who do not keep up with important innovations, those whose testimony can be purchased in court, and so on. Here one is speaking of the normative ideal of the doctor or physician, an ideal by no means always actualized by the profession.

Or one can speak of the profession as it actually is, that is, as it is sociologically, historically, or descriptively, a profession made up of persons of all sorts, persons with different aims and commitments, and certainly with different concerns for the norms and ideals of the medical profession—so long as they possess the objective prerequisites for being recognized as doctors and function in society in that role. Certainly they are in *that* sense "doctors"; they are not lawyers, brokers, professors, or clergymen—nor are they paid on the scale of the latter!

Correspondingly, one can speak of *real* Christianity or *real* Christians, "those who *do* Christianity"; and then one omits a goodly number, and in fact probably most, of the members of churches, of the clergy, of the officials of the historical churches, and of the profession of theologians. Surely the churches of, say, Sicily and Appalachia, not to mention southern California and Chicago, are to be named "Christian"—as is even the Moral Majority. On the other hand, it is abundantly clear that these groups (at least to many of us) are not "doing Christianity." They possess all the objective credentials of Christians; they function in society in that role; they proclaim themselves to be such—and certainly they do not represent forms either of Islam or of Buddhism. Deviant as they may be and unpalatable as it is to say so, undeniably they represent forms of Christianity.

In the same way, just as the less-exalted doctors, who now abound around us, are a *type* of physician, and as the less-than-noble clergymen are nevertheless a *form* of priest or minister, so people with scientific degrees and scientific positions in academic institutions or in research laboratories are *types* of "scientists," whether in fact they are "doing" science or not. It is part of the problem of becoming "established," as we will argue in Chapter 7, that institutions and the professionals within them have to face the widespread appearance of radically non-normative, in fact deviant and often corrupt, forms of themselves—and have to understand themselves anew in the light of that unwelcome appearance. As this happened to the unhappy Church in the fourth, fifth, and sixth centuries, so it is now happening to the scientific community in advanced scientific cultures.

3. The data in the text were taken (1) from the list of witnesses for the defense announced and called by the lawyers for the defense, and (2) from the pamphlet entitled "Twenty-one Scientists Who Believe in Creation," produced by Creation Life Publishers, San Diego, 1974 and 1977.

   The list of witnesses for the defense (the creationist cause) included the following: Dr. William Scott Morrow, professor of biochemistry, Wofford College, South Carolina; Dr. Wayne Triar, professor of biology at the King's College, Briarcliff Manor, New York; Dr. Margaret Hilder, retired professor of biology at Broch University, St. Cathedral, Ontario; Dr. Daniel Chittick, professor of chemistry, University of Puget Sound and George C. Fox University; Dr. Ariel Roth, director of the Geoscience Research Institute, Loma Linda University, California, a former professor of biology at the University of Michigan; Dr. N. Chandra Wichranasinghe, professor of applied mathematics and astronomy, University College, Cardiff, Wales.

   On a visit to the Westinghouse Research Laboratory in Pittsburgh, I asked the assembled research scientists (about 300) how many regarded themselves as creationists. To the amazement of their colleagues about thirty raised their hands. Subsequently on a visit to Purdue University, I was told that four tenured members of the faculties in the natural sciences identified themselves as creationists. Interestingly, no member of the Religion Department at Purdue was a creationist.

4. It is interesting and ironic that another form of this same challenge, namely that science cannot know past, unrepeatable events—a challenge made in this instance by the creationists against the natural sciences—has frequently been made by representatives of natural science, that is, by philosophers of science, against *history* as a theoretical inquiry. In his famous, or infamous, article in the *Journal of Philosophy*, 1942, entitled "The Function of General Laws in History," Carl Hempel argued that historical inquiry could neither be "theoretical" nor contribute to knowledge. The reasons he gave were that history dealt with unique events in the past which could not be repeated in the present. Thus the events to which historical theory attended could not be observed, nor could a theory about them be tested by experiment. As a result, he argued, because history produced no testable theories, it could hardly be called a theoretical discipline at all (as could natural science). On the contrary, history was an inquiry based solely on the imagination, at best an example of art, and its hypotheses merely statements of preference.

Needless to say, historians reacted to this accusation with about the same sort of disbelief and horror as natural scientists have reacted to the creationists' challenge based on what is essentially the same argument. For Hempel's article, see P. Gardiner, ed., *Theories of History* (New York: The Free Press, 1959), pp. 345-346. For one extremely effective reply, see Gordon Leff, *History and Social Theory* (New York: Doubleday Anchor, 1971).

5. It has been a surprise to me—though a fascinating one—to find that in practice, if not in explicit theory, a surprisingly similar view of science seems to be prevalent in at least some aspects of contemporary medical education. A relative of mine in her second year at a well-respected medical school reported that in most of her scientific courses in this school the instruction was composed of the recitation of facts, accompanied by graphs and slides, but with little discourse on the theories involved. Correspondingly, tests were almost invariably true-false tests,

or multiple-choice tests—again concerned only with the knowledge of *facts* and not with the understanding of the theories binding the facts together. Thus can a scientific culture tend to descend, by its own lack of self-understanding, from the level of science to that of *techne*, from (as Aristotle put it) knowledge *why* to mere knowledge *that*, and its practitioners from theorists ("scientists") to artisans and craftspersons.

6. This argument was used by the defense at the trial. According to the full and careful report in *The Pea Ridge Country Times* ("Official newspaper for Avoca, Garfield, Little Flock, and Pea Ridge") of Pea Ridge, Arkansas (December 20, 1981, p. 11), Judge Overton "interrupted the examination by State's Attorney Williams to ask whether Friar [a professor of biology and a witness for the Creationists] could show positive evidence for creation-science, not just negative evidence against 'evolution-science.' Williams responded that since the two are mutually exclusive, whatever is evidence against one is automatically evidence for the other."

7. This point came to me in a debate with Dr. Walter T. Brown, Jr. (Ph.D. in physics from M.I.T.), at Albion College, Michigan, in January of 1984. Dr. Brown denied that creation science had any religious content to it because, said he, the theory did not, as specified for scientific classes, make any reference at all to the Bible—"and the Bible is what contains religious ideas. If there is no reference to the Bible, there is no religion there." I recall wondering how he would classify ideas about the Hindu and Shinto gods and goddesses, a typical gospel hymn, a Catholic sacramental rite or symbol, an image or statue of the Buddha, and so on, all of which are clearly "religious" and yet none of which has any explicit referential relation to our Bible.

8. To continue the theme of the last footnote. One of the major puzzles for me as for others about the creationist case was how creationists could really believe that their model was not religious, especially when they admitted —as these texts show—that "God" was a necessary agent within that model. Were they not then admitting our case from the start? We can now suggest an answer: that it is for them the Bible, not the character of ideas, rites, laws,

and so on, that constitutes what is and what is not religion. Thus an idea—like that of creation—which is Biblical, if it be set amid *Biblical references*, is considered to be
religious; the same idea, set in the context of "science,"
that is, as an explanation of facts of scientific inquiry, is
for them a secular idea and not religious at all.

Chapter 3—Deposition

1. These conversations with Tony Siano were, of course, not
   recorded. There is, therefore, no footnoting them, except
   to report that I wrote careful notes after each one about its
   substance.
2. The record of the deposition of each witness is, of course,
   one of the official court documents available to each side
   of the case. The record of the conversation here described
   (*Deposition of Langdon Gilkey*, No. LR-C-81-322, 150 pp.,
   Bull & Associates [sic!], 4651 Roswell Road, Atlanta) was
   sent to me shortly after the deposition took place to be
   corrected, signed, and returned to the court. As a literary
   document, namely as one seeking to state clearly and
   unequivocally what was in fact said, it was (I felt with
   horror) a total disaster. Among other things, proper
   names were wildly misheard and misunderstood. For
   example, Reinhold Niebuhr and Paul Tillich appeard as
   Ryan O'Neal and Paul Tiller; and I could not for the
   longest time make out why I had on a number of occasions apparently referred to a law firm named Birch &
   Russell—until I realized this was what the reporter had
   heard when I said Bertrand Russell! The description in
   the present text has, of course, been checked with this
   deposition—but more in order to correct, amend, and
   clarify the official record than my own chapter!
3. This is the crucial role for metaphysics which Whitehead
   envisioned when he called it "the critic of the abstrac-
   tions" represented by the different specialized disciplines of culture. Metaphysics is, he said, that rational
   and yet imaginative speculation that articulates in universal categories the "general and yet infinite background lying behind each specific sentence" in ordinary
   cultural life. See especially *Science and the Modern World*
   (New York: Macmillan, 1925), pp. 122, 197; *Adventures of*

Ideas (New York: Macmillan, 1933), pp. 180-181, 187, 285; *Process and Reality* (New York: Macmillan, 1929), pp. vii, 4, 25; *Religion in the Making* (Cambridge, Massachusetts: University Press, 1926), p. 84.

4. Interestingly, as "unscientific" a thinker as Sören Kierkegaard (1813-1855), was one of the first to formulate clearly this characteristic of all scientific and historical—and commonsense—"truth" about the world, a world of continual becoming, as an "approximation process" whose conclusions are at best temporary and hypothetical and by no means final and absolute. See *Philosophical Fragments*, tr. by D. Swenson (Princeton, 1946), pp. 60-71; and *Concluding Unscientific Postscript*, tr. by W. Lowrie (Princeton, 1944), pp. 169ff.

5. It is now widely recognized that falsification of evidence, suppression of counter-factual data, and distortion of procedures represent a *corruption* of science, and their spread a *threat* to the integrity of science. Thus does science have a *moral* base, and thus does its continuation depend on the moral integrity of the scientific community and, of course, on that of the wider cultural community. One of the reasons this moral base for science is now so universally apparent, even if it is not yet universally acknowledged, is that, with what we will call later the "establishment" of science, vast funds of money and a great deal of prestige accrue to anyone "successful" in scientific inquiry. As a result, not only are scientists now more tempted than previously; even more, a different sort of person, perhaps one with more of an eye to advancement than with a commitment to the truth, appears with increasing frequency in scientific and medical circles.

   The recent rash of cases of falsification of evidence and of procedures vividly proves that without the moral (and even "religious") "*eros* towards truth," science can hardly exist as science. (*Eros* is the Greek word for "*love* for truth"; we would probably put this "*commitment* to truth"). See, as indications of the moral predicament of a now-established scientific community, the volume by William Broad and Nicholas Wade, *Betrayers of the Truth* (New York: Simon and Schuster), and, as another example, the strange case of Dr. Joseph H. Cort of Mount Sinai

Hospital and elsewhere as reported in *The New York Times*,
December 27, 1982.

Chapter 4—The Trial:
Religious and Historical Backgrounds

1. This brief summary of elements within Professor Geisler's deposition can of course be checked in the offical
   records of the case, the *Deposition of Norman Geisler*.
2. The complete report of Mr. Cearley's statement—of
   which that in the text represents excerpts and a summary
   —is to be found in the "Transcript" or *Court Record*, U.S.
   District Court, Eastern District of Arkansas, Western Division, Reverend Bill McLean, et. al., Plaintiffs vs. Arkansas
   Board of Education, etc., Defendants, Little Rock, Decem
   ber 7-16, 1981, published (in part) by Sandra Smith, CVR,
   Official Court Reporter, vol. 1, pp. 4-11 (henceforth *Court
   Record*).
3. The Attorney-General's statement—of which the above
   represents excerpts and a summary—is to be found in
   Court Record, vol. I, pp. 12ff.
4. Bishop Hicks' testimony can be found in *Court Record*,
   vol. I, pp. 22-36; the above is a summary of what the
   author regarded as the central thrust of that well-articu-
   lated statement.
5. Father Vawter's testimony occupies pp. 31-58 of *Court Record*, vol. I. The above is an excerpt and summary of the
   relevant parts of that testimony. One humorous note
   about the otherwise excellent transcript provided by the
   Court was that the word "exegesis," used twice by Professor Vawter, was transcribed as "text of Jesus" (see pp.
   37-38). ("Exegesis" is the word for the scholarly investigation into the original meaning of a particular passage in a
   given text.)
6. To my surprise this interchange, which is recorded
   clearly in my notes, does not appear in the account of
   Professor Marsden's testimony found in the *Court Record*,
   vol. I, pp. 58-112. On several other occasions, humorous
   incidents or asides that delighted the spectators were also
   absent from this otherwise-excellent record. This is not a

complaint; it is stated merely to explain why some things I have here related cannot be found in the official text.

7. Henry M. Morris, *The Troubled Waters of Evolution* (San Diego: CLP, 1974), p. 10; and Morris, *Studies in the Bible and Science* (Philadelphia: Presbyterian and Reformed Publishing Company, 1966), p. 102 (see *Court Record*, vol. I, pp. 79-83).
8. For example, Duane Gish, *Evolution: The Fossils Say No* (San Diego: CLP, 1972), p. 42.
9. Or, as the *Court Record* itself puts this point in Judge Overton's words, " . . . I don't think the writers can call it religion for one purpose and science for another, if that is what they've done in these writings. And [if] they underpin it with religious writings, then I don't think they can just take the hat off and say 'Well, we're talking about science now.'" *Court Record*, vol. I, p. 86.
10. *Court Record*, vol. I, p. 146.

Chapter 5—The Trial: Theological and Philosophical Issues

1. This document is of course one of the official documents of the case, like the depositions and the *Court Record*, and is therefore available for research.
2. The official record of this testimony is in *Court Record*, vol. I, pp. 172-239. Reading over that record of my own testimony, competently as it was done considering the difficulties of reporting and then transcribing often complex and frequently esoteric matters, I realize how much of what was actually said is inevitably omitted from such an official record.
3. My insistence upon a distinction between the logic and the language of natural science from that of philosophy and also, in this case, theology should not be construed as an insistence upon their final separation. One major point of this volume as a whole is to argue for an interrelationship, certainly an interconnection, between science and theology, a coherent and unified understanding of *both* in their distinction from and yet their relations to each other. Such an understanding is the task of philosophy and of philosophical theology, and it is absolutely

essential to our culture, our personal, and our professional university life (for these arguments, see Chapters 7 and 8). As the present creationist case shows, however, it is also important to distinguish them, lest as in the creationist movement, religion encroach upon science, or lest also from the other side science swallow religion.

In the same way it is also important to distinguish the methods, criteria, and language of natural science from those of history, possibly psychology and the social sciences, and certainly hermeneutics (the study of texts), though again a unified view of these diverse realms of being is also vital. Chemical, biological, and physiological language about a person is quite distinct from psychological language, and both are distinct from personal, philosophical, or religious language about that person. The "object" in each case is the same, but the perspective in which it is viewed and "known" is significantly different. The same difference in many cases appears between scientific, philosophical, and theological language as each approaches "experienced actuality" from its own unique perspective.

Chapter 6—The Trial:
The Overwhelming Weight of Scientific Evidence

1. Professor Ruse's complete testimony is to be found in the Court Record, vol. II, pp. 224-278.
2. See for example, ibid., vol. II, pp. 317, 373.
3. Ibid., pp. 293.
4. In the Court Record the account of this matter is found in vol. II, pp. 359-367, especially pp. 363 and 365.
5. Other examples could be cited: Malthus' theory of population that Darwin used analogously in his conception of natural selection and Paley's understanding of adaptation which Darwin also employed. In the present case Ruse refers to Marx's theory of sudden revolutionary change which Gould is here said to have used in his new view of "punctuated equilibrium," i.e., of evolution as characterized by sudden, "revolutionary" leaps or changes.
6. For example, the fact that both Kierkegaard and Nietzsche were unusual, not to say strange, personalities, both

always close to the edge of sanity, is very significant for the origins of their respective views but utterly irrelevant to the question of the universal validity of those views.

7. As we have noted, despite the judge's opening remarks, most scientific observers of the trial (see the article in *Science*, January 1982, and in *Discovery*, February 1982) did not seem clearly to understand this crucial legal point or, in fact, the logic of the ACLU case. In reporting on the case and its outcome, they considered the trial essentially to represent a debate between "evolutionary theory" on the one hand and "creation science" on the other, in which an impressive team of scientists successfully proved the former to be science and thus valid, and the latter to be pseudo-science and as a consequence invalid. Such an interpretation forgot that there is nothing unconstitutional about not teaching science or even teaching something that is not science. For example, the headline over the article in *Science* stated: "A High Powered Battery of Lawyers and Scientists Challenges Arkansas' 'Creation-Science' Law." In such a scenario, of course, the arguments of the "religious experts" neither made nor could make any theoretical or legal contribution; or, as Ruse puts this point in a later address, they provided an interesting "religious introduction" or "a general religious background" to the main burden of the case, which was the argument that creation science is neither science nor true.

The article on the trial in *Chemical and Engineering News* (January 18, 1982) does not even record the participation of any religious institutions, persons, or witnesses on the side of ACLU. Not only did the numerous representatives of religion have for that observer no role in the case on the "right side"; obviously, their presence remained quite invisible. To the ACLU and Skadden, Arps lawyers, however, this reading of the case was simply erroneous—and, as one remarked to me, "woefully biased." The main thrust of our case, and of the judge's later ruling, was that creation science represent precisely *a religious theory of origins* and thus, when mandated in public education, contravenes the First Amendment. Correspondingly, to validate this claim in court required that arguments be given as to why and in what ways it represents in fact a *religious*, and not a scientific, theory, which arguments only experts in the field of religious sources, history, and conceptuality could muster. The elegant, hilarious, and perceptive exception to this faulty reporting of the trial was the article by Gene Lyons in *Harpers*, April 1982, entitled "Repealing the Enlightenment."

8. For some obscure reason, the present official *Court Record* skips the testimony of Professor Ayala. At first, this omitted testimony was promised to appear in a continuation of the record still to be transcribed (see vol. II, p. 378). As a consequence of its omission in the presently published materials, the account in this chapter of Professor Ayala's testimony, as with that of Professors Morowitz and Gould, must depend entirely on my own notes, carefully but hastily scribbled. Furthermore, because in February 1982 the state of Arkansas decided *not* to appeal the judge's ruling in January against them and for the plaintiffs, the promised publication of this further testimony has never been made. Thus for the latter half of the trial there is no transcribed *Court Record*; as a consequence, except for newspaper reports, there is no way of reviewing in any official source what was said in this latter half.

9. A report on the major portion of Professor Dalrymple's testimony is included in the *Court Record*, vol. II, pp. 406-445.

10. Ibid., p. 410.

11. Ibid., pp. 410-411.

12. Ibid., pp. 436.

13. As noted above, the *Court Record* ceases prior to this testimony and to that of Professor Gould.

14. The creationists frequently claim that the reasoning of the "evolutionists" is here circular, the dating of the geological column being dependent on the fossil record, and the latter in turn being determined by the place of the relevant fossils in the column of rocks. Dalrymple effectively showed that on the contrary the dating of the rocks is quite independent of the paleontological record, being itself dependent entirely on the procedures and theories within the science of physics, namely radiometric dating. See ibid., pp. 411-417.

15. It is basic to the "theory" of creation science that the stars have never changed their positions, a view which runs

directly counter to the now almost universally acknowledged thesis of an expanding universe. On an even more fundamental level, the entire methodology for mapping the stellar and galactic content of the astronomical universe by means of calculating distance and speed via the speed of light breaks down completely in a radically *recent* universe. In such a universe, light from "distant" stars could not have taken hundreds of thousands of years to get here. In a creationist pamphlet designed for high-school students, the creationist father replied to a question on this issue from his high-school son: "Dad, how do you explain the light from the stars that my teacher said took eons of time to get here if the world was created only ten thousand years ago?" by saying, "Son, God created that light on its way." If that *were* the case, no current astronomical measurement would make sense, and every bit of astronomical mapping—not to mention the analysis of the spectrum by which the properties of each star are known—would become utterly without ground.

16. The text at this point represents excerpts from and a summary of the testimony as recorded in vol. II, pp. 380-406.
17. Ibid., vol. II, p. 397.
18. See the full article on Judge Overton's ruling in *The New York Times*, Jan. 6, 1983, pp. 1 and 10, as well as the official document of the ruling printed here in Appendix B.
19. See the notice in *The New York Times*, Feb. 5, 1983.

Chapter 7—Science and Religion in an Advanced Scientific Culture

1. For some time I have found illuminating this comparison of the social movement of science in modern culture (from roughly the seventeenth century on) with the social status and power of an established religious community (e.g., the Christian Church). Both communities in their history have moved from "outside" the established forces of the wider society to "inside" it, to *establishment* at the intellectual and power center of the society in question. The Christian Church achieved this position of dominance and influence in the period from 300 to 500 A.D., an establishment that lasted until modern times; the

scientific community achieved this prominence beginning in the seventeenth century, moving through the eighteenth and nineteenth centuries, and has finally achieved dominance in the twentieth century.

Correspondingly, so I have found, each of these two communities on "establishment" has found itself faced with strikingly similar problems: problems of a new self-understanding and interpretation; of becoming "watered down," so to speak, in its integrity and inner power; of new ignorance within its own ranks of what it stands for; of creeping corruption, moral ambiguity, and actual dishonesty; of the appearance of "popular" forms of Christianity and now even of science; and so on.

This comparison, however, frequently offends scientists as an insult to the purity and grandeur of science. In an address to a number of Nobel Laureates at Gustavus Adolphus College in October of 1975, I used this comparison of the problems of present science to those of established religions in order to point out in a convincing and, I thought, humble way (after all, I *do* represent religion) some of the risks and dangers ahead in "the future of science" (the title given each speaker). A Nobel Laureate from Stanford University was so offended by all of this that he came up to me afterwards and said just before he stalked off, "The critical things you said about science were bad enough; but to compare it to religion is unendurable." This address was published in the volume for the Nobel conference entitled *The Future of Science* (New York: John Wiley & Sons, 1977), and then republished as "The Creativity and Ambiguity of Science" in the author's *Society and the Sacred* (New York: Crossroad, 1981, Chapter 6).

2. This "myth" of the continual warfare between religion and science—or perhaps "conventional and anachronistic view of the issue" is better—is well illustrated by the reports of the media in general, by most of the accounts in scientific journals of the controversy and the trial, and by many (but not all) of the representatives of the scientific community associated with this controversy. Typical of the latter is William Moyer, Director of the Biological Sciences Curriculum Study in Louisville, Colorado. A doughty and tireless fighter against creationism and a

-249-

fellow witness at Little Rock, Moyer is one who interprets the contemporary controversy purely in what are, to me, the quite out-of-date terms of the struggle of religious obscurantism against scientific enlightenment.

He rightly characterizes the creationists as "fundamentalists," but there is no recognition at all of the part their new participation in scientific training and knowledge plays in the current movement, no recognition or awareness of the resistance of most religious groups and institutions to creation science; nor is there any awareness at all of the role the larger scientific community has, sometimes consciously, sometimes unconsciously, played in the development of the controversy as a whole.

He is, as he says, worried about the lack of understanding of science in the wider nonscientific community, and he is irritated at the lethargy of his scientific colleagues in the face of this threat to science from the forces of religion. But there is no hint at all of concern for a similar lack of the understanding of science in the scientific community itself, or of any failure in the scientific community to understand better its relations to religion, or of its even more unfortunate tendency to assume that science has now replaced religious beliefs. See the quotations from him in an article on the trial in *Chemical and Engineering News*, January 18, 1982.

3. I was heartened to find this correlation of *scientific certainty* and *scientific forms of thinking* with the characteristics of recent fundamentalism spelled out irrefutably in James Barr's excellent study, *Fundamentalism* (Philadelphia: Westminster Press, 1978), especially pp. 93ff.

4. Perhaps the prime example of this union of religious truth seen as fact with scientific truth also seen as fact is to be found in the most influential fundamentalist interpreter of modern culture and the most revered "theologian" of contemporary fundamentalism, the late Francis Schaeffer. The influence of this man's writings and teachings on younger fundamentalists, both American and European (he lived in Switzerland), has been immense. One of the main themes he stressed is the identity at the most fundamental level of the truths of revelation with the truths of science, both being propositional statements of facts that are known with certitude.

It follows that these two kinds of truths are convertible; that is, that religious revelation can inform us of matters of fact and thus can become the basis of scientific conclusions.

While most of us in the community of theology find strange, even bizarre, Schaeffer's interpretations of modern philosophy and theology—and frequently wonder how much of either one he had actually read himself—and while we thoroughly disagree with his understanding of scientific truth and of religious truth, still there can be no question of his intention to reflect strenuously on both culture and on Christian faith from the point of view of the Christian tradition. Thus I have called him a "theologian" of fundamentalism. See footnote 5, Chapter 2, for the same problem vis-à-vis the title "scientists." For Francis Schaeffer's representative works, see A Christian Manifesto, 1981; Escape from Reason, 1968; Genesis in Space and Time: The Flow of Biblical History, 1972.

5. See our own definition of religion in Chapter 5, pp. 99-100. For an example of the critique of the word religion, see the work of Wilfred Cantwell Smith, which faults the usual use of that word to name the traditions of Buddhism, Christianity, Islam, etc. The Meaning and End of Religion (San Francisco: Harper and Row, 1978), especially Chapters 2 and 6.

6. This usage of the category "the religious" to cover other, secular elements in culture is often criticized on the grounds that since such usage seems to encompass everything, it signifies nothing. More specifically, so it is argued, by making no distinctions between religion and the religious on the one hand and other aspects of cultural life on the other, these categories so used no longer point to or mean anything specific. If everyone and everything is "religious," what does the category then refer to?

This critcism is at fault for two reasons. First, it assumes a priori that religion is always (as it is, to be sure, in our present culture) represented by definite and quite distinquishable, "separate" elements (institutions or groups) in a culture—an historically unwarrantable assumption. In ancient and traditional culture (or in current Iran) *every-thing* is "religious," and yet the word clearly has a specifiable meaning. Secondly, this criticism makes, again on a priori grounds, no room for the important distinction proffered in the text: the distinction between "religions" and "the religious." On the one hand, there are "religions," those institutions (e.g., churches and synagogues) legitimately separable in analysis (at least in modern culture!) from the political, economic, and social institutions of society. These institutions (e.g., churches) we have called institutions "of religion," or "religions" (e.g., Christianity and Judaism). They are (except where a religion rules and penetrates *all* of culture) clearly separable and distinct from other aspects of or institutions in the culture (for example, from the Stock Exchange).

In contrast to religion so defined, on the other hand, there is "the religious," pointing to *aspects* or *dimensions* of cultural life as a whole and so also of the other "secular" aspects of culture—for example its politics, its economics, art, and literature. It is probable, in fact almost certain, that the critics mentioned above do not recognize such dimensions of the secular aspects of culture—as many persons have refused to see the sexual or the economic aspects of *every* aspect of cultural life.

To object to this wide usage in cultural analysis as a whole on the grounds that it is meaningless is, I suggest, sheer prejudice. It represents in fact a dogged insistence against massive amounts of evidence that such aspects or dimensions labelled "religious" do not in fact exist. No one, I take it, objects in principle to Freud's interpretation of the realms of art, literature, philosophy, politics, and religion as saturated with and perhaps even determined by psychological determinants, nor is his theory that in a parallel way there is a *psychological* ingredient to all aspects of individual and social life (whether the persons concerned are aware of this ingredient or not) regarded as "meaningless." In the same way, no exception is taken in principle to Marx's view that "the economic" dominates political, social, moral, and religious affairs alike. These critics do not complain that this sort of psychological or economic interpretation of the *whole* of culture makes the

-252-

special categories of psychology or of economics "empty."

Our present point is that in somewhat the same way, "the religious dimension" appears throughout individual and social life, affecting both in various important ways. This is not to say that this is the *only* effective factor present—as Freud and Marx were apt to say about *their* factors. It is only to say that this factor is present and is effective enough to require an analysis on its own terms as well as in the more widely accepted terms of psychological, sociological, political, economic, and historical interpretation.

7. For other discussions of this "religious aura" granted to science in modern culture, see the author's *Religion and the Scientific Future* (Macon, Ga.: Mercer University Press [formerly Harper and Row], 1970), Chapter 3, and *Society and the Sacred*, Chapters 6-8.

8. We may take, as an example of this view, the new book of readings in evolutionary theory edited by C. Leon Harris, *Evolution, Genesis and Revelations* (Albany: State University of New York Press, 1981). While this volume assuredly contains a rich set of historical writings on evolution and kindred subjects, still it clearly reflects the scientistic—or modern secular—interpretation of intellectual history: religion as pre-science and therefore as anti-science, and science as an accumulating and unified progression towards validity. For example, Chapter 1 is titled "Pre-scientific Concepts of the Origin of Species: Genesis" and concludes with a section on modern fundamentalism. Chapter 3 is called "The Infanticide of Science: Rome and the Middle Ages," and its first section is entitled "Augustine and the Dark Ages." This is a strange reading of Augustine—on science as well as on everything else—about as far removed from what Augustine (or Genesis) was seeking to say as would be an interpretation of Einstein or Fermi that set them (as one *could* do if one wished) within a chapter on "Modern Developments of Destructive Weaponry." As a potent example of the latter interpretation of these great scientists, see Jonathan Schell's respectful but deeply troubled assessment of Einstein's role in the "creation" of the nuclear *nemesis*, and

thus as a possible "father" of the final extinction of life, in *The Fate of the Earth* (New York: Knopf, 1982), pp. 104-105.

9. For an explication of these "religious" dilemmas of modern scientific and technical culture, see Chapter 7 of *Society and the Sacred*.

10. The literature criticizing this totally "objectivist" interpretation of modern science is by now impressive. Prominent in it is the following very select list: E. A. Burtt, *The Metaphysical Foundations of Modern Physical Science*; A. N. Whitehead, *Science and the Modern World*; Stephen Toulmin, *The Philosophy of Science, Foresight and Understanding, Human Understanding*, Vols. I and II; Michael Polanyi, *Personal Knowing*; Thomas A. Kuhn, *The Structure of Scientific Revolutions*; Herbert O. Butterfield, *The Origins of Modern Natural Science*; Bernard J. Lonergan, *Insight*; Norwood R. Hanson, *Patterns of Discovery*; Harold J. Brown, *Perception, Theory and Commitment: A New Philosophy of Science*.

11. Another example: When recently I made an exceedingly pleasant visit to Purdue University, I was asked to speak about the creationist controversy to a class in the theory and history of science. After I began, I could see from the baffled faces of the students that something was amiss; soon it became evident that the young instructor of that class had assumed—and announced to the class—that, since I was a visiting *theologian*, I must have represented the creationist cause at Little Rock. She confirmed that she knew little or nothing of the existence of non-fundamentalist religion, of non-fundamentalist seminaries or Divinity Schools, and, above all, of non-fundamentalist theologians! What was ironical about these easy, quite inaccurate, and yet common assumptions was that while it was quite *in*conceivable that any member of Purdue's excellent philosophy or religious studies departments would be a creationist, four tenured professors in Purdue's divisions of the sciences, and in the fields of biology and genetics, are in fact active supporters of the creationist cause!

12. For an example of the argument that *history* can be understood only in so far as this religious dimension of history and politics is admitted and analyzed—and that in turn that dimension can be made intelligible only in terms of a theory of the religious as a response—see the author's

Reaping the Whirlwind (New York: Crossroad, 1976), Chapter 2. Despite the importance of the category of the "sacred" in the sociological tradition (see Robert Nesbit's excellent book, *The Sociological Tradition* [New York: Basic Books, 1966]), a goodly number of social scientists insist that no social theories that interpret the category of the sacred "realistically," that is *as* a response, can be considered legitimate social scientific theories. To do so, say they, is to leave the ground of science and to be perpetuating anachronistic "myths." For example, see the article by Michael Cavanaugh, professor of sociology at the University of Pittsburgh, "Pagan and Christian: Sociological Euhemerism versus American Sociology of Religion," *Sociological Analysis* 43, No. 2 (1982): 109-130.

I agree with Professor Cavanaugh that a distinction must be made between the discrimination of the presence of *sacrality* in social relations and communities (as Durkheim showed) on the one hand and the (metaphysical or ontological) conclusion on the other that this category must be realistically explained, that is as a response. The first represents an aspect of sociological analysis; but the conclusion represents a "leap" beyond the methodological limits of sociology. And this "leap" or step should be freely admitted by the sociologists who make this argument (Bellah and Berger especially). However, Professor Cavanaugh makes the same mistake when he disallows any such conclusion on the part of a sociologist as "myth" or "fideism" and implies that the inquiries of sociological sciences, what he terms "objective reflection," show how silly in fact all this is. Sociology does not and cannot *itself* answer the question whether this undoubted presence of the "sacred" in all society represents a *projection* out of human subjectivity and thus (as most projectionists have agreed) springs from some form of alienation; or whether it represents a *response*—though (to me) the continuing and mounting evidence of its universality and of its vast significance, even ultimate significance, points clearly to the latter interpretation as more "realistic."

13. Take, for example, the remarkable role that Mikhail A. Suslov (deceased January 25, 1982), the primary theorist of Marxist dogma, enjoyed in the Kremlin. As *The New York Times* (Jan. 30, 1982) declared on his death, he was

universally recognized as *the* official interpreter of the "theory" (ideology) basic to Soviet society, and in that crucial role he had for several decades "possessed a continuing authority equalled only by that of Stalin himself." In effect, Suslov was the official "theologian" of that society's "religious substance."

14. Arnold J. Toynbee, *A Study of History* (London: Oxford University Press, 1945), especially Vol. 1, p. 53, and Vol. 4, pp. 91, 105, etc. Toynbee in the text speaks both of "times of trouble" and "time of troubles."

15. One can see how dramatic a shift in sensibility this represents if one compares *this* point (that the locus of the human problem is in the self, and hence the resolution of that problem lies in self-knowledge and self-control) with much early twentieth-century philosophical and social scientific reflection on this issue. For examples of the latter, John Dewey cites as *the* hope of modern culture the increasingly widespread acceptance of science and technology; Kenneth Boulding mentions the development of scientific knowledge as *the* main determinant of "civilization"; and cultural evolutionist Julian H. Steward cites the accumulation of scientific knowledge as the key element of historical advance. (John Dewey, "Science and the Future of Society," address at the Harvard Tercentary, 1936; Kenneth Boulding, *The Meaning of the Twentieth Century* [New York: Harper Colophon, 1965], pp. 27 and 35; Julian Steward, "Cultural Evolution Today"). By *their* estimate our present culture is, through its incredibly accumulating scientific knowledge, rapidly approaching "civilization," that is to say, stability, order, and justice.

In contrast, many present estimates view the same accumulation of knowledge and techniques, despite the obvious "benefits" they have brought us all, nevertheless *also* as engendering increased social instability, as posing the threat of a dehumanizing rationalization and organization of social life, and in the end threatening an ultimate extinction through nuclear holocaust. Thus, if these very negative results of "progress" are to be avoided, new levels of self-understanding and self-control are utterly necessary. As examples of this latter view of our situation, see Robert Heilbroner, *An Inquiry into the Human*

Prospect (New York: Norton, 1974), and Jonathan Schell, *The Fate of the Earth* (New York: Knopf, 1982).

Chapter 8—The Shape of a Religious Symbol and the Meaning of Creation

1. The identification of religious discourse with what lies beyond, and appears through, the *"limits"* of human experience and of ordinary human cognition has enjoyed of course a long history. It begins, one might say, with St. Thomas's distinction between natural knowledge through philosophy on the one hand and supernatural knowledge through revelation and grace on the other. It continues in another form with Kant's *limiting ideas* of God, the soul, and immortality, and was reworked in another way by Sören Kierkegaard in the *Philosophical Fragments.*

In the middle of the present century it has become a very important theme in religious reflection. The first case, to my knowledge, of this designation in recent theology was Reinhold Niebuhr's description of permanent religious myths as concerned with limits (see "The Truth in Myth" in *The Nature of Religious Experience* [New York: Harper and Row, 1937], and *Beyond Tragedy*, Chapters 1 and 2 [New York: Scribner's, 1937]; and *The Nature and Destiny of Man* [New York: Scribner's, 1941, Part 1]).

Later, in this same tradition of theology, I sought to define religious language as concerned with the ultimate and the sacred that appeared *at the limits of human knowledge and power*, first in 1959 in *Maker of Heaven and Earth* (New York: Doubleday), Chapter 10, and then in the late 1960s in a fashion finally formulated in *Naming the Whirlwind* (New York: Bobbs-Merrill, 1969), Part 2, Chapter 2. Somewhat earlier and in a philosophical rather than theological context, Stephen Toulmin had in his *An Examination of the Place of Reason in Ethics* (Cambridge: Cambridge University Press, 1950), uncovered and described—from a starting point in philosophical reflection—what he called "limit questions," questions that appear at the boundary of a discipline, often as its presuppositions;

there were, therefore, questions which cannot by definition be dealt with *within* that discipline. Following that
philosophical lead, the combining of these two traditions, one theological and the other philosophical, Schu-
bert Ogden in *The Reality of God* (New York: Harper and
Row, 1966), pp. 30ff. and 114-15, and David Tracy in his
Blessed Rage for Order (New York: Seabury, 1976), especially Chapters 5-9, have in their excellent and full discussions of the character of religious discourse made this
rubric well-nigh universal.

2. As examples of this relation of theological discourse
about *God* with modern "cultural" discourse about nature
and history, see this author's two works on the theological concepts of creation and of providence, namely, *Making of Heaven and Earth* and *Reaping the Whirlwind*.

3. The necessity of a unity between religious speech and
"secular" experience was the central theme of *Naming the
Whirlwind: The Renewal of God Language*.

4. Quoted in Loren Eiseley, *Darwin's Century* (Garden City,
N.J.: Doubleday, 1958), p. 2.

5. Quoted in John C. Greene, *The Death of Adam* (Ames: Iowa
State University Press, 1959), p. 128. This is a remarkable
treatise giving the most complete, unbiased, and richly
illustrated account of the history of the idea of evolution
that this writer knows.

6. See Father Vawter's helpful discussion of the two sets of
"meanings" in the book of Genesis, the "proto-scientific"
meanings and the "religious" meanings, and the clear
dominance of the latter, Chapter 4, pp. 85-87.

7. For a detailed discussion of the *meanings* of the symbol of
creation, and of the continuity of these religious meanings throughout the entire theological tradition, see
Maker of Heaven and Earth.

8. For a more comprehensive discussion of this process of
the reinterpretation of religious symbols—especially that
of creation—as modern science has developed, see the
author's *Religion and the Scientific Future* (New York:
Harper and Row, 1970), Chapter 1.

9. For this dependence of many fundamental attitudes of
modern culture, including those basic for modern empirical science, on the traditional religious symbol of creation, see A. N. Whitehead, *Science and the Modern World*

(New York: The Macmillan Co., 1925), pp. 17-22, R. B. Collingwood, *An Essay on Metaphysics* (London: Oxford University Press, 1940), Chapter 21, and Gilkey, *Maker of Heaven and Earth*, Chapter 5.

10. For a more detailed treatment of the relation of the modern sense of history to the Christian and Hebrew understandings of creation and providence, see *Reaping the Whirlwind*, Chapters 7-9.

11. For a representative interpretation of nature as both to be understood and evaluated solely in terms of its use for our human purposes, see John Dewey, *Reconstruction in Philosophy* (New York: Henry Holt & Co., 1920), especially pp. 54-66, 67-74, 85, 111-116.

Appendix A:
Arkansas Act 590

State of Arkansas
73rd General Assembly
Regular Session. 1981

Act 590 of 1981

"AN ACT TO REQUIRE BALANCED TREATMENT OF CREATION-SCIENCE AND EVOLUTION-SCIENCE IN PUBLIC SCHOOLS; TO PROTECT ACADEMIC FREEDOM BY PROVIDING STUDENT CHOICE; TO ENSURE FREEDOM OF RELIGIOUS EXERCISE; TO GUARANTEE FREEDOM OF BELIEF AND SPEECH; TO PREVENT ESTABLISHMENT OF RELIGION; TO PROHIBIT RELIGIOUS INSTRUCTION CONCERNING ORIGINS; TO BAR DISCRIMINATION ON THE BASIS OF CREATIONISTS OR EVOLUTIONIST BELIEF; TO PROVIDE DEFINITIONS AND CLARIFICATIONS; TO DECLARE THE LEGISLATIVE PURPOSE AND LEGISLATIVE FINDINGS OF FACT; TO PROVIDE FOR SEVERABILITY OF PROVISIONS; TO PROVIDE FOR REPEAL OF CONTRARY LAWS; AND TO SET FORTH AN EFFECTIVE DATE."

BE IT ENACTED BY THE GENERAL ASSEMBLY OF THE STATE OF ARKANSAS:

SECTION 1. Requirement for Balanced Treatment. Public schools within this State shall give balanced treatment to creation-science and to evolution-science. Balanced treatment to these two models shall be given in classroom lectures taken as a whole for each course, in textbook materials taken as a whole for each course, in library materials taken as a whole for the sciences and taken as a whole for the humanities, and in other educational programs in public schools, to the extent that such lectures, textbooks, library materials, or educational programs deal in any way with the subject of the origin of man, life, the earth, or the universe.

SECTION 2. Prohibition against Religious Instruction. Treatment of either evolution-science or creation-science shall be limited to scientific evidences for each model and inferences from those scientific evidences, and must not include any religious instruction or references to religious writings.

SECTION 3. Requirement for Nondiscrimination. Public schools within this State, or their personnel, shall not discriminate, by reducing a grade of a student or by singling out and making public criticism, against any student who demonstrates a satisfactory understanding of both evolution-science and creation-science and who accepts or rejects either model in whole or part.

SECTION 4 Definitions. As used in this Act:
(a) "Creation-science" means the scientific evidences for creation and inferences from those scientific evidences. Creation-science includes the scientific evidences and related inferences that indicate: (1) Sudden creation of the universe, energy, and life from nothing; (2) The insufficiency of mutation and natural selection in bringing about development of all living kinds from a single organism; (3) Changes only within fixed limits of originally created kinds of plants and animals; (4) Separate ancestry for man and apes; (5) Explanation of the earth's geology by catastrophism, including the occurrence of a worldwide flood; and (6) A relatively recent inception of the earth and living kinds.
(b) "Evolution-science" means the scientific evidences for evolution and inferences from those scientific evidences. Evolution-science includes the scientific evidences and

related inferences that indicate: (1) Emergence by naturalistic processes of the universe from disordered matter and emergence of life from nonlife; (2) The sufficiency of mutation and natural selection in bringing about development of present living kinds from simple earlier kinds; (3) Emergency [sic] by mutation and natural selection of present living kinds from simple earlier kinds; (4) Emergence of man from a common ancestor with apes; (5) Explanation of the earth's geology and the evolutionary sequence by uniformitarianism; and (6) An inception several billion years ago of the earth and somewhat later of life.

(c) "Public schools" mean public secondary and elementary schools.

SECTION 5. Clarifications. This Act does not require or permit instruction in any religious doctrine or materials. This Act does not require any instruction in the subject of origins, but simply requires instruction in both scentific models (of evolution-science and creation-science) if public schools choose to teach either. This Act does not require each individual textbook or library book to give balanced treatment to the models of evolution-science and creation-science; it does not require any school books to be discarded. This Act does not require each individual classroom lecture in a course to give such balanced treatment, but simply requires the lectures as a whole to give balanced treatment; it permits some lectures to present evolution-science and other lectures to present creation-science.

SECTION 6. Legislative Declaration of Purpose. This Legislature enacts this Act for public schools with the purpose of protecting academic freedom for students' differing values and beliefs; ensuring neutrality toward students' diverse religious convictions; ensuring freedom of religious exercise for students and their parents; guaranteeing freedom of belief and speech for students; preventing establishment of Theologically Liberal, Humanist, Nontheist, or Atheist religions; preventing discrimination against students on the basis of their personal beliefs concerning creation and evolution; and assisting students in their search for truth. This Legislature does not have the purpose of causing instruction in religious concepts or making an establishment of religion.

-262-

SECTION 7. Legislative Findings of Fact. This Legislature finds that:

(a) The subject of the origin of the universe, earth, life, and man is treated within many public school courses, such as biology, life science, anthropology, sociology, and often also in physics, chemistry, world history, philosophy, and social studies.

(b) Only evolution-science is presented to students in virtually all of those courses that discuss the subject of origins. Public schools generally censor creation-science and evidence contrary to evolution.

(c) Evolution-science is not an unquestionable fact of science, because evolution cannot be experimentally observed, fully verified, or logically falsified, and because evolution-science is not accepted by some scientists.

(d) Evolution-science is contrary to the religious convictions or moral values or philosophical beliefs of many students and parents, including individuals of many different religious faiths and with diverse moral values and philosophical beliefs.

(e) Public school presentation of only evolution-science without any alternative model of origins abridges the United States Constitution's protections of freedom of religious exercise and of freedom of belief and speech for students and parents, because it undermines their religious convictions and moral or philosophical values, compels their unconscionable professions of belief, and hinders religious training and moral training by parents.

(f) Public school presentation of only evolution-science furthermore abridges the Constitution's prohibition against establishment of religion, because it produces hostility toward many Theistic religions and brings preference to Theological Liberalsim, Humanism, Nontheistic religions, and Atheism, in that these religious faiths general include a religious belief in evolution.

(g) Public school instruction in only evolution-science also violates the principle of academic freedom, because it denies students a choice between scientific models and instead indoctrinates them in evolution-science alone.

(h) Presentation of only one model rather than alternative scientific models of origins is not required by any compelling interest of the State, and exemption of such students from a course or class presenting only evolution-science does not provide an adequate remedy because of teacher influence and student pressure to remain in that course or class.

(i) Attendance of those students who are at public schools is compelled by law, and school taxes from their parents and other citizens are mandated by law.

(j) Creation-science is an alternative scientific model of origins and can be presented from a strictly scientific standpoint without any religious doctrine just as evolution-science can, because there are scientists who conclude that scientific data best support creation-science and because scientific evidences and inferences have been presented for creation-science.

(k) Public school presentation of both evolution-science and creation-science would not violate the Constitution's prohibition against establishment of religion, because it would involve presentation of the scientific evidences and related inferences for each model rather than any religious instruction.

(l) Most citizens, whatever their religious beliefs about origins, favor balanced treatment in public schools of alternative scientific models of origins for better guiding students in their search for knowledge, and they favor a neutral approach toward subjects affecting the religious and moral and philosophical convictions of students.

SECTION 8. Short Title. This Act shall be known as the "Balanced Treatment for Creation-Science and Evolution-Science Act."

SECTION 9. Severability of Provisions. If any provision of this Act is held invalid, that invalidity shall not affect other provisions that can be applied in the absence of the invalidated provisions, and the provisions of this Act are declared to be severable.

SECTION 10. Repeal of Contrary Laws. All State laws or parts of State laws in conflict with this Act are hereby repealed.

Section 11. Effective Date. The requirements of the Act shall be met by and may be met before the beginning of the next school year if that is more than six months from the date of enactment, or otherwise one year after the beginning of the next school year, and in all subsequent school years.

3-19-81   (signed: Frank White)
APPROVED   GOVERNOR

Appendix B:
Judgment by the Federal Court

IN THE UNITED STATES DISTRICT COURT
EASTERN DISTRICT OF ARKANSAS
WESTERN DIVISION

REV. BILL McLEAN, ET AL.   PLAINTIFFS

VS.   NO. LR C 81 322

THE ARKANSAS BOARD OF EDUCATION,

ET AL.   DEFENDANTS

JUDGMENT
Pursuant to the Court's Memorandum Opinion filed this date, judgment is hereby entered in favor of the plaintiffs and against the defendants. The relief prayed for is granted.
Dated this January 5, 1982.

(SIGNED: WILLIAM R. OVERTON)
UNITED STATES DISTRICT JUDGE

IN THE UNITED STATES DISTRICT COURT
EASTERN DISTRICT OF ARKANSAS
WESTERN DIVISION

REV. BILL McLEAN, ET AL.   PLAINTIFFS

VS.   NO. LR C 81 322

THE ARKANSAS BOARD OF EDUCATION,

ET AL.   DEFENDANTS

INJUNCTION

Pursuant to the Court's Memorandum Opinion filed this date, the defendants and each of them and all their servants and employees are hereby permanently enjoined from implementing in any manner Act 590 of the Acts of Arkansas of 1981.

It is so ordered this January 5, 1982.

(SIGNED: WILLIAM R. OVERTON)
UNITED STATES DISTRICT JUDGE

IN THE UNITED STATES DISTRICT COURT
EASTERN DISTRICT OF ARKANSAS
WESTERN DIVISION

REV. BILL McLEAN, ET AL.   PLAINTIFFS

VS.   NO. LR C 81 322

THE ARKANSAS BOARD OF EDUCATION,

ET AL.   DEFENDANTS

MEMORANDUM OPINION

Introduction

On March 19, 1981, the Governor of Arkansas signed into law Act 590 of 1981, entitled the "Balanced Treatment for Creation-Science and Evolution-Science Act." The Act is codified as Ark. Stat. Ann. S80-1663, *et seq.*, (1981 Supp.). Its essential mandate is stated in its first sentence: "Public schools within this State shall give balanced treatment to creation-science and to evolution-science." On May 27, 1981, this suit was filed[1] challenging the constitutional validity of Act 590 on three distinct grounds.

First, it is contended that Act 590 constitutes an establishment of religion prohibited by the First Amendment to the Constitution, which is made applicable to the states by the Fourteenth Amendment. Second, the plaintiffs argue the Act violates a right to academic freedom which they say is guaranteed to students and teachers by the Free Speech Clause of the First Amendment. Third, plaintiffs allege the Act is

-268-

impermissibly vague and thereby violates the Due Process Clause of the Fourteenth Amendment.

The individual plaintiffs include the resident Arkansas Bishops of the United Methodist, Episcopal, Roman Catholic and African Methodist Episcopal Churches, the principal official of the Presbyterian Churches in Arkansas, other United Methodist, Southern Baptist and Presbyterian clergy, as well as several persons who sue as parents and next friends of minor children attending Arkansas public schools. One plaintiff is a high school biology teacher. All are also Arkansas taxpayers. Among the organizational plaintiffs are the American Jewish Congress, the Union of American Hebrew Congregations, the American Jewish Committee, the Arkansas Education Association, the National Association of Biology Teachers and the National Coalition for Public Education and Religious Liberty, all of which sue on behalf of members living in Arkansas.[2]

The defendants include the Arkansas Board of Education and its members, the Director of the Department of Education, and the State Textbooks and Instructional Materials Selecting Committee.[3] The Pulaski County Special School District and its Directors and Superintendent were voluntarily dismissed by the plaintiffs at the pre-trial conference held October 1, 1981.

The trial commenced December 7, 1981, and continued through December 17, 1981. This Memorandum Opinion constitutes the Court's findings of fact and conclusions of law. Further orders and judgment will be in conformity with this opinion.

There is no controversy over the legal standards under which the Establishment Clause portion of this case must be judged. The Supreme Court has on a number of occasions expounded on the meaning of the clause, and the pronouncements are clear. Often the issue has arisen in the context of public education, as it has here. In *Everson v. Board of Education*, 330 U.S. 1, 15-16 (1947), Justice Black stated:

"The 'establishment of religion' clause of the First Amendment means at least this: Neither a state nor the Federal Government can set up a church. Neither can pass laws which aid one religion, aid all religions, or prefer one religion over another. Neither can force nor influence a person to go to or to remain away from church against his will or force him to profess a belief or disbelief in any religion. No person can be punished for entertaining or professing religious beliefs or disbeliefs, for church-attendance or non-attendance. No tax, large or small, can be levied to support any religious activities or institutions, whatever they may be called, or whatever form they may adopt to teach or practice religion. Neither a state nor the Federal Government can, openly or secretly, participate in the affairs of any religious organizations or groups and *vice versa*. In the words of Jefferson, the clause . . . was intended to erect 'a wall of separation between church and State.'"

The Establishment Clause thus enshrines two central values: voluntarism and pluralism. And it is in the area of the public schools that these values must be guarded most vigilantly.

"Designed to serve as perhaps the most powerful agency for promoting cohesion among a heterogeneous democratic people, the public school must keep scrupulously free from entanglement in the strife of sects. The preservation of the community from divisive conflicts, of Government from irreconcilable pressures by religious groups, of religion from censorship and coercion however subtly exercised, requires strict confinement of the State to instruction other than religious, leaving to the individual's church and home, indoctrination in the faith of his choice."

McCollum v. Board of Education, 333 U.S. 203, 216-217 (1948), (Opinion of Frankfurter, J., joined by Jackson, Burton and Rutledge, J.J.).

The specific formulation of the establishment prohibition has been refined over the years, but its meaning has not varied from the principles articulated by Justice Black in *Everson*. In *Abbington School District v. Schempp*, 374 U.S. 203, 222 (1963), Justice Clark stated that "to withstand the strictures of the Establishment Clause there must be a secular legislative purpose and a primary effect that neither advances nor inhibits religion." The Court found it quite clear that the First Amendment does not permit a state to require the daily reading of the Bible in public schools, for "[s]urely the place of the Bible as an instrument of religion cannot be gainsaid." *Id.* at 224. Similarly, in *Engel v. Vitale*, 370 U.S. 421 (1962), the Court held that the First Amendment prohibited the New York Board of Regents from requiring the daily recitation of a certain prayer in the schools. With characteristic succinctness, Justice Black wrote, "Under [the First] Amendment's prohibition against governmental establishment of religion, as reinforced by the provisions of the Fourteenth Amendment, government in this country, be it state or federal, is without power to prescribe by law any particular form of prayer which is to be used as an official prayer in carrying on any program of governmentally sponsored religious activity." *Id.* at 430. Black also identified the objective at which the Establishment Clause was aimed: "Its first and most immediate purpose rested on the belief that a union of government and religion tends to destroy government and to degrade religion." *Id.* at 431.

Most recently, the Supreme Court has held that the clause prohibits a state from requiring the posting of the Ten Commandments in public school classrooms for the same reasons that officially imposed daily Bible reading is prohibited. *Stone v. Graham*, 449 U.S. 39 (1980). The opinion in *Stone* relies on the most recent formulation of the Establishment Clause test, that of *Lemon v. Kurtzman*, 403 U.S. 602, 612-613 (1971):

"First, the statute must have a secular legislative purpose; second, its principal or primary effect must be one that neither advances nor inhibits religion . . .; finally, the statute must not foster 'an excessive government entanglement with religion.'"

Stone v. Graham, 449 U.S. at 40.

It is under this three part test that the evidence in this case must be judged. Failure on any of these grounds is fatal to the enactment.

II.

The religious movement known as Fundamentalism began in nineteenth century America as part of evangelical Protestantism's response to social changes, new religious thought and Darwinism. Fundamentalists viewed these developments as attacks on the Bible and as responsible for a decline in traditional values. The various manifestations of Fundamentalism have had a number of common characteristics,[4] but a central premise has always been a literal interpretation of the Bible and a belief in the inerrancy of the Scriptures. Following World War I, there was again a perceived decline in traditional morality, and Fundamentalism focused on evolution as responsible for the decline. One aspect of their efforts, particularly in the South, was the promotion of statutes prohibiting the teaching of evolution in public schools. In Arkansas, this resulted in the adoption of Initiated Act 1 of 1929.[5]

Between the 1920's and early 1960's, anti-evolutionary sentiment had a subtle but pervasive influence on the teaching of biology in public schools. Generally, textbooks avoided the topic of evolution and did not mention the name of Darwin. Following the launch of the Sputnik satellite by the Soviet Union in 1957, the National Science Foundation funded several programs designed to modernize the teaching of science in the nation's schools. The Biological Sciences Curriculum Study (BSCS), a nonprofit organization, was among those receiving grants for curriculum study and revision. Working with scientists and teachers, BSCS developed a series of biology texts which, although emphasizing different aspects of biology, incorporated the theory of evolution as a major theme. The success of the BSCS effort is shown by the fact that fifty percent of American school children currently use BSCS books directly and the curriculum is incorporated indirectly in virtually all biology texts. (Testimony of Mayer; Nelkin, Px 1)[6]

In the early 1960's, there was again a resurgence of concern among Fundamentalists about the loss of traditional values and a fear of growing secularism in society. The Fundamentalist movement became more active and has steadily grown in numbers and political influence. There is an emphasis among current Fundamentalists on the literal interpretation of the Bible and the Book of Genesis as the sole source of knowledge about origins.

The term "scientific creationism" first gained currency around 1965 following publication of The Genesis Flood in 1961 by Whitcomb and Morris. There is undoubtedly some connection between the appearance of the BSCS texts emphasizing evolutionary thought and efforts by Fundamentalists to attack the theory. (Mayer)

In the 1960's and early 1970's, several Fundamentalist organizations were formed to promote the idea that the Book of Genesis was supported by scientific data. The terms "creation science" and "scientific creationism" have been adopted by these Fundamentalists as descriptive of their study of creation and the origins of man. Perhaps the leading creationist organization is the Institute for Creation Research (ICR), which is affiliated with the Christian Heritage College and supported by the Scott Memorial Baptist Church in San Diego, California. The ICR, through the Creation-Life Publishing Company, is the leading publisher of creation science material. Other creation science organizations include the Creation Science Research Center (CSRC) of San Diego and the Bible Science Association of Minneapolis, Minnesota. In 1963, the Creation Research Society (CRS) was formed from a schism in the American Scientific Affiliation (ASA). It is an organization of literal Fundamentalists[7] who have the equivalent of a master's degree in some recognized area of science. A purpose of the organization is "to reach all people with the vital message of the scientific and historical truth about creation." Nelkin, *The Science Textbook Controversies and the Politics of Equal Time*, 66. Similarly, the CSRC was formed in 1970 from a split in the CRS. Its aim has been "to reach the 63 million children of the United States with the scientific teaching of Biblical creationism." *Id.* at 69.

Among creationist writers who are recognized as authorities in the field by other creationists are Henry M. Morris, Duane Gish, G. E. Parker, Harold S. Slusher, Richard B. Bliss, John W. Moore, Martin E. Clark, W. L. Wysong, Robert E. Kofahl and Kelly L. Segraves. Morris is Director of ICR, Gish is Associate Director and Segraves is associated with CSRC.

Creationists view evolution as a source of society's ills, and the writings of Morris and Clark are typical expressions of that view.

"Evolution is thus not only anti-Biblical and anti-Christian, but it is utterly unscientific and impossible as well. But it has served effectively as the pseudo-scientific basis of atheism, agnosticism, socialism, fascism, and numerous other false and dangerous philosophies over the past century."
Morris and Clark, *The Bible Has The Answer*, (Px 31 and Pretrial Px 89).

Creationists have adopted the view of Fundamentalists generally that there are only two positions with respect to the origins of the earth and life: belief in the inerrancy of the Genesis story of creation and of a worldwide flood as fact, or belief in what they call evolution.

Henry Morris has stated, "It is impossible to devise a legitimate means of harmonizing the Bible with evolution." Morris, "Evolution and the Bible," ICR *Impact Series* Number 5 (undated, unpaged), quoted in Mayer, Px 8, at 3. This dualistic approach to the subject of origins permeates the creationist literature.

The creationist organizations consider the introduction of creation science into the public schools part of their ministry. The ICR has published at least two pamphlets[9] containing suggested methods for convincing school boards, administrators and teachers that creationism should be taught in public schools. The ICR has urged its proponents to encourage school officials to voluntarily add creationism to the curriculum.[10]

Citizens For Fairness In Education is an organization based in Anderson, South Carolina, formed by Paul Ellwanger, a respiratory therapist who is trained in neither law nor science. Mr. Ellwanger is of the opinion that evolution is the forerunner of many social ills, including Nazism, racism and abortion. (Ellwanger Depo. at 32-34). About 1977, Ellwanger collected several proposed legislative acts with the idea of preparing a model state act requiring the teaching of creationism as science in opposition to evolution. One of the proposals he collected was prepared by Wendell Bird, who is now a staff attorney for ICR.[11] From these various proposals, Ellwanger prepared a "model act" which calls for "balanced treatment" of "scientific creationism" and "evolution" in public schools. He circulated the proposed act to various people and organizations around the country.

Mr. Ellwanger's views on the nature of creation science are entitled to some weight since he personally drafted the model act which became Act 590. His evidentiary deposition with exhibits and unnumbered attachments (produced in response to a subpoena *duces tecum*) speaks to both the intent of the Act and the scientific merits of creation science. Mr. Ellwanger does not believe creation science is a science. In a letter to Pastor Robert E. Hays he states, "While neither evolution nor creation can qualify as a scientific theory, and since it is virtually impossible at this point to educate the whole world that evolution is not a true scientific theory, we have freely used these terms - the evolution theory and the theory of scientific creationism - in the bill's text." (Unnumbered attachment to Ellwanger Depo., at 2.) He further states in a letter to Mr. Tom Bethell, "As we examine evolution (remember, we're not making any scientific claims for creation, but we are challenging evolution's claim to be scientific) . . . " (Unnumbered attachment to Ellwanger Depo. at 1.)

Ellwanger's correspondence on the subject shows an awareness that Act 590 is a religious crusade, coupled with a desire to conceal this fact. In a letter to State Senator Bill Keith of Louisiana, he says, "I view this whole battle as one between God and anti-God forces, though I know there are a large number of evolutionists who believe in God." And further, ". . . . it behooves Satan to do all he can to thwart our efforts and confuse the issue at every turn." Yet Ellwanger suggests to Senator Keith, "If you have a clear choice between having grassroots leaders of this statewide bill promotion effort to be ministerial or non-ministerial, be sure to opt for the non-ministerial. It does the bill effort no good to have ministers out there in the public forum and the adversary will surely pick at this point . . . Ministerial persons can accomplish a tremendous amount of work from behind the scenes, encouraging their congregations to take the organizational and P.R. initiatives. And they can lead their churches in storming Heaven with prayers for help against so tenacious an adversary." (Unnumbered attachment to Ellwanger Depo. at 1.)

Ellwanger shows a remarkable degree of political candor, if not finesse, in a letter to State Senator Joseph Carlucci of Florida:

"2. It would be very wise, if not actually essential, that all of us who are engaged in this legislative effort be careful not to present our position and our work in a religious framework. For example, in written communications that might somehow be shared with those other persons whom we may be trying to convince, it would be well to exclude our own personal testimony and/or witness for Christ, but rather, if we are so moved, to give that testimony on a separate attached note." (Unnumbered attachment to Ellwanger Depo. at 1.)

The same tenor is reflected in a letter by Ellwanger to Mary Ann Miller, a member of FLAG (Family, Life, America under God) who lobbied the Arkansas Legislature in favor of Act 590:

". . . we'd like to suggest that you and your co-workers be very catious about mixing creation-science with creation-religion . . . Please urge your co-workers not to allow themselves to get sucked into the 'religion' trap of mixing the two together, for such mixing does incalculable harm to the legislative thrust. It could even bring public opinion to bear adversely upon the higher courts that will eventually have to pass judgment on the constitutionality of this new law." (Ex. 1 to Miller Depo.)

Perhaps most interesting, however, is Mr. Ellwanger's testimony in his deposition as to his strategy for having the model act implemented:

Q. You're trying to play on other people's religious motives.

A. I'm trying to play on their emotions, love, hate, their likes, dislikes, because I don't know any other way to involve, to get humans to become involved in human endeavors. I see emotions as being a healthy and legitimate means of getting people's feelings into action, and . . . I believe that the predominance of population in America that represents the greatest potential for taking some kind of action in this area is a Christian community. I see the Jewish community as far less potential in taking action . . . but I've seen a lot of interest among Christians and I feel, why not exploit that to get the bill going if that's what it takes. (Ellwanger Depo. at 146-147.)

Mr. Ellwanger's ultimate purpose is revealed in the closing of his letter to Mr. Tom Bethell: "Perhaps all this is old hat to you, Tom, and if so, I'd appreciate your telling me so and perhaps where you've heard it before—the idea of killing evolution instead of playing these debating games that we've been playing for nigh over a decade already." (Unnumbered attachment to Ellwanger Depo. at 3.)

It was out of this milieu that Act 590 emerged. The Reverend W. A. Blount, a Biblical literalist who is pastor of a church in Little Rock area and was, in February, 1981, chairman of the Greater Little Rock Evangelical Fellowship, was among those who received a copy of the model act from Ellwanger.[12]

At Reverend Blount's request, the Evangelical Fellowship unanimously adopted a resolution to seek introduction of Ellwanger's act in the Arkansas Legislature. A committee composed of two ministers, Curtis Thomas and W. A. Young, was appointed to implement the resolution. Thomas obtained from Ellwanger a revised copy of the model act which he transmitted to Carl Hunt, a business associate of Senator James L. Holsted, with the request that Hunt prevail upon Holsted to introduce the act.

Holsted, a self-described "born again" Christian Fundamentalist, introduced the act in the Arkansas Senate. He did not consult the State Department of Education, scientists, science educators or the Arkansas Attorney General.[13] The Act was not referred to any Senate committee for hearing and was passed after only a few minutes' discussion on the Senate floor. In the House of Representatives, the bill was referred to the Education Committee which conducted a perfunctory fifteen minute hearing. No scientist testified at the hearing, nor was any representative from the State Department of Education called to testify.

Ellwanger's model act was enacted into law in Arkansas as Act 590 without amendment or modification other than minor typographical changes. The legislative "findings of fact" in Ellwanger's act and Act 590 are identical, although no meaningful fact-finding process was employed by the General Assembly.

Ellwanger's efforts in preparation of the model act and campaign for its adoption in the states were motivated by his opposition to the theory of evolution and his desire to see the Biblical version of creation taught in the public schools. There is no evidence that the pastors, Blount, Thomas, Young or The Greater Little Rock Evangelical Fellowship were motivated by anything other than their religious convictions when proposing its adoption or during their lobbying efforts in its behalf. Senator Holsted's sponsorship and lobbying efforts in behalf of the Act were motivated solely by his religious beliefs and desire to see the Biblical version of creation taught in the public schools.[14]

The State of Arkansas, like a number of states whose citizens have relatively homogeneous religious beliefs, has a

long history of official opposition to evolution which is motivated by adherence to Fundamentalist beliefs in the inerrancy of the Book of Genesis. This history is documented in
Justice Fortas' opinion in *Epperson v. Arkansas*, 393 U.S. 97
(1968), which struck down Initiated Act 1 of 1929, Ark. Stat.
Ann. SS80-1627-1628, prohibiting the teaching of the theory
of evolution. To this same tradition may be attributed Initiated Act 1 of 1930, Ark. Stat. Ann. S80-1606 (Repl. 1980),
requiring "the reverent daily reading of a portion of the
English Bible" in every public school classroom in the State.[15]

It is true, as defendants argue, that courts should look to
legislative statements of a statute's purpose in Establishment
Clause cases and accord such pronouncements great defer-
ence. See, e.g., *Committee for Public Education & Religious Liberty v. Nyquist*, 413 U.S. 756, 773 (1973) and *McGowan v.
Maryland*, 366 U.S. 420, 445 (1961). Defendants also correctly
state the principle that remarks by the sponsor or author of a
bill are not considered controlling in analyzing legislative
intent. See, e.g., *United States v. Emmons*, 410 U.S. 396 (1973)
and *Chrysler Corp. v. Brown*, 441 U.S. 281 (1979).

Courts are not bound, however, by legislative statements
of purpose or legislative disclaimers. *Stone v. Graham*, 449 U.S.
39 (1980); *Abbington School Dist. v. Schempp*, 374 U.S. 203
(1963). In determining the legislative purpose of a statute,
courts may consider evidence of the historical context of the
Act, *Epperson v. Arkansas*, 393 U.S. 97 (1968), the specific
sequence of events leading up to passage of the Act, depar-
tures from normal procedural sequences, substantive depar-
tures from the normal, *Village of Arlington Heights v.
Metropolitan Housing Corp.*, 429 U.S. 252 (1977), and contemporaneous statements of the legislative sponsor, *Fed. Energy
Admin. v. Algonquin SNG, Inc.*, 426 U.S. 548, 564 (1976).

The unusual circumstances surrounding the passage of Act
590, as well as the substantive law of the First Amendment,
warrant an inquiry into the stated legislative purposes. The
author of the Act had publicly proclaimed the sectarian purpose of the proposal. The Arkansas residents who sought
legislative sponsorship of the bill did so for a purely sectarian
purpose. These circumstances alone may not be particularly
persuasive, but when considered with the publicly

announced motives of the legislative sponsor made contemporaneously with the legislative process; the lack of any legislative investigation, debate or consultation with any educators or scientists; the unprecedented intrusion in school curriculum;[16] and official history of the State of Arkansas on the subject, it is obvious that the statement of purposes has little, if any, support in fact. The State failed to produce any evidence which would warrant an inference or conclusion that at any point in the process anyone considered the legitimate educational value of the Act. It was simply and purely an effort to introduce the Biblical version of creation into the public school curricula. The only inference which can be drawn from these circumstances is that the Act was passed with the specific purpose by the General Assembly of advancing religion. The Act therefore fails the first prong of the three-pronged test, that of secular legislative purpose, as articulated in Lemon V. Kurtzman, supra, and Stone v. Graham, supra.

III.

If the defendants are correct and the Court is limited to an examination of the language of the Act, the evidence is overwhelming that both the purpose and effect of Act 590 is the advancement of religion in the public schools.

Section 4 of the Act provides:

Definitions. As used in this Act:

(a) "Creation-science" means the scientific evidences for creation and inferences from those scientific evidences. Creation-science includes the scientific evidences and related inferences that indicate: (1) Sudden creation of the universe, energy, and life from nothing; (2) The insufficiency of mutation and natural selection in bringing about development of all living kinds from a single organism; (3) Changes only within fixed limits of originally created kinds of plants and animals; (4) Separate ancestry for man and apes; (5) Explanation of the earth's geology by catastrophism, including the occurrence of a worldwide flood; and (6) A relatively recent inception of the earth and living kinds.

(b) "Evolution-science" means the scientific evidences for evolution and inferences from those scientific evidences. Evolution-science includes the scientific evidences and related inferences that indicate: (1) Emergence by naturalistic processes of the universe from disordered matter and emergence of life from non-life; (2) The sufficiency of mutation and natural selection in bringing about development of present living kinds from simple earlier kinds; (3) Emergence by mutation and natural selection of present living kinds from simple earlier kinds; (4) Emergence of man from a common ancestor with apes; (5) Explanation of the earth's geology and the evolutionary sequence by uniformitarianism; and (6) An inception several billion years ago of the earth and somewhat later of life.

(c) "Public schools" mean public secondary and elementary schools.

The evidence establishes that the definition of "creation science" contained in 4(a) has as its unmentioned reference the first 11 chapters of the Book of Genesis. Among the many creation epics in human history, the account of sudden creation from nothing, or *creatio ex nihilo*, and subsequent destruction of the world by flood is unique to Genesis. The concepts of 4(a) are the literal Fundamentalists' view of Genesis. Section 4(a) is unquestionably a statement of religion, with the exception of 4(a)(2) which is a negative thrust aimed at what the creationists understand to be the theory of evolution.[17]

Both the concepts and wording of Section 4(a) convey an inescapable religiosity. Section 4(a)(1) describes "sudden creation of the universe, energy and life from nothing." Every theologian who testified, including defense witnesses, expressed the opinion that the statement referred to a supernatural creation which was performed by God.

Defendants argue that: (1) the fact that 4(a) conveys ideas similar to the literal interpretation of Genesis does not make it conclusively a statement of religion; (2) that reference to a creation from nothing is not necessarily a religious concept since the Act only suggests a creator who has power, intelligence and a sense of design and not necessarily the attributes of love, compassion and justice;[18] and (3) that simply teaching about the concept of a creator is not a religious exercise unless the student is required to make a commitment to the concept of a creator.

The evidence fully answers these arguments. The ideas of 4(a)(1) are not merely similar to the literal interpretation of Genesis; they are identical and parallel to no other story of creation.[19]

The argument that creation from nothing in 4(a)(1) does not involve a supernatural deity has no evidentiary or rational support. To the contrary, "creation out of nothing" is a concept unique to Western religions. In traditional Western religious thought, the conception of a creator of the world is a conception of God. Indeed, creation of the world "out of nothing" is the ultimate religious statement because God is the only actor. As Dr. Langdon Gilkey noted, the Act refers to one who has the power to bring all the universe into existence from nothing. The only "one" who has this power is God.[20]

The leading creationist writers, Morris and Gish, acknowledge that the idea of creation described in 4(a)(1) is the concept of creation by God and make no pretense to the contrary.[21] The idea of sudden creation from nothing, or creatio ex nihilo, is an inherently religious concept. (Vawter, Gilkey, Geisler, Ayala, Blount, Hicks.)

The argument advanced by defendants' witness, Dr. Norman Geisler, that teaching the existence of God is not religious unless the teaching seeks a commitment, is contrary to common understanding and contradicts settled case law. Stone v. Graham, 449 U.S. 39 (1980); Abbington School District v. Schempp, 374 U.S. 203 (1963).

The facts that creation science is inspired by the Book of Genesis and that Section 4(a) is consistent with a literal interpretation of Genesis leave no doubt that a major effect of the Act is the advancement of particular religious beliefs. The legal impact of this conclusion will be discussed further at the conclusion of the Court's evaluation of the scientific merit of creation science.

The approach to teaching "creation science" and "evolution science" found in Act 590 is identical to the two-model approach espoused by the Institute for Creation Research and is taken almost verbatim from ICR writings. It is an extension of Fundamentalists' view that one must either accept the literal interpretation of Genesis or else believe in the godless system of evolution.

The two model approach of the creationists is simply a contrived dualism[22] which has no scientific factual basis or legitimate educational purpose. It assumes only two explanations for the origins of life and existence of man, plants and animals: It was either the work of a creator or it was not. Application of these two models, according to creationists, and the defendants, dictates that all scientific evidence which fails to support the theory of evolution is necessarily scientific evidence in support of creationism and is, therefore, creation science "evidence" in support of Section 4(a).

The emphasis on origins as an aspect of the theory of evolution is peculiar to creationist literature. Although the subject of origins of life is within the province of biology, the scientific community does not consider origins of life a part of evolutionary theory. The theory of evolution assumes the existence of life and is directed to an explanation of *how* life evolved. Evolution does not presuppose the absence of a creator or God and the plain inference conveyed by Section 4 is erroneous.[23]

As a statement of the theory of evolution, Section 4(b) is simply a hodgepodge of limited assertions, many of which are factually inaccurate. For example, although 4(b)(2) asserts, as a tenet of evolutionary theory, "the sufficiency of mutation and natural selection in bringing about the existence of present living kinds from simple earlier kinds," Drs. Ayala and Gould both stated that biologists know that these two processes do not account for all significant evolutionary change. They testified to such phenomena as recombination, the founder effect, genetic drift and the theory of punctuated equilibrium, which are believed to play important evolutionary roles. Section 4(b) omits any reference to these. Moreover, 4(b) utilizes the term "kinds" which all scientists said is not a word of science and has no fixed meaning. Additionally, the Act presents both evolution and creation science as "package deals." Thus, evidence critical of some aspect of what the creationists define as evolution is taken as support for a theory which includes a worldwide flood and a relatively young earth.[24]

IV.(C)

In addition to the fallacious pedagogy of the two model approach, Section 4(a) lacks legitimate educational value because "creation science" as defined in that section is simply not science. Several witnesses suggested definitions of science. A descriptive definition was said to be that science is what is "accepted by the scientific community" and is "what scientists do." The obvious implication of this description is that, in a free society, knowledge does not require the imprimatur of legislation in order to become science.

More precisely, the essential characteristics of science are:

(1) It is guided by natural law;

(2) It has to be explanatory by reference to natural law;

(3) It is testable against the empirical world;

(4) Its conclusions are tentative, i.e., are not necessarily the final word; and

(5) It is falsifiable. (Ruse and other science witnesses.)

Creation science as described in Section 4(a) fails to meet these essential characteristics. First, the section revolves around 4(a)(1) which asserts a sudden creation "from nothing." Such a concept is not science because it depends upon a supernatural intervention which is not guided by natural law. It is not explanatory by reference to natural law, is not testable and is not falsifiable.[25]

If the unifying idea of supernatural creation by God is removed from Section 4, the remaining parts of the section explain nothing and are meaningless assertions.

Section 4(a)(2), relating to the "insufficiency of mutation and natural selection in bringing about development of all living kinds from a single organism", is an incomplete negative generalization directed at the theory of evolution.

Section 4(a)(3) which describes "changes only within fixed limits of originally created kinds of plants and animals" fails to conform to the essential characteristics of science for several reasons. First, there is no scientific definition of "kinds" and none of the witnesses was able to point to any scientific authority which recognized the term or knew how many "kinds" existed. One defense witness suggested there may be 100 to 10,000 different "kinds". Another believes there were "about 10,000, give or take a few thousand." Second, the assertion appears to be an effort to establish outer limits of changes within species. There is no scientific explanation for these limits which is guided by natural law and the limitations, whatever they are, cannot be explained by natural law.

The statement in 4(a)(4) of "separate ancestry of man and apes" is a bald assertion. It explains nothing and refers to no scientific fact or theory.[26]

Section 4(a)(5) refers to "explanation of the earth's geology by catastrophism, including the occurrence of a worldwide flood." This assertion completely fails as science. The Act is referring to the Noachian flood described in the Book of Genesis.[27] The creationist writers concede that *any* kind of Genesis Flood depends upon supernatural intervention. A worldwide flood as an explanation of the world's geology is not the product of natural law, nor can its occurrence be explained by natural law.

Section 4(a)(6) equally fails to meet the standards of science. "Relatively recent inception" has no scientific meaning. It can only be given meaning by reference to creationist writings which place the age at between 6,000 and 20,000 years because of the genealogy of the Old Testament. See, e.g. Px 78, Gish (6,000 to 10,000); Px 87, Segraves (6,000 to 20,000). Such a reasoning process is not the product of natural law; not explainable by natural law; nor is it tentative.

Creation science, as defined in Section 4(a), not only fails to follow the canons defining scientific theory, it also fails to fit the more general descriptions of "what scientists think" and "what scientists do." The scientific community consists of individuals and groups, nationally and internationally, who work independently in such varied fields as biology, paleontology, geology and astronomy. Their work is published and subject to review and testing by their peers. The journals for publication are both numerous and varied. There is, however, not one recognized scientific journal which has published an article espousing the creation science theory described in Section 4(a). Some of the State's witnesses suggested that the scientific community was "close-minded" on the subject of creationism and that explained the lack of acceptance of the creation science arguments. Yet no witness produced a scientific article for which publication had been refused. Perhaps some members of the scientific community are resistant to new ideas. It is, however, inconceivable that such a loose knit group of independent thinkers in all the varied fields of science could, or would, so effectively censor new scientific thought.

The creationists have difficulty maintaining among their ranks consistency in the claim that creationism is science. The author of Act 590, Ellwanger, said that neither evolution nor creationism was science. He thinks both are religion. Duane Gish recently responded to an article in *Discover* critical of creationism by stating:

"Stephen Jay Gould states that creationists claim creation is a scientific theory. This is a false accusation. Creationists have repeatedly stated that neither creation nor evolution is a scientific theory (and each is equally religious)." Gish, letter to editor of *Discover*, July, 1981, app. 30 to Plaintiffs' Pretrial Brief.

The methodology employed by creationists is another factor which is indicative that their work is not science. A scientific theory must be tentative and always subject to revision or abandonment in light of facts that are inconsistent with, or falsify, the theory. A theory that is by its own terms dogmatic, absolutist and never subject to revision is not a scientific theory.

The creationists' methods do not take data, weigh it against the opposing scientific data, and thereafter reach the conclusions stated in Section 4(a). Instead, they take the literal wording of the Book of Genesis and attempt to find scientific support for it. The method is best explained in the language of Morris in his book (Px 31) *Studies in The Bible and Science* at page 114:

". . . it is . . . quite impossible to determine anything about Creation through a study of present processes, because present processes are not creative in character. If man wishes to know anything about Creation (the time of Creation, the duration of Creation, the order of Creation, the methods of Creation, or anything else) his sole source of true information is that of divine revelation. God was there when it happened. We were not there . . . Therefore, we are completely limited to what God has seen fit to tell us, and this information is in His written Word. This is our textbook on the science of Creation!"

The Creation Research Society employs the same unscientific approach to the issue of creationism. Its applicants for membership must subscribe to the belief that the Book of Genesis is "historically and scientifically true in all of the original autographs."[28] The Court would never criticize or discredit any person's testimony based on his or her religious beliefs. While anybody is free to approach a scientific inquiry in any fashion they choose, they cannot properly describe the methodology used as scientific, if they start with a conclusion and refuse to change it regardless of the evidence developed during the course of the investigation.

IV.(D)

In efforts to establish "evidence" in support of creation science, the defendants relied upon the same false premise as the two model approach contained in Section 4, i.e., all evidence which criticized evolutionary theory was proof in support of creation science. For example, the defendants established that the mathematical probability of a chance chemical combination resulting in life from non-life is so remote that such an occurrence is almost beyond imagination. Those mathematical facts, the defendants argue, are scientific evidences that life was the product of a creator. While the statistical figures may be impressive evidence against the theory of chance chemical combinations as an explanation of origins, it requires a leap of faith to interpret those figures so as to support a complex doctrine which includes a sudden creation from nothing, a worldwide flood, separate ancestry of man and apes, and a young earth.

The defendants' argument would be more persuasive if, in fact, there were only two theories or ideas about the origins of life and the world. That there are a number of theories was acknowledged by the State's witnesses, Dr. Wickramasinghe and Dr. Geisler. Dr. Wickramasinghe testified at length in support of a theory that life on earth was "seeded" by comets which delivered genetic material and perhaps organisms to the earth's surface from interstellar dust far outside the solar system. The "seeding" theory further hypothesizes that the earth remains under the continuing influence of genetic material from space which continues to affect life. While Wickramasinghe's theory[29] about the origins of life on earth has not received general acceptance within the scientific community, he has, at least, used scientific methodology to produce a theory of origins which meets the essential characteristics of science.

The Court is at a loss to understand why Dr. Wickramasinghe was called in behalf of the defendants. Perhaps it was because he was generally critical of the theory of evolution and the scientific community, a tactic consistent with the strategy of the defense. Unfortunately for the defense, he demonstrated that the simplistic approach of the two model analysis of the origins of life is false. Furthermore, he corroborated the plaintiffs' witnesses by concluding that "no rational scientist" would believe the earth's geology could be explained by reference to a worldwide flood or that the earth was less than one million years old.

The proof in support of creation science consisted almost entirely of efforts to discredit the theory of evolution through a rehash of data and theories which have been before the scientific community for decades. The arguments asserted by creationists are not based upon new scientific evidence or laboratory data which has been ignored by the scientific community.

Robert Gentry's discovery of radioactive polonium haloes in granite and coalified woods is, perhaps, the most recent scientific work which the creationists use as argument for a "relatively recent inception" of the earth and a "worldwide flood." The existence of polonium haloes in granite and coalified wood is thought to be inconsistent with radiometric dating methods based upon constant radioactive decay rates. Mr. Gentry's findings were published almost ten years ago and have been the subject of some discussion in the scientific community. The discoveries have not, however, led to the formulation of any scientific hypothesis or theory which would explain a relatively recent inception of the earth or a worldwide flood. Gentry's discovery has been treated as a minor mystery which will eventually be explained. It may deserve further investigation, but the National Science Foundation has not deemed it to be of sufficient import to support further funding.

The testimony of Marianne Wilson was persuasive evidence that creation science is not science. Ms. Wilson is in charge of the science curriculum for Pulaski County Special

School District, the largest school district in the State of Arkansas. Prior to the passage of Act 590, Larry Fisher, a science teacher in the District, using materials from the ICR, convinced the School Board that it should voluntarily adopt creation science as part of its science curriculum. The District Superintendent assigned Ms. Wilson the job of producing a creation science curriculum guide. Ms. Wilson's testimony about the project was particularly convincing because she obviously approached the assignment with an open mind and no preconceived notions about the subject. She had not heard of creation science until about a year ago and did not know its meaning before she began her research.

Ms. Wilson worked with a committee of science teachers appointed from the District. They reviewed practically all of the creationist literature. Ms. Wilson and the committee members reached the unanimous conclusion that creationism is not science; it is religion. They so reported to the Board. The Board ignored the recommendation and insisted that a curriculum guide be prepared.

In researching the subject, Ms. Wilson sought the assistance of Mr. Fisher who initiated the Board action and asked professors in the science departments of the University of Arkansas at Little Rock and the University of Central Arkansas[30] for reference material and assistance, and attended a workshop conducted at Central Baptist College by Dr. Richard Bliss of the ICR staff. Act 590 became law during the course of her work so she used Section 4(a) as a format for her curriculum guide.

Ms. Wilson found all available creationists' materials unacceptable because they were permeated with religious references and reliance upon religious beliefs.

It is easy to understand why Ms. Wilson and other educators find the creationists' textbook material and teaching guides unacceptable. The materials misstate the theory of evolution in the same fashion as Section 4(b) of the Act, with emphasis on the alternative mutually exclusive nature of creationism and evolution. Students are constantly encouraged to compare and make a choice between the two models, and the material is not presented in an accurate manner.

A typical example is *Origins* (Px 76) by Richard B. Bliss, Director of Curriculum Development of the ICR. The presentation begins with a chart describing "preconceived ideas about origins" which suggests that some people believe that evolution is atheistic. Concepts of evolution, such as "adaptive radiation," are erroneously presented. At page 11, figure 1.6, of the text, a chart purports to illustrate this "very important" part of the evolution model. The chart conveys the idea that such diverse mammals as a whale, bear, bat and monkey all evolved from a shrew through the process of adaptive radiation. Such a suggestion is, of course, a totally erroneous and misleading application of the theory. Even more objectionable, especially when viewed in light of the emphasis on asking the student to elect one of the models, is the chart presentation at page 17, figure 1.6. That chart purports to illustrate the evolutionists' belief that man evolved from bacteria to fish to reptile to mammals and, thereafter, into man. The illustration indicates, however, that the mammal from which man evolved was a rat.

Biology, A Search For Order in Complexity[31] is a high school biology text typical of creationists' materials. The following quotations are illustrative:

"Flowers and roots do not have a mind to have purpose of their own; therefore, this planning must have been done for them by the Creator." - at page 12.

"The exquisite beauty of color and shape in flowers exceeds the skill of poet, artist, and king. Jesus said (from Matthew's gospel), 'Consider the lilies of the field, how they grow; they toil not, neither do they spin . . .'"
Px 129 at page 363.

The "public school edition" texts written by creationists simply omit Biblical references but the content and message remain the same. For example, *Evolution - The Fossils Say No!*[32] contains the following:

Creation. By creation we mean the bringing into being by a supernatural Creator of the basic kinds of plants and animals by the process of sudden, or fiat, creation. We do not know how the Creator created, what processes He used, *for He used processes which are not now operating anywhere in the natural universe.* This is why we refer to creation as Special Creation. We cannot discover by scientific investigation anything about the creative processes used by the Creator." - page 40

Gish's book also portrays the large majority of evolutionists as "materialistic atheists or agnostics."

Scientific Creationism (Public School Edition) by Morris, is another text reviewed by Ms. Wilson's committee and rejected as unacceptable. The following quotes illustrate the purpose and theme of the text:

Forword [*sic*]

- - - - -

"Parents and youth leaders today, and even many scientists and educators, have become concerned about the prevalence and influence of evolutionary philosophy in modern curriculum. Not only is this system inimical to orthodox Christianity and Judaism, but also, as many are convinced, to a healthy society and true science as well."
at page iii

* * * * *

"The rationalist of course finds the concept of special creation insufferably naive, even 'incredible'. Such a judgment, however, is warranted only if one categorically dismisses the existence of an omnipotent God."
at page 17.

Without using creationist literature, Ms. Wilson was unable to locate one genuinely scientific article or work which supported Section 4(a). In order to comply with the mandate of the Board she used such materials as an article from *Readers Digest* about "atomic clocks" which inferentially suggested that the earth was less than 4 1/2 billion years old. She was unable to locate any substantive teaching material for some parts of Section 4 such as the worldwide flood. The curriculum guide which she prepared cannot be taught and has no educational value as science. The defendants did not produce any text or writing in response to this evidence which they claimed was usable in the public school classroom.[33]

The conclusion that creation science has no scientific merit or educational value as science has legal significance in light of the Court's previous conclusion that creation science has, as one major effect, the advancement of religion. The second part of the three-pronged test for establishment reaches only those statutes having as their *primary* effect the advancement of religion. Secondary effects which advance religion are not constitutionally fatal. Since creation science is not science, the conclusion is inescapable that the *only* real effect of Act 590 is the advancement of religion. The Act therefore fails both the first and second portions of the test in *Lemon v. Kurtzman*, 403 U.S. 602 (1971).

IV.(E)

Act 590 mandates "balanced treatment" for creation science and evolution science. The Act prohibits instruction in any religious doctrine or references to religious writings. The Act is self-contradictory and compliance is impossible unless the public schools elect to forego significant portions of subjects such as biology, world history, geology, zoology, botany, psychology, anthropology, sociology, philosophy, physics and chemistry. Presently, the concepts of evolutionary theory as described in 4(b) permeate the public school textbooks. There is no way teachers can teach the Genesis account of creation in a secular manner.

The State Department of Education, through its textbook selection committee, school boards and school administrators will be required to constantly monitor materials to avoid using religious references. The school boards, administrators and teachers face an impossible task. How is the teacher to respond to questions about a creation suddenly and out of nothing? How will a teacher explain the occurrence of a worldwide flood? How will a teacher explain the concept of a relatively recent age of the earth? The answer is obvious because the only source of this information is ultimately contained in the Book of Genesis.

References to the pervasive nature of religious concepts in creation science texts amply demonstrate why State entanglement with religion is inevitable under Act 590. Involvement of the State in screening texts for impermissible religious references will require State officials to make delicate religious judgments. The need to monitor classroom discussion in order to uphold the Act's prohibition against religious instruction will necessarily involve administrators in questions concerning religion. These continuing involvements of State officials in questions and issues of religion create an excessive and prohibited entanglement with religion. *Brandon v. Board of Education*, 487 F.Supp 1219, 1230 (N.D.N.Y.), *aff'd.*, 635 F.2d 971 (2nd Cir. 1980).

V.

These conclusions are dispositive of the case and there is no need to reach legal conclusions with respect to the remaining issues. The plaintiffs raised two other issues questioning the constitutionality of the Act and, insofar as the factual findings relevant to these issues are not covered in the preceding discussion, the Court will address these issues. Additionally, the defendants raised two other issues which warrant discussion.

V.(A)

First, plaintiff teachers argue the Act is unconstitutionally vague to the extent that they cannot comply with its mandate of "balanced" treatment without jeopardizing their employment. The argument centers around the lack of a precise definition in the Act for the word "balanced." Several witnesses expressed opinions that the word has such meanings as equal time, equal weight, or equal legitimacy. Although the Act could have been more explicit, "balanced" is a word subject to ordinary understanding. The proof is not convincing that a teacher using a reasonably acceptable understanding of the word and making a good faith effort to comply with the Act will be in jeopardy of termination. Other portions of the Act are arguably vague, such as the "relatively recent" inception of the earth and life. The evidence establishes, however, that relatively recent means from 6,000 to 20,000 years, as commonly understood in creation science literature. The meaning of this phrase, like Section 4(a) generally, is, for purposes of the Establishment Clause, all too clear.

V.(B)

The plaintiffs' other argument revolves around the alleged infringement by the defendants upon the academic freedom of teachers and students. It is contended this unprecedented intrusion in the curriculum by the State prohibits teachers from teaching what they believe should be taught or requires them to teach that which they do not believe is proper. The evidence reflects that traditionally the State Department of Education, local school boards and administration officials exercise little, if any, influence upon the subject matter taught by classroom teachers. Teachers have been given freedom to teach and emphasize those portions of subjects the individual teacher considered important. The limits to this discretion have generally been derived from the approval of textbooks by the State Department and preparation of curriculum guides by the school districts.

Several witnesses testified that academic freedom for the teacher means, in substance, that the individual teacher should be permitted unlimited discretion subject only to the bounds of professional ethics. The Court is not prepared to adopt such a broad view of academic freedom in the public schools.

In any event, if Act 590 is implemented, many teachers will be required to teach material in support of creation science which they do not consider academically sound. Many teachers will simply forego teaching subjects which might trigger the "balanced treatment" aspects of Act 590 even though they think the subjects are important to a proper presentation of a course.

Implementation of Act 590 will have serious and untoward consequences for students, particularly those planning to attend college. Evolution is the cornerstone of modern biology, and many courses in public schools contain subject matter relating to such varied topics as the age of the earth, geology and relationships among living things. Any student who is deprived of instruction as to the prevailing scientific thought on these topics will be denied a significant part of science education. Such a deprivation through the high school levels would undoubtedly have an impact upon the quality of education in the State's colleges and universities, especially including the pre-professional and professional programs in the health sciences.

V.(C)

The defendants argue in their brief that evolution is, in effect, a religion, and that by teaching a religion which is contrary to some students' religious views, the State is infringing upon the student's free exercise rights under the First Amendment. Mr. Ellwanger's legislative findings, which were adopted as a finding of fact by the Arkansas Legislature in Act 590, provides:

"Evolution-science is contrary to the religious convictions or moral values or philosophical beliefs of many students and parents, including individuals of many different religious faiths and with diverse moral and philosophical beliefs." Act 590, S7(d).

The defendants argue that the teaching of evolution alone presents both a free exercise problem and an establishment problem which can only be redressed by giving balanced treatment to creation science, which is admittedly consistent with some religious beliefs. This argument appears to have its genesis in a student note written by Mr. Wendell Bird, "Freedom of Religion and Science Instruction in Public Schools," 87 Yale L.J. 515 (1978). The argument has no legal merit.

If creation science is, in fact, science and not religion, as the defendants claim, it is difficult to see how the teaching of such a science could "neutralize" the religious nature of evolution.

Assuming for the purposes of argument, however, that evolution is a religion or religious tenet, the remedy is to stop the teaching of evolution; not establish another religion in opposition to it. Yet it is clearly established in the case law, and perhaps also in common sense, that evolution is not a religion and that teaching evolution does not violate the Establishment Clause, *Epperson v. Arkansas, supra, Willoughby v. Stever*, No. 15574-75 (D.D.C. May 18, 1973); *aff'd.* 504 F.2d 271 (D.C. Cir. 1974), *cert. denied*, 420 U.S. 924 (1975); *Wright v. Houston Indep. School Dist.*, 366 F.Supp. 1208 (S.D. Tex. 1978), *aff'd.* 486 F.2d 137 (5th Cir. 1973), *cert. denied* 417 U.S. 969 (1974).

V.(D)

The defendants presented Dr. Larry Parker, a specialist in devising curricula for public schools. He testified that the public school's curriculum should reflect the subjects the public wants taught in schools. The witness said that polls indicated a significant majority of the American public thought creation science should be taught if evolution was taught. The point of this testimony was never placed in a legal context. No doubt a sizeable majority of Americans believe in the concept of a Creator or, at least, are not opposed to the concept and see nothing wrong with teaching school children about the idea.

The application and content of First Amendment principles are not determined by public opinion polls or by a majority vote. Whether the proponents of Act 590 constitute the majority or the minority is quite irrelevant under a constitutional system of government. No group, no matter how large or small, may use the organs of government, of which the public schools are the most conspicuous and influential, to foist its religious beliefs on others.

The Court closes this opinion with a thought expressed eloquently by the great Justice Frankfurter:

"We renew our conviction that 'we have staked the very existence of our country on the faith that complete separation between the state and religion is best for the state and best for religion.'" *Everson v. Board of Education*, 330 U.S. at 59. If nowhere else, in the relation between Church and State, 'good fences make good neighbors.'" *McCollum v. Board of Education*, 333 U.S. 203, 232 (1948).

An injunction will be entered permanently prohibiting enforcement of Act 590.

It is so ordered this January 5, 1982.

(signed: William R. Overton)
UNITED STATES DISTRICT JUDGE

NOTES

1. The complaint is based on 42 U.S.C. S1983, which provides a remedy against any person who, acting under color of state law, deprives another of any right, privilege or immunity guaranteed by the United States Constitution or federal law.

This Court's jurisdiction arises under 28 U.S.C. SS1331, 1343(3) and 1343(4). The power to issue declaratory judgments is expressed in 28 U.S.C. SS2201 and 2202.

2. The facts necessary to establish the plaintiff's standing to sue are contained in the joint stipulation of facts, which is hereby adopted and incorporated herein by reference.

There is no doubt that the case is ripe for adjudication.

3. The State of Arkansas was dismissed as a defendant because of its immunity from suit under the Eleventh Amendment. *Hans v. Louisiana*, 134 U.S. 1 (1890).

4. The authorities differ as to generalizations which may be made about Fundamentalism. For example, Dr. Geisler testified to the widely held view that there are five beliefs characteristic of all Fundamentalist movements, in addition, of course, to the inerrancy of Scripture: (1) belief in the virgin birth of Christ, (2) belief in the deity of Christ, (3) belief in the substitutional atonement of Christ, (4) belief in the second coming of Christ, and (5) belief in the physical resurrection of all departed souls. Dr. Marsden, however, testified that this generalization, which has been common in religious scholarship, is now thought to be historical error. There is no doubt, however, that all Fundamentalists take the Scriptures as inerrant and probably most take them as literally true.

5. Initated Act 1 of 1929, Ark. Stat. Ann. S80-1627 *et seq.*, which prohibited the teaching of evolution in Arkansas schools, is discussed *infra* at text accompanying note 26.

6. Subsequent references to the testimony will be made by the last name of the witness only. References to documentary exhibits will be by the name of the author and the exhibit number.

7. Applicants for membership in the CRS must subscribe to the following statement of belief: "(1) The Bible is the written Word of God, and because we believe it to be inspired thruout (sic), all of its

assertions are historically and scientifically true in all of the original autographs. To the student of nature, this means that the account of origins in Genesis is a factual presentation of simple historical truths. (2) All basic types of living things, including man, were made by direct creative acts of God during Creation Week as described in Genesis. Whatever biological changes have occurred since Creation have accomplished only changes within the original created kinds. (3) The great Flood described in Genesis, commonly referred to as the Noachian Deluge, was an historical event, world-wide in its extent and effect. (4) Finally, we are an organization of Christian men of science, who accept Jesus Christ as our Lord and Savior. The account of the special creation of Adam and Eve as one man and one woman, and their subsequent Fall into sin, is the basis for our belief in the necessity of a Savior for all mankind. Therefore, salvation can come only thru (sic) accepting Jesus Christ as our Savior." (Px 115)

8. Because of the voluminous nature of the documentary exhibits, the parties were directed by pre-trial order to submit their proposed exhibits for the Court's convenience prior to trial. The numbers assigned to the pre-trial submissions do not correspond with those assigned to the same documents at trial and, in some instances, the pre-trial submissions are more complete.

9. Px 130, Morris, *Introducing Scientific Creationism Into the Public Schools* (1975), and Bird, "Resolution for Balanced Presentation of Evolution and Scientific Creationism," *ICR Impact Series* No. 71, App. 14 to Plaintiffs' Pretrial Brief.

10. The creationists often show candor in their proselytization. Henry Morris has stated, "Even if a favorable statute or court decision is obtained, it will probably be declared unconstitutional, especially if the legislation or injunction refers to the Bible account of creation." In the same vein he notes, "The only effective way to get creationism taught properly is to have it taught by teachers who are both willing and able to do it. Since most teachers now are neither willing nor able, they must first be both persuaded and instructed themselves." Px 130, Morris, *Introducing Scientific Creationism Into the Public Schools* (1975) (unpaged).

11. Mr. Bird sought to participate in this litigation by representing a number of individuals who wanted to intervene as defendants. The application for intervention was denied by this Court. *McLean v. Arkansas*, _____ F.Supp _____, (E.D. Ark. 1981), aff'd. *per curiam*, Slip Op. No. 81-2023 (8th Cir. Oct. 16, 1981).

12. The model act had been revised to insert "creation science" in lieu of creationism because Ellwanger had the impression people thought creationism was too religious a term. (Ellwanger Depo. at 79.)

13. The original model act had been introduced in the South Carolina Legislature, but had died without action after the South Carolina Attorney General had opined that the act was unconstitutional.

14. Specifically, Senator Holsted testified that he holds to a literal interpretation of the Bible; that the bill was compatible with his religious beliefs; that the bill does favor the position of literalists; that his religious convictions were a factor in his sponsorship of the bill; and that he stated publicly to the *Arkansas Gazette* (although not on the floor of the Senate) contemporaneously with the legislative debate that the bill does presuppose the existence of a divine creator. There is no doubt that Senator Holsted knew he was sponsoring the teaching of a religious doctrine. His view was that the bill did not violate the First Amendment because, as he saw it, it did not favor one denomination over another.

15. This statute is, of course, clearly unconstitutional under the Supreme Court's decision in *Abbington School Dist. v. Schempp*, 374 U.S. 203 (1963).

16. The joint stipulation of facts establishes that the following areas are the only *information* specifically required by statute to be taught in all Arkansas schools: (1) the effects of alcohol and narcotics on the human body, (2) conservation of national resources, (3) Bird Week, (4) Fire Prevention, and (5) Flag etiquette. Additionally, certain specific courses, such as American history and Arkansas history, must be completed by each student before graduation from high school.

17. Paul Ellwanger stated in his deposition that he did not know why Section 4(a)(2) (insufficiency of mutation and natural selection) was included as an evidence supporting creation science. He indicated that he was not a scientist, "but these are the postulates that have been laid down by creation scientists." Ellwanger Depo. at 136.

18. Although defendants must make some effort to cast the concept of creation in non-religious terms, this effort surely causes discomfort to some of the Act's more theologically sophisticated supporters. The concept of a creator God distinct from the God of love and mercy is closely similar to the Marcion and Gnostic heresies, among the

deadliest to threaten the early Christian church. These heresies had much to do with development and adoption of the Apostle's [sic] Creed as the official creedal statement of the Roman Catholic Church in the West. (Gilkey.)

19. The parallels between Section 4(a) and Genesis are quite specific: (1) "sudden creation from nothing" is taken from Genesis, 1:1-10 (Vawter, Gilkey); (2) destruction of the world by a flood of divine origin is a notion peculiar to Judeo-Christian tradition and is based on Chapters 7 and 8 of Genesis (Vawter); (3) the term "kinds" has no fixed scientific meaning, but appears repeatedly in Genesis (all scientific witnesses); (4) "relatively recent inception" means an age of the earth from 6,000 to 10,000 years and is based on the genealogy of the Old Testament using the rather astronomical ages assigned to the patriarchs (Gilkey and several of the defendants' scientific witnesses); (5) Separate ancestry of man and ape focuses on the portion of the theory of evolution which Fundamentalists find most offensive, *Epperson v. Arkansas*, 393 U.S. 97 (1968).

20. "[C]oncepts concerning . . . a supreme being of some sort are manifestly religious . . . These concepts do not shed that religiosity merely because they are presented as philosophy or as a science . . . " *Malnak v. Yogi*, 440 F.Supp. 1284, 1322 (D.N.J. 1977); *aff'd per curiam*, 592 F.2d 197 (3d Cir. 1979).

21. See, e.g., Px 76, Morris, *et al, Scientific Creationism*, 203 (1980) ("If creation really is a fact, this means there is a *Creator*, and the universe is His creation.") Numerous other examples of such admissions can be found in the many exhibits which represent creationist literature, but no useful purpose would be served here by a potentially endless listing.

22. Morris, the Director of ICR and one who first advocated the two model approach, insists that a true Christian cannot compromise with the theory of evolution and that the Genesis version of creation and the theory of evolution are mutually exclusive. Px 31, Morris, *Studies in the Bible & Science*, 102-103. The two model approach was the subject of Dr. Richard Bliss's doctoral dissertation. (Dx 35). It is presented in Bliss, *Origins: Two Models-Evolution, Creation* (1978). Moreover, the two model approach merely casts in educationalist language the dualism which appears in all creationist literature - creation (i.e. God) and evolution are presented as two alternative and mutually exclusive theories. See, e.g., Px 75, Morris, *Scientific Creationism* (1974) (public school edition); Px 59, Fox, *Fossils: Hard Facts from the Earth*. Particularly illustrative is Px 61, Boardman, *et al,*

Worlds Without End (1971), a CSRC publication: "One group of scientists, known as creationists, believe that God, in a miraculous manner, created all matter and energy . . .

"Scientists who insist that the universe just grew, by accident, from a mass of hot gases without the direction or help of a Creator are known as evolutionists."

23. The idea that belief in a creator and acceptance of the scientific theory of evolution are mutually exclusive is a false premise and offensive to the religious views of many. (Hicks) Dr. Francisco Ayala, a geneticist of considerable renown and a former Catholic priest who has the equivalent of a Ph.D. in theology, pointed out that many working scientists who subscribed to the theory of evolution are devoutly religious.

24. This is so despite the fact that some of the defense witnesses do not subscribe to the young earth or flood hypotheses. Dr. Geisler stated his belief that the earth is several billion years old. Dr. Wickramasinghe stated that no rational scientist would believe the earth is less than one million years old or that all the world's geology could be explained by a worldwide flood.

25. "We do not know how God created, what processes He used, for *God used processes which are not now operating anywhere in the natural universe.* This is why we refer to divine creation as Special Creation. We cannot discover by scientific investigation anything about the creative processes used by God." Px 78, Gish, *Evolution? The Fossils Say No!*, 42 (3d ed. 1979) (emphasis in original).

26. The evolutionary notion that man and some modern apes have a common ancestor somewhere in the distant past has consistently been distorted by anti-evolutionists to say that man descended from modern monkeys. As such, this idea has long been most offensive to Fundamentalists. See, *Epperson v. Arkansas*, 393 U.S. 97 (1968).

27. Not only was this point acknowledged by virtually all the defense witnesses, it is patent in the creationist literature. See, e.g., Px 89, Kofahl & Segraves, *The Creation Explanation*, 40: "The Flood of Noah brought about vast changes in the earth's surface, including vulcanism, mountain building, and the deposition of the major part of sedimentary strata. This principle is called 'Biblical catastrophism.'"

28. See n. 7, *supra*, for the full text of the CRS creed.

29. The theory is detailed in Wickramasinghe's book with Sir Fred Hoyle, *Evolution from Space* (1981), which is Dx 79.

30. Ms. Wilson stated that some professors she spoke with sympathized with her plight and tried to help her find scientific materials to support Section 4(a). Others simply asked her to leave.

31. Px 129, published by Zondervan Publishing House (1974), states that it was "prepared by the Textbook Committee of the Creation Research Society." It has a disclaimer pasted inside the front cover stating that it is not suitable for use in public schools.

32. Px 77, by Duane Gish.

33. The passage of Act 590 apparently caught a number of its supporters off guard as much as it did the school district. The Act's author, Paul Ellwanger, stated in a letter to "Dick," (Apparently Dr. Richard Bliss at ICR): "And finally, if you know of any textbooks at any level and for any subjects that you think are acceptable to you and also constitutionally admissible, these are things that would be of *enormous* [sic—help?] to these bewildered folks who may be caught, as Arkansas now has been, by the sudden need to implement a whole new ball game with which they are quite unfamiliar." (sic) (Unnumbered attachment to Ellwanger depo.)